Innovative
Management

Innovative Management

A Pragmatic Guide to
New Techniques

NICOLA PHILLIPS

FINANCIAL TIMES

PITMAN PUBLISHING

Pitman Publishing
128 Long Acre , London WC2E 9AN

A Division of Longman Group UK Limited

First published in 1993

© Nicola Phillips 1993

A CIP catalogue record for this book can be obtained from the
British Library.

ISBN 0 273 60025 7

Typeset by PanTek Arts, Maidstone, Kent
Printed and bound in Great Britain by
Biddles Ltd, Guildford and King's Lynn

CONTENTS

FOREWORD

It is frequently a source of puzzlement to me, and perhaps to you too, that so much time, effort and money should be devoted to strategic planning and, relatively speaking, so little to an understanding of the factors which govern and drive implementation of strategies and so determine their success or failure.

In a sense, of course, strategic planning is by definition more amenable to the application of intellect and logic; it is one level removed from people. Conversely, at the implementation stage, subjectivity creeps in. People are involved; people who do not always react in a rational or predictable manner. They include suppliers, employees, customers and consumers. It is upon them that our ability to make our strategy work will ultimately depend.

All too often, I believe, the best strategies founder on the rocks of culture, structure and attitude. The objective of this book, largely by using real examples to illustrate its message, is to provide some guidance to navigation.

Many companies have been through processes of de-layering and restructuring in a drive to improve or defend margins by reducing overheads and thus to enhance their competitive positions. Several, I believe, may have gone too far. The demands of implementing new strategies can be considerable. They require change-management skills, improved levels of internal communications and training; training not just in normal functional skills but in accepting and adapting to change. They require new skills not found in the custodial cultures of companies which have operated in a static, or only slowly-changing environment.

So if there is a single message which can be crystallised from this book, it is perhaps this: successful implementation of strategies demands changes in the way people work. It is as important to research and plan for those as it is to construct the strategy itself. And change needs people. People who own the strategy, people who not only communicate it and explain it but who act as leaders of change, people who coach others to understand and to adapt.

In short, new strategies often demand sophisticated change management skills if they are to be successfully implemented. It is a truism to say that the pace of change is accelerating; we all know it. But what are we doing about it?

Can you introduce a new system into a traditional, hierarchical, bureaucratic organisation? Perhaps, but probably not. However, can you do it if it will require review and modification every year or so? Certainly not. We require organisations capable of evolution and adaptation as the environment in which we compete changes, and the behaviour of our competitors adjusts. The faster the environment changes, the more quickly we must evolve to compete successfully. The dinosaurs, as ever, will fail.

A.D.Portno
Chief Executive
Bass Brewers
December 1992

ACKNOWLEDGEMENTS

The publishing of this book owes much to Katherine Adams, my sub-editor, for tolerance, and an ability to understand the unwritten and to stick to unrealistic deadlines. Thanks to Dee Hahn Rollins for inspiration, introductions and a warm study. This book was written with many sacrifices and much support and faith from Lauren and Peter.

My special thanks to those organisations who gave me insights into their innovative management practices. In particular, Evelyn Lee Barber, 'la reine des networks', and to all the Personnel team at Bass Taverns; Steve Bourne at 3M; and to Dr. Portno and all his management team at Bass Brewers. Many thanks to Gillian Scholes and Digital for a glimpse of their future.

1 INTRODUCTION

The real quest isn't where ideas come from. It's where they go and how they get there.

The future is hidden, even from the men who made it.
Anatole France

Anyone who can only spell a word one way is an idiot.
W C Fields

Walking on water was not built in a day.
Jack Kerouac

Different rules, new competition and changing structures in business all mean that new approaches to management are constantly being thought up. But this creates an immediate set of problems for busy managers, who are faced with the following questions:

- What are these new approaches?
- Which ones should I use?
- How can I use some of the more exciting ideas without appearing 'cranky'?
- How can I find out which are just 'flavour of the month', and which are sound, tried and tested business practices?

This book attempts to answer these questions by looking at some of the innovative techniques now being used to address business issues around the world. It looks at where the ideas come from, how they are communicated, and, most importantly, how they are applied.

A PROLIFERATION OF NEW IDEAS

'New wave', 'New Age', 'Paradigm shift', 'Learning organisation': managers could be forgiven for a degree of bewilderment at some of the terms now being used to describe their trade. What do these terms mean, and how are they connected to the day-to-day job of managing? Do these new ideas really improve business productivity, or do they do no more than line the pockets of the people who thought them up? In this book, we shall examine some of the new concepts now being used to discuss the task of management. We shall be asking how useful each of them is, and whether they have any application in the real world of business.

The process of writing this book only served to emphasise the need for such a critical assessment of the current ideas and jargon. The plethora of ideas, initiatives, and theories are enough to make the head reel, and the more one looks, the more new ideas seem to emerge from the woodwork.

A classic example of the proliferation of new management ideas is the career of Tom Peters, the American management guru. Peters' initial argument was that senior managers should reject the traditional model of the dispassionate, analytical manager, and focus on serving the customer instead. Tens of thousands of business people in the US, Europe and the Far East accepted these teachings, and have used them to inform their management styles.

In his latest book, though, Peters seems to make a remarkable about turn, casting doubt on his own earlier theories. His latest idea is that in order to be competitive, today's companies must free themselves from traditional organisational structures and go 'bonkers', constantly shifting their systems in response to markets that change as swiftly and unexpectedly as the weather.

It is surely a demonstration of the power of management gurus that few business organisations during the 1980s did *not* use the word 'excellence' in their strategic plans, in honour of Peters' first two books, *In Search of Excellence* and *A Passion for Excellence*.

So how is the manager to begin to find a way through this maze of management ideas, some of which seem to have such a short shelf-life? The starting point for any manager must be, of course, what he or she wants to achieve. This is the benchmark by which to measure the usefulness of any theory or new idea. In this book, we shall start from this premise, and examine the usefulness of a number of management theories to real, living companies.

MANAGEMENT AND CHANGE

Economically, politically and socially, the world is changing so fast that by the time this volume gets into print, a whole new set of concepts, as yet unthought of, may be joining those mentioned above. As people's values and priorities change, this has a profound effect on business practices. We can see that worldwide recession has affected company structures and practices, while global management has brought companies face-to-face with complex cross-cultural issues.

Without exception, all of the innovative management ideas and practices described in this book have been developed in response to change. Change was a buzzword of the 1980s, and looks set to continue its influence into the 1990s and beyond. But, more importantly, recent global political upheavals and the worldwide recession do genuinely seem to have persuaded organisations into thinking another way. While in the 1980s there was simply too much money to be made for serious long-term thinking, the 1990s may see the coming of age of genuine strategies for change.

Energy for change is generally born of a mixture of hope and dissatisfaction. It requires tension between what is and what could be. And most change is stressful, and produces resistance, especially during the uncomfortable transitional stages. Many of the new ideas in this book may, of course, founder at this stage, especially if there are problems in the way they are implemented.

In the chapters that follow, we shall be looking at how changes in the international business environment are affecting the way managers manage, and how they are changing our view of what management is about. And we shall examine some of the barriers that can face the effective implementation of innovative management techniques.

HUMAN RESOURCES – THE KEY TO MANAGEMENT

Some people would argue that since 1928 the principal source of new or added national income has been human resources. Power and profit used to come from property, but now it comes from people. And productivity is measured not so much by the *quantity* of human resources, but by the *quality*. But although there is plenty of lip service to the importance of this human aspect of business, the behaviour of large corporations scarcely seems to bear it out. While there is talk of partnership, there are few signs of employees sharing real power with their managements.

Even in young, growing companies, some of the old hierarchical habits seem to have maintained their hold. Many start off in the right direction, but as they grow, these organisations start to look more and more like the big dinosaurs, and the same divisions appear between staff and management.

Take the example of one British company widely regarded as innovative and offering real equality to its employees. This company describes itself in 'New age' terms, as consultative and communicative. However, whilst being taken on a tour of the new catering facilities, the chairman asked what hours the canteen was open. The manager replied that, after carrying out much research and consultation, the whole unit had decided that the most cost effective times were over a three hour period in the middle of the day. The chairman replied that that was all well and good, but he wanted it to be open all day, and would brook no argument. The hours were changed immediately. In spite of the company's 'New age' credentials, this sounds very much like the good old autocratic style of management.

Throughout this book, we shall be examining the central role played by the management of human resources in the process of change and innovation.

DEFINING WHAT YOU WANT TO ACHIEVE

Defining what it is that needs to be achieved is critical to successful innovation. You can think of the manager as a mountaineer looking up from the foot of the mountain to the summit, attempting to map the route of the ascent. The experienced mountaineer actually plans the route in reverse, from the summit to the start. He or she will first decide at which point below the summit to begin the final climb to the top, and then where to begin the stage of the climb before that, and so on, step by step, downwards to the starting point. The alternative is starting from the bottom and discovering after several hours of strenuous climbing that the expedition has reached an impasse.

By planning 'backwards' from the desired solution to the present problem the manager may well succeed where previous attempts have failed, and come up with a truly innovative strategy. Of course, the manager's problem-solving skills cannot stop there. There is also the major task of convincing other people even to consider using a strategy that is new and different.

Writers, teachers, and other gurus like to think that when they have identified a problem and offered some solutions, the problem is on its way to being solved. But, of course, a crucial factor will be the way in which these 'solutions' are.applied in real organisations.

Because no two organisations are identical, any 'miracle cures' have to be read in the context of the particular firms that have used them successfully. What works for one company is unlikely to work in exactly the same way for another. Any new management techniques will have to be adapted to the situation current in your own organisation. By providing case studies of real organisations that have attempted innovative solutions to the demands of change, we aim only to show how some of the current thinking and values have worked for particular organisations, with particular needs.

In a world of change, it is tempting to seek out definite solutions. But in a time of change, the last thing you really need is over-definite answers. The organisations that survive in a changing world are very often those who learn not the answers, but what questions they need to ask in order to progress.

In conclusion, let us not forget the biologist Ludwig von Bertalanffy's theory of 'equifinality' (1950). Bertalanffy stressed the fact that there are often many different paths leading to one point. Put colloquially, we could summarise his theory by saying that there is more than one way to skin a cat. Such a simplistic notion might at first appear to have no place in management, but if nature arrives at the same place from many directions, people, being part of nature, are likely to do much the same thing. In management, as much as anywhere, we should always remember that there is unlikely to be one best way to do anything.

This book looks at some of the ways being used to manage in today's turbulent 'whitewater'. We would claim none of them as *the only* way, just one organisation's solution – for them, it was *a way*.

2 VISION – FOCUSING THE FUTURE

The tendency of modern organisations to become bigger and more centralised makes a clear, common sense of direction increasingly urgent for many organisations. Worldwide recession, and the increasing emphasis on getting value for money from expensive workforces has also led to greater interest in the question of motivating an organisation's people. Increasingly, innovative organisations are responding to these pressures by developing a distinctive 'vision' of the kind of company they would like to be.

But what is a 'corporate vision', and how should it be achieved? In this chapter we take a close look at some of the elements making up an effective vision, and examine some good and some bad examples from real companies.

We argue that, in order to be truly pro-active in a rapidly-changing marketplace, an organisation needs to have a clear vision of its role. Much more than just a 'mission statement', a corporate vision is made up of two vital elements: the organisation's fundamental values, and a strong image of the organisation it would like to be.

A company's fundamental values can touch on its employees, its customers, its profit, its products, its ethics, and its view of society. They should form the basis of its overall sense of purpose, of its view of its own role in the world. Clearly, if they are to motivate an organisation's people, they must be able to inspire and uplift.

The ubiquitous mission statement does come into its own, however, when it comes to the second element of a company's vision: the inspiring image. Narrower in scope than the organisation's overall purpose, the mission statement should allow an organisation to visualise what it aims to achieve. We look at some effective mission statements, which set achievable and practical aims, whilst being couched in the vivid language of the emotions. The chapter concludes with a consideration of some of the barriers to effective vision faced by many organisations.

Everything you see or hear or experience in any way, is specific to you. You create a universe by perceiving it, so everything in the universe you perceive is specific to you.

Douglas Adams

One of the most crucial tasks for the senior managers of any organisation is to decide the overall direction for the company. They, and they alone, are charged with providing the 'vision' for the rest of the organisation.

A vision is something that can shape a way of working, and colour actions and policies. A vision needs to take account of intellectual and economic arguments, but at the same time to transcend them.

A vision may be easier to recognise than to explain. As Louis Armstrong is said to have said, when asked to define jazz, 'Man, if you've gotta ask, you'll never know'. Equally, it could be said that if you don't understand your firm's 'vision', perhaps you should not be working there at all. However, the responsibility for ensuring that the company's vision is widely recognised lies firmly with the senior managers. If your people don't understand that vision, there is little chance that they will be able to help the company to progress in the way you hope for.

An increasingly important aspect of the art of innovative management is to recognise how important a clear vision can be to an organisation's effectiveness. By creating such a vision, a company is much more likely to be able to have a say in its own future, and less likely to be merely reactive.

One reason for the growing importance of vision has been the trend towards decentralisation and globalisation. Organisations which are both widening their geographical scope and decentralising their centres of control increasingly need to find a unifying principle to inspire their far-flung employees. Developing a shared vision is essential for co-ordinated, coherent policies in this new kind of organisation.

Worldwide recession has been another important reason for the importance of a clear vision. More and more, companies are reviewing the way they treat their most costly overhead – their staff. Creating a company vision is seen as one way of getting more out of expensive workforces by providing something that each employee can subscribe to.

In this chapter, we will look at some of the ways in which successful organisations are using the idea of a vision to provide a clear direction for their businesses in the future.

VISION: MORE THAN JUST A 'MISSION STATEMENT'

A vision is a difficult thing to describe. By explaining it, you run the risk of destroying the 'magic' which is an essential part of its power. Nevertheless, there are some things which many effective corporate visions have in common.

Perhaps the most important aspect of any vision is that it should 'grab' people. At a time when companies are asking employees to take pay cuts or to accept freezes in their salaries, a vision needs to be especially inspiring. A good vision should be able to motivate people to work towards a common goal. It has to focus attention, and to galvanise employees into putting their heart and soul into the enterprise.

Not surprisingly, many executives find it difficult to formulate a clear vision for their organisations. In frustration, many respond by creating a 'mission statement'. Whilst this is certainly a step in the right direction, most mission statements fail to provide a truly compelling vision. Here are some examples:

> *We provide our customers with retail banking, finance and corporate banking products which will meet their credit investment, security and liquidity needs.*

> *[The company] is in the business of applying micro-electronics and computer technology in two areas: computer-related hard-*

*ware and computer enhancing services, which include infor-
mation education and finance.*

These mission statements are, of course, merely a straightforward
description of the company's products and services. Here is a
rather better example:

*We are made a unique company through employee involve-
ment. We promote from within regardless of race, religion,
creed, or educational background. Only through Attitude,
Pride and Enthusiasm will both our employees and our company prosper and grow.*

This mission statement uses more inspirational words, and sounds
more enthusiastic. However, what it lacks is a clear overall idea of
what the company is about. Instead, it conjures up a hodge-podge
of different values and beliefs.

Many of the words used to describe corporate visions are poorly
defined and confused. But to be effective, an organisation must
have a system of values that is clear and explicit. In this, the company is no different from individuals, who also have to make up
their own minds about their principles, and what is important to
them, before they can achieve their full potential.

In trying to arrive at a coherent vision, it can help to think of it
in terms of two major components, *fundamental values* and *an
inspiring image*. Much of the rest of this chapter will be devoted to
looking at each of these components in turn.

FUNDAMENTAL VALUES

The fundamental values are where a vision begins. They should be
capable of permeating an organisation's decisions, policies, and
actions, and colouring everything it does. These values should
form a system, rather like an individual person's system of values.
They will cover what the company regards as important in busi-

ness and community life, how it thinks the business should be conducted, the way the company is to respond to external issues, and what should be held to be inviolable.

Fundamental values can be expressed in one- or two-liners, like the American multifaceted 3M's:

> *The 11th commandment:*
> *Thou shalt not kill a new product idea*

or the outdoor equipment and clothing manufacturer, Patagonia's:

> *I believe in blurring the distinction between work and play. If*
> *you can't get up in the morning and look forward to going to*
> *work, then you're doing something wrong.*

Alternatively, a company can decide that it has several fundamental values. The Exxon Chemical corporation has created a system of 12 core values:

- Safety, health and environment
- Teamwork and partnership
- Leadership
- Ethics and integrity
- Quality and continuous improvement
- Diversity and international focus
- Enthusiastic pursuit of profit
- Candid and open communications
- External and community involvement
- Individual growth and development
- Innovation
- Enjoyment and fun.

In describing these values to the company's employees, Exxon's President used the words of Thomas Watson Jr, son of the founder of IBM:

Any organisation, in order to survive and achieve success, must have a sound set of beliefs on which it premises all its policies and actions ... The most important single factor in corporate success is faithful adherence to those beliefs. If an organisation is to meet the challenges of a changing world, it must be prepared to change everything about itself except those beliefs.

Herman Miller Company, the innovative furniture manufacturer, prefaces each of its company values with 'We believe':

- *We believe in good design in every aspect of our business.*
- *We believe that we should make a contribution to society.*
- *We believe in helping our people realise their full potential.*
- *We believe that profit, which is essential, is an outgrowth of making that contribution.*

As the examples quoted above have shown, there are many things that a company's values can touch on, including its own people, its customers, profit, products, as well as concepts like 'ethics' and 'society'.

If the vision is to be effective as a guiding force, however, it is essential that these values should be not only clear but also *authentic*. Rather than espousing the values it *thinks* it should have, an organisation should ask, 'What values do we *actually* hold dear?' Otherwise, people will respond with justifiable cynicism.

Once it has decided upon its fundamental values, an organisation will be in a much better position to describe its overall *purpose*. Ideally, it should be able to do this in just one or two sentences. These sentences should clearly and unequivocally convey how the organisation fulfils basic human needs. In this way, the purpose statement should aim to be both inspirational and enduring.

The purpose need not necessarily involve a description of products or customers. In fact, it should only mention either of these if they can be directly linked to a more fundamental need.

Here are some examples of inspirational corporate purpose statements:

> *We are in the business of preserving and improving human life.*
> *All of our actions must be measured by our success in*
> *achieving this.*
> Merck

> *To make people happy.*
> Disney

> *To serve as both a role model and a tool for social change.*
> Lost Arrow Corporation

> *To make a contribution to the world by making tools for*
> *the mind that advance humankind.*
> Apple

An effective purpose statement does more than just reflect the importance people attach to the company's work; it captures the organisation's soul. To produce such a statement, an organisation should ask itself questions like the following:

- *What would happen if we ceased to exist?*
- *Why don't we just sell off our assets?*
- *Why do we direct our energies in the way we do?*
- *How do the organisation's goals fit with our own personal goals?*

Vision is important at all levels of an organisation, and some organisations are now encouraging each function or department to devise their own purpose statements.

Two consultants recently described[1] how they helped one department to devise, and then to refine, a purpose statement. The departmental manager's first attempt at a purpose statement was:

> *To be the undisputed leader in providing the best estimating,*
> *project control and management support services.*

[1] Collins and Porras, *California Management Review*, Fall 1991.

The consultants asked the manager to consider *why* it was important to provide the best services to the organisation. After some discussion, the manager's answer reflected a deeper sense of purpose:

> *To provide the best estimating, project control, and management services so that we can help our company deliver high quality completed works to our customers.*

A further series of questions yielded an even better purpose statement:

> *To be the lifeblood and conscience of all those we serve.*

This example illustrates the fact that it can take a good deal of time, and several attempts, to arrive at a purpose statement that can really inspire people.

The importance of a well-defined purpose can hardly be overstated. It can help to determine who joins the company, and who succeeds inside it. It can attract those people whose personal values are in tune with the company's, and serve to deter those who do not espouse the same values.

The primary purpose of the purpose statement is to excite people *within* the organisation; it should not be seen as a marketing ploy. If the purpose statement does, in fact, inspire those outside the company as well, then that is an added bonus, but the main aim is to motivate an organisation's employees to commit themselves to its success.

AN INSPIRING IMAGE

We have been focusing on the part played by fundamental values in the development of a corporate vision. The second important component of any effective vision is an inspiring image which sums up these values, and makes them concrete.

We argued earlier that many organisations, struggling to formulate a vision, came up instead with a mission statement. Although a mission statement is not the whole of the story, it is, nevertheless an important part of any corporate vision. Indeed, an effective mission statement can go some way to providing just the concrete image that is needed.

A mission can be defined as the goal that focuses the organisation's efforts. It is narrower in scope than the organisation's purpose, and thus more concrete and easily visualised. If you like, the mission is the path to the purpose.

Like any other goal or objective, a company's mission should require effort, involve some risk, but at the same time be achievable. The aim of a mission statement is to translate the company's overall purpose or 'soul' into something that can be done. Consequently, it has to be crystal clear, and need no second explanation.

A mission statement needs to set a definite timescale for completion. However, over-emphasising *quantity* can dilute the strength of the message. Henry Ford's very picturesque mission, to 'democratise the automobile', would have lost its punch if he had reduced it to the exact number of automobiles to be produced. A good mission statement will often be based on the hunch that something is possible. President Kennedy's 1961 description of the NASA moon mission is a good example:

> *Achieving the goal, before this decade is out, of landing a man on the moon and returning him safely to earth.*

Frequently, organisations will define their mission in terms of their 'enemies'. This is a classic way to fire up the company troops. Pepsi's mission at one time was to 'Beat Coke!'. When Yamaha overtook Honda as the number one motorcycle manufacturer, Honda came up with this mission statement:

> *Yamaha wo tsubusu! (We will crush Yamaha).*

Nike, the leisure shoe manufacturer, has thrived on 'enemy' missions. It first set out to beat Adidas in the United States. As soon as it had achieved this, the company went into decline, and did not rally until faced with a new challenge from Reebok.

Although it taps into a very human desire to compete and to win, the 'enemy' mission does have disadvantages. It tends to foster short-term, reactive behaviour. Missions should be pro-active. Identifying the competition really belongs to the area of strategy (see Chapter 2), and should be tackled only after the mission statement has been   established.

One of the ways that a good mission statement can help an organisation to create a clear image of its vision is by picturing what things will be like once the mission is accomplished. In this way, it can provoke the necessary emotion and generate excitement about the organisation. In devising its mission statement, the company's executives need to think about what being successful means to them. Do they want the firm's picture on the cover of a magazine? Do they want state-of-the-art facilities? Or would they rather achieve recognition in their local communities?

Some managers feel uncomfortable about using the language of the emotions as part of their mission statements. But if an organisation wants to inspire excitement and commitment, then that is the language it will have to use. It is passion and conviction that motivates people, not bald factual statements.

Most importantly of all, a mission statement needs to be couched in vivid language. A good example comes from General Motors' mission statement:

> *As we succeed in ridding ourselves of the tentacles of ritual and bureaucracy ...*

Here, you can almost see the tentacles squeezing the lifeblood out of the company.

And, of course, the picture that is painted has to be something that the company genuinely wants to achieve, whether that is:

People will come to work because they would rather be here than anywhere else

or:

People will feel that they have contributed to the community in a positive way.

A CLEAR VISION

In this chapter, we have been looking closely at the different components making up a company vision. If these are tackled effectively, the organisation should be able to arrive at a clear, well-integrated corporate vision.

The following extracts[2] from the corporate vision statement of Giro Sport Design, a small sports goods manufacturer, provide a good example of such a vision.

- **Values and beliefs:**

Integrity is not to be compromised; be honest, consistent and fair.

Never cut corners; get the details right.

Style is important; all of our products should look great.

Teamwork should prevail; use 'we', not 'I'.

- **Purpose:**

Giro exists to make a positive impact on society – to make people's lives better – through innovative high quality products.

- **Mission:**

Our mission is ... to be to the bicycling industry what Nike is to athletic shoes, and Apple is to computers.

[2] Ibid

● **Description:**

The best riders in the world will be using our products in world class competition ... Our employees will feel that this is the best place they have ever worked ... We will receive unsolicited phone calls and letters from customers who say, 'Thank you for being in business: one of your helmets saved my life' ...

WHEN THE VISION FAILS

Often, after much agonising, organisations come up with quite ineffective vision statements. One of the chief causes of this failure is that companies are unable to approach the question of values from the point of view of the company's employees. Just as you don't sell washing machines by telling the customer how many knobs they have, but by describing what they will do, an effective mission statement does not enumerate the facts about the company, but rather its benefits to the employee. The result of an ineffective vision statement of this kind is that the workforce pays mere lipservice to it, and the chance of gaining real commitment is lost.

Sometimes the very words used in describing a company's vision show how out of touch senior managers can be with the people they want to reach. Jargon will only alienate those the vision is designed to motivate.

Even very effective vision statements can fail, of course, if they are not seen to be acted upon at the highest levels of an organisation. If a company's vision involves empowering its staff, and allowing them to make their own decisions, then the vision will fall into disrepute the moment it becomes clear that senior managers are in fact overturning these decisions for no apparent reason.

THE LEADERS AND THE LED

One of the most potent myths surrounding the concept of vision is the idea that a visionary organisation requires a charismatic leader blessed with near-mystical powers of charm and persuasion. But in fact, truly charismatic leaders can sometimes be quite destructive. Very often, they will have a strong personal vision, one which they are reluctant to share, and particularly unwilling to see diluted by debate and consensus.

Of course, strong leadership is an important aspect of developing a vision. An organisation's fundamental values often stem from its first leaders, who shape it and imprint it with their personal philosophies of life and business. Generally, they achieve this by their actions, rather than through pronouncements from on high. Richard Branson of Virgin and Anita Roddick of The Body Shop are good examples of leaders who have imbued their organisations with their own distinctive approaches to business.

As long as these leaders are active in the enterprise, the fundamental values they have established tend to be maintained. But as the organisation matures, and the leader's presence diminishes, these values can easily be dissipated. To become an organisation with vision, rather than just an organisation with a single visionary leader, these values must transcend the founders, and be understood by the masses. One of the biggest challenges for many successful small companies is to lessen their dependence on one or two individuals at the top. Only when values become identified with the company as a whole, rather than with particular individuals, can it evolve into a lasting, self-renewing organisation.

Another barrier to the effective implementation of a corporate vision is the well-documented phenomenon of chief executives retiring before the long-term process of instilling a vision into a company can be completed. Often, they are succeeded by a new chief with a quite different vision, who will set about dismantling much of the work done by his or her predecessor. Once again, these cases illustrate the dangers of entrusting a vision to particular individuals, rather than to the organisation as a whole.

For all the reasons described above, the process of formulating and acting upon a vision is a difficult one. Despite the difficulties, though, it is likely that a corporate vision will increasingly be seen as a vital tool in the armoury of innovative management. Without it, organisations are reduced to merely reacting to their ever-changing environments. With it, they stand at least a chance of creating their own futures.

3 STRATEGY FOR OPERATIONALISTS

In this chapter we discuss a new approach to strategic planning, the *future search conference*.

The rapid rate of change in the current business environment requires strategic planning to be considerably more flexible than it has been in the past. In particular, strategic thinking will have to rely less and less on the 'quick fix' and more and more on the idea of a 'learning organisation', in which every employee is involved in the development and refinement of strategic issues.

We examine what is meant by strategic thinking, and argue that a strategy is useless without the commitment of all those in the organisation, or a clear plan of how it is to be implemented. One of the major barriers to effective strategy making is the attitude of those senior managers whose responsibility it is. Very often, the very characteristics that have propelled a manager to the top of an organisation will prevent him or her from being a truly effective strategic thinker.

A common approach to strategic planning in many organisations is to compile a list of problems to be solved. A major disadvantage of this approach is that many of the problems may prove to be quite outside the control of the organisation.

One innovative alternative to this approach now being adopted by some organisations is to concentrate their efforts, instead, on coming up with a common picture of a preferred future, and 'working backwards' through the stages involved in getting to this ideal point. The idea of a future search conference draws on this basic concept. It involves drawing together a diverse group of those connected with the organisation to form a *learning community* whose task is to produce such a common vision of a preferred future. We look at the way such a conference can be designed and run.

Although the idea behind future search conferences is rooted in common sense, we see that there are pitfalls for those who only half understand its principles.

A search conference is a method for bringing whole systems in one room and focusing on the future.
Marvin Weisbord

The leaner, more demanding economy that seems set to be a permanent feature of the next decade means that many organisations are going to have to change their thinking about strategy planning. The annual planning cycle, and the 'ivory tower' of the corporate planning department are unlikely to be flexible enough to react to the likely changes in the business environment over the next few years.

Too many monolithic, prestigious companies around the world have demonstrated the fact that the mere existence of a pristine 'corporate strategy' does not ensure excellence, or even survival in the new climate. There is a growing awareness of the importance of linking strategy to issues of effective resource management. The expert's report and the 'quick fix', so beloved in the past by organisations   facing difficulties, are now widely acknowledged to be a waste of time and money.

So what kind of new approach is required? There is growing recognition of the need to link the so-called 'hard' issues of business direction to the so-called 'soft' issues of organisation development. In particular, business strategists need to be able to draw on the idea, developed by human resource specialists, of the 'learning organisation'. As well as continuous learning, ownership, commitment and understanding are the cornerstones of this concept.

In the context of business strategy, this approach means that strategic thinking should no longer be seen as the exclusive province of the board, but rather as a requirement of all employees. Adapting to changing circumstances needs to be seen as a continuous process, undertaken by all the members of an organisation. Of course, tackling entrenched attitudes, especially amongst senior management, is no easy task. Nevertheless, it seems increasingly likely that the capacity to learn quickly will be the hallmark of successful organisations in the future.

WHAT IS STRATEGIC MANAGEMENT?

There are many myths surrounding the phrases 'strategic management' and 'strategic planning'. One of the biggest myths is that these things can only be done by two kinds of people: either the top managers in an organisation, or external consultants. Senior managers are seen as prime movers in this area because it is thought that they are the only ones who really know the direction the company needs to take. External consultants are thought to have a role in what is seen as a highly theoretical exercise because of their understanding of the theories, and awareness of the possible options.

Perhaps it would be helpful first of all to define what we mean by a strategy. In very general terms, a strategy deals with how an organisation should behave in relation to its environment. We can see that the two crucial terms in this definition – the organisation, and the environment – will have a lot to do with the 'vision' the organisation has for itself, which will often be expressed by the company's mission statement (see Chapter 1).

A strategy, then, is a declaration of intent, which governs what will be done in particular circumstances. A strategy involves *reasoned* choices which have been arrived at after thought and discussion. It needs to be constantly reviewed in the light of changing circumstances.

The opposite of strategic thinking is expediency, a knee-jerk reaction to events (although, of course, some strategies may advocate ad hoc decision-making as the appropriate response to certain circumstances).

Many senior managers like to think of strategic planning as something they do, and then pass on to their managers for implementation. This, of course, is why so many strategic initiatives fail. Even if this approach was acceptable once, in the current climate of change it is a recipe for disaster. A strategic plan is meaningless without the following:

● Plans for implementation, including ways of generating commitment and dealing with contingencies

- Consultation with those who will be responsible for implementing the strategy.

BARRIERS TO EFFECTIVE STRATEGY-MAKING

Peter Vaill, in his recent book *Management as a Performing Art* (Jossey Bass 1992), uses three simple terms to describe the processes involved in strategic management:

- *Inward*: the feelings, values, energies and commitments of senior management
- *Outward*: the environment in which the organisation is working
- *Forward*: the future development of the organisation.

We can use these definitions to understand some of the major problems that can occur with strategic planning in many organisations. Let us start first with the problems associated with the inward dimension.

This dimension concerns the feelings, values, energies and commitments of an organisation's senior management. One of the major hurdles to effective strategic thinking is the fact that many members of this group will have values which are quite unsuited to good strategy-making.

Many, for instance, will be preoccupied with the need for action, at any cost. Indeed, some will have been promoted to their senior positions just because they have a strong desire to achieve, to *do*. On their way up the corporate ladder, many senior managers will have developed a competitive streak, and learned how to win at company politics. They may also have learned to base all their decisions on firm supporting evidence, and be unwilling to take decisions in the absence of such evidence.

Sound as they may be in other respects, these habits of mind are strongly at odds with the ability to think strategically. Managers who are strongly action-orientated will often take an overly 'hands-on' approach to the implementation of a strategy. They may refuse to let those with responsibility for implementing the strategy have a full say in how it is done. Senior managers of this kind may be better at doing, than at communicating their thoughts, and may become impatient with those who do not grasp the strategy easily.

On the other hand, the strong political instincts of some senior managers mean that they can become too engrossed in the impact of any strategy on their own plans and aspirations. This may lead to short-termism, and a strategy which takes inadequate account of the wider business arena.

A strong political streak also often explains the reluctance of many senior strategy-makers to see themselves as a team. Executives tend to become protective of their own interests, making any collaboration or sharing of resources impossible. An autocratic chief executive can further worsen the situation by use of the divide and rule tactic amongst his or her senior managers.

Strategic thinking is severely compromised by a competitive rather than co-operative approach. Trying new ideas is a risk, and if senior managers are unwilling to put the performance of their own staff in jeopardy, innovative approaches may die a premature death. Highly political senior managers can develop ingenious ways of avoiding responsibility for risk taking. A very common one is to fill up strategic meetings with discussion of the fine detail of implementation, rather than concentrating on truly strategic issues.

Finally, the tendency of senior managers to emphasis the need for concrete evidence to support any decisions they make can also hamper effective strategic thinking. Strategic planning often requires the development of quite new approaches, which have no precedent in the business, and this can make it hard to provide empirical evidence of their likely effects. Risk taking is part and parcel of the strategy-making process. Effective strategic thinking relies rather on the senior manager's intuitive business sense than on a thorough analysis of the current situation in the organisation.

For all of these reasons, it is very easy for genuine strategic planning to be hijacked by the attitudes of senior managers.

We have seen how barriers to effective strategy-making can

arise from the inward dimension – the values and attitudes of those senior managers responsible for strategic planning. But there are other problems, too, and these can be seen as arising from the outward dimension – the very environment in which the organisation is operating.

Russell Ackoff of the University of Pennsylvania said that corporate planning was like rain dancing: although it was unlikely to bring rain, it made the dancers feel better. This cynical view of strategic planning is based on the quite valid observation that attempting to predict the future on the basis of past trends is an uncertain business.

The environment in which many organisations operate is particularly uncertain at present, and becoming rapidly more so. Attempting to predict a company's circumstances even five years ahead in today's rapidly changing business climate is becoming more and more perilous.

A common approach to strategic planning is to build a long list of 'problems' to be tackled. These problems are then prioritised, and solutions proposed. Although this is an obvious way to set about the task, there is a danger that depression will set in as people identify problems which are beyond their control. In reaction to the frustration this produces, organisations will sometimes turn to short-term solutions, designed to deal with the symptoms rather than the causes of problems, and to reduce anxiety.

AN INNOVATIVE APPROACH

We have been examining some of the barriers and problems that can arise when an organisation attempts to think strategically. For the rest of this chapter, we will look at a new approach to the development of strategy, one that attempts to sidestep some of these difficulties.

The essence of this approach is to start, not from a list of perceived 'problems', but from a picture of a desired future situation. Its exponents argue that when conditions are in a constant state of flux, listing and prioritising 'old' problems do not help. Rather, what is required is a leap of the imagination.

The origins of this idea can be found in the work of Ronald Lippitt, founder of the NTL (National Training Laboratory) Institute and 'futurist' Edward Lindaman, who directed planning for the Apollo moon shot. In 1979, Lippitt and Lindaman argued that when people plan their actions by working backwards from a desired goal, they are more likely to show high levels of energy, enthusiasm, optimism and commitment.

One of the main reasons given for this finding is that by envisaging a concrete goal, people can see their aspirations as realistic and achievable. By thinking backwards from such a concrete, achievable goal, tackling the likely problems as they arise, people become more motivated to succeed. Starting with an achievable goal, rather than a list of 'problems', can lead to higher levels of optimism and enthusiasm.

This idea, of working backwards from a desired goal, was developed by a number of social psychologists and others who used it to develop the idea of a *future search conference* or *strategic futures conference*. Other versions of the idea are called *collaborative communities* or *visioning meetings*.

Future search conferences for strategic thinking

When it is applied to the development of organisational strategy, the idea of the future search conference involves drawing up a picture of the future that a wide range of those concerned with the organisation can subscribe to. This means getting together not just senior managers but also internal and external consultants, the company's suppliers, distributors; in short, anyone who has anything to do with the company's future development. The idea is to develop an outward-looking network of people, all of whom have the same goal in mind, but who may have very different ideas of how to get there, and widely varying skills and resources to achieve this end.

All the evidence is that using a future search conference to build a sense of common values and purpose can be particularly helpful to organisations facing significant change, whether this be changes in their markets, a merger, the introduction of new technology, or new leadership. It is perhaps at its most useful when organisations are at a turning point, knowing that they have to do something new, but unsure about precisely what this might be.

Marvin Weisbord has written[1] with great enthusiasm about the use of future search conferences as a strategic planning tool for organisations. Helped by some visionary chief executives, Weisbord has managed strategy conferences for organisations in banking, manufacturing, publishing, communications and the public sector. His view is that the way to improve strategic thinking is to move away from the use of experts to solve particular problems. Instead, *all* the interested parties should be brought in to tackle the revision of whole organisational systems. This, he argues, is the only way to achieve a sense of community and long-term commitment.

Increasing business globalisation means that organisations are having to bridge the gaps of culture, race, and hierarchy. Future search conferences – events that bring people together across diverse boundaries for the purposes of joint planning – seem to be ideally suited to bridging these gaps. The essence of these events can be summed up in the current business buzz word: partnership, empowerment, and learning.

The future search conference aims to combine a new way of doing things with a method people know only too well: holding meetings. Managers, of course, spend a large portion of their time either running or attending meetings. And, very often, managers will express dissatisfaction with the meetings they attend. Future search conferences are not primarily about better ways to run meetings. However, some proponents of this method argue that if future search conferences were held regularly – say once a quarter – they would obviate the need for more frequent, smaller meetings.

1 Weisbord, Marvin *Productive Workplaces*, (Jossey Bass, 1987).

Designing a future search conference

The design of a future search conference relies on the creative interplay between two key decisions: who is invited, and what they are asked to discuss. There is also a third factor implicit in the design of any such event, namely how it is conducted.

Typically, between 20 and 40 people will meet for up to two-and-a-half days. It is important that these people should be drawn from a wide variety of different backgrounds. They should generally be people whose work directly or indirectly affects that of the other participants, although they may never meet in the course of their normal work.

During the conference, the participants complete a series of tasks. Typically, there might be five tasks, each taking around three hours to complete. The idea behind these tasks is to explore the past, present, and future of their organisation, its environment, and the role they themselves play in it.

The focus of future search is the whole organisation, and its circumstances, its history and ideals, and the constraints and opportunities open to it. The aim is to focus as widely as possible on national and global trends, rather than on the parochial and close to home. Throughout the conference, everybody is encouraged to contribute information and ideas, to discuss them, and to make joint decisions.

The participants are encouraged to form a 'learning community'. There are no chairpersons, although discussions are structured, and parameters set in terms of behaviour, subject matter, time limits, and so on. The discussions generally take place in mixed groups, usually of about eight people. The groups can be made up of those drawn from similar functions, or those with a common 'stake' in the organisation, or participants can decide on their own groupings.

Each group has to manage its own tasks of dialogue, learning and planning. These groups report their findings back to the conference, where they are preserved and recorded. The conference is facilitated, but not led, by either the organisation's senior managers, or members of the human resource department. There is little that these managers can do directly to influence the rate of learning in the community, other than to maintain and display faith in its willingness and ability to learn at all.

It is important that the 'learning community' should dig into its own resources of expertise and experience, rather than turn to experts, in order to encourage confidence and commitment. For this reason, future search conferences avoid 'key-note speakers', and, although experts may be invited to the conference, their input is seen as being of no greater importance than anyone else's.

Participants are allowed to express their differences during the discussions. Indeed, it is often a feature of really effective conferences, ones where the 'right' people have been invited, that there are plenty of unresolved conflicts and disagreements. However, the aim of the conference is to find common ground and establish joint aspirations, rather than to rework old problems. Of course, conflicts do not magically disappear overnight, but the aim is to encourage a more constructive and co-operative approach, where differences can be appreciated, because there is no attempt to reconcile them.

A typical plan for a future search conference might be as follows:

Task 1   Review of the past:
Milestones in society, in oneself, and in the organisation over a set number of years.

Task 2   View of the present (i):
The external forces that shape our lives and the organisation now.

Task 3   View of the present (ii):
Positives and negatives in terms of the way we relate to the future of the organisation, i.e. things that we need to leave behind, and things that we need to take forward.

Task 4   View of the future (i):
An ideal scenario or scenarios.

Task 5   View of the future (ii):
              Action planning in groups.

A matter of common sense?

The founding principle of the future search conference is that, given the right task, and the right people, in the right setting, unprecedented decisions can be made and effective action taken. This sounds just like common sense, so the question has to be why it is not done always, and by everybody. One reason why this approach is not more widely adopted may be that in many organisations strategic planning and strategic meetings aim less for breakthroughs than for control. That is, the political will, and fear of losing control of the leaders of organisations often takes over from the desire to try a new approach.

Many organisations may grasp part of the equation but fatally forget other parts. For instance, they may organise strategic planning with the right group of people, but give them the wrong task. Indeed, many organisations divide their strategic thinkers into small task forces which have no shared appreciation of the organisation's strategy as a whole. This narrow, operational, problem-solving approach is likely to focus on detail, and may keep a lot of people busy, without improving the organisation's effectiveness. This is one reason why quality circles may fail to work. By dividing strategic thinking up into small parcels, they miss the big picture. By limiting their strategic thinking to solving problems and managing conflict, they miss the common ground.

Some facilitators have tried to run shorter future search conferences for single functions within an organisation. But attempts like these reveal a fundamental lack of understanding of the principles behind such a conference; working with too narrow a group, in too short a time frame, with too closed an objective is unlikely to achieve any kind of breakthrough.

If implementation is the key to effective strategy-making, then it is essential that everyone with a role in it should have a personal commitment to, and understanding of, the wider picture. It is this insight which forms the basis of the future search approach, and provides its distinctive contribution to the art of strategic management.

CASE STUDY

Digital's strategy for merger

In this case study we look at the way an American computer company, Digital, has used a future search conference to help develop a strategy for its new merged user information business.

In January 1992, the organisation development department of Digital Equipment Corporation was asked to consult with the managers of two Digital groups, the Corporate User Information and Publications Group (CUIP), and the Documentation and Course Development Group, (DCD).

CUIP was part of the engineering department and was responsible for developing all the manuals and other documentation that accompanied Digital's computer products and services. Their goal was to help Digital's customers to install, use and maintain their Digital computers. Similarly DCD's role was to help users of Digital's products by developing and teaching technical courses that would help users of Digital's products to learn about the hardware and the software.

Both organisations were funded by other Digital groups, who contracted with them to develop documentation and training for new products and services. They would typically collaborate on various projects. In 1991, the management teams of CUIP and DCD proposed that the two organisations merge, to make contracting and communication easier for their internal clients. The proposal was approved, and the combined organisation of 1200 people consolidated under a Vice President in the Engineering Department.

Although the merger was generally assumed to be a good idea, it was not clear how the combined business should be run, to build on the strengths of both groups, as they had different organisational structures and very different cultures. Consequently, a new team was created to drive the process of the merger. The Organisation Design Team (ODT) was made up of eight people in different positions across the organisations. Team members temporarily left their normal positions in order to work full time on the team. The team's goals were to:

- Define a strategy for the new merged businesses
- Design an appropriate organisation for the new business

The consultants proposed that the ODT should first look at how they planned to focus their new business, having combined both documentation and course development functions. To do this it was decided that a future search conference should be a major part of the overall reorganisation process.

The idea was to provide a forum for people to challenge the accepted ways of doing things, to openly debate the needs of the organisation, and, most importantly, to create a vision of how computer users would want to access information about products and services in the future. What was unique about the search conference was that it would involve participation from people outside the two merging organisations, and even from outside the company.

In addition to the future search conference, the team was to use a wide range of methods in order to design the new, merged organisation's structure, its people and reward systems, its information and decision-making systems, and a system for organisational 'renewal'.

The ODT's first task was to talk to the users, sponsors and customers of the two groups' services, so that they developed a first-hand understanding of the needs and issues of their stakeholders. On the basis of this investigation, they started to plan the future search conference.

The future search conference

The conference was called *Creating the future of information – no more lessons, no more books, no more user's dirty looks,* and was held at the Boston Computer Museum in April 1992. The conference topic was chosen specifically so that participants could explore how computer users receive information and support, and they coined the term 'user information support', to encompass product documentation and support.

Forty participants or 'stakeholders' were invited to the conference. They included funders from other Digital groups, representatives from CUIP and DCD, and the ODT themselves. A third of the participants came from outside Digital and were either customers who used Digital's product information and training, or product information experts from other high technology companies and from the academic world.

Each participant received a briefing package with materials to help them prepare for the conference. They were invited to bring along to the conference a newspaper or magazine article on an issue of importance for the future, and an information 'artefact' relating to their own experience with computer product information. The conference facilitators were drawn from members of Digital's consultancy group.

The conference was designed to achieve three goals:

- To create a collective vision of the future of user information support
- To build a sense of community among the people who could make this vision happen
- To set the stage for the future of the new, merged organisation.

The conference agenda included three kinds of exercises. The first kind, focused on the businesses' *history*, aimed to develop a shared perspective of a common past. The second type focused on *current* external events, trends, and developments that were shaping the future of the business.

The third kind of exercise focused on creating ideal but feasible *future* scenarios for the year 2012. These were designed to disconnect the participants from the constraints of the present, allowing a free flow of ideas and creating a vision for the future.

All the participants would be involved in all the exercises, while the facilitators managed the process and the time. The participants were seated at round tables. For some of the exercises, they were in mixed groups, and for others, they were with their stakeholder groups. Before beginning any of the exercises, the facilitators laid down certain ground rules:

- All ideas should be accepted as valid
- All ideas should be written up on flip charts
- Time must be strictly managed
- Participants should seek to discover common ground and possibilities for action
- Differences and problems should be acknowledged, explored, and understood, but no attempt should be made to resolve them.

The facilitator also explained what it should be possible to achieve during the conference:

- To compile information that could become the basis for a shared understanding
- To acknowledge, understand and explore differences and problems
- To create visions of the future
- To seek, confirm and document emerging consensus.

Setting out clearly from the outset what could be achieved and explaining the ground rules of behaviour were crucial to the success of the event. By doing this, the facilitators provided a benchmark against which to measure the effectiveness of the event and established norms of acceptable behaviour.

Exercise 1

In order to gain a common appreciation of the history of the businesses, and the changes people in those businesses had experienced, the first exercise focused the participants on three major topics:

- **Global society**
  What has happened and why it is significant

- **User information and support**
  Products and services in general
  Computer products
  Digital's products

- **Individuals**

  Professional experience

  Major career events

  Personal involvement in user information support.

Initially, each individual noted their own ideas, and then copied them on to sheets of paper taped to the wall. When the exercise was complete there was over 12 feet of flip chart paper covered with ideas. This bank of information served as the basis for future tasks and discussions. In fact, it served as a graphical representation, not only of the history of information technology, but also of the diversity and richness of the experience and backgrounds of the participants. While creating this 'database', it became apparent that the participants were already beginning to discover common ground and common viewpoints.

Exercise 2

The next task set for the participants was to interpret themes and patterns from the database taped to the wall. The participants were divided into five mixed groups, and each group focused on one section of the database.

Group 1 was asked to produce an analysis of *global society*. On one side of a flip chart, they drew up two tables. One characterised the changes which had taken place during three time periods, the 1960s, the 1970s, and the 1980s/1990s. The other table described the elements that would make up an ideal future over the next decade.

Group 2 focused on the history of *user information support*. They looked at milestones and critical changes, at the development of user information support in the three time periods, and projected an ideal future for user information support.

Group 3 analysed developments in *user information support in the computer industry*, and decided on the most desirable future for this activity.

Group 4 analysed developments in the way that *Digital* has provided user information support, and identified milestones and critical changes over the three time periods.

Group 5 looked at the professional experience present at the conference, examined similarities and differences between the participants, and described the potential of the group.

By the time this task was completed, the conference had a clear picture of their collective view of the past. This was a firm foundation, and one that they needed in order to start building a common vision of the future. It had also encouraged the participants to talk to each other, discovering common ground in an unthreatening way.

Exercise 3

The next task involved dividing the participants into groups of those with a similar 'stake' in the organisation. Each stakeholder group prepared a two-to-three minute report addressing the following questions:

- Of the themes raised so far, which are the most significant for your stakeholder group?
- With which of those themes do you believe the other stakeholder groups will agree and with which will they disagree?

Common themes emerging from many of the presentations included:

- The trend towards a global society
- Technological advances, and their effect on the creation of information
- Increased diversity in the experience, background and function of information technology users
- A desire for the needs of product users to become an integral part of the information produced about those products.

The internal 'clients' discussed the need for more customer-orientated, effective targeting of product information, and the need to maintain cost and quality standards. The discussions of the customer group were quite passionate. They felt dissatisfied because they felt that Digital and other stakeholders were not listening to their needs. They argued that Digital had not made the transition from being a computer engineering company to a greater emphasis on the needs of its information technology users. They also claimed that the company needed to provide better, customer-driven training.

Exercise 4

When it came to the fourth task, focusing on the events and trends affecting behaviour today, many of the participants' comments were influenced by the problems identified by the customer group in the previous task. Some of the learning and insights gained from this session were as follows:

- The product information that Digital provided needed to be *tailored* to the customers' needs, and delivered in a more directed fashion. Some people felt that the business provided either too little or too much information.
- Previous restructuring at Digital had reduced customer access to people at Digital. Many customers missed the personal contact they had previously had. To give the customers what they needed, 'the walls would have to come down'.
- Digital needed to adopt a more global perspective when considering the future, and to see whether any of its successful solutions could be shared with parts of the world at an earlier stage of development.

As part of this exercise, the participants created a 'mind map' to capture the main points of the discussions so far. Mind mapping is a way of recording and connecting all the ideas and feelings that occur to a group, using the members' own words. The facilitator does not screen or evaluate any contribution, and the person naming the issue decides where the issue gets placed on the map. In this case, the facilitator started the mind map off with some phrases that had emerged in the course of the previous two days' discussions.

After the mind map was completed, each stakeholder group was asked to put colour-coded stickers against the parts of the map that seemed most important to them. This involved adding some new themes to the mind map, such as the need for the organisation to move away from a hierarchical structure to the use of mixed teams. Another message was that if user information support is valued as part of a Digital computer product, then information designers must be seen as equal members of the product team.

Exercise 5

In this exercise, each stakeholder group was asked to address three or more themes from the mind map. Among the themes chosen were:

- Customer- and user-focused information
- Delivery of real quality
- Partnerships
- Delivery of information through new media.

Each stakeholder group took each of their chosen themes, and identified what they were doing about it now, and what they should do about it in the future. One of the themes chosen by the customer group, for example, was partnership. The group felt that Digital's customers wanted to move beyond a traditional vendor relationship, where they only dealt with the marketing and sales departments, but were finding it difficult to do this. For the future, these customers wanted to deal directly with subject experts and to share in the development of new ways to support the information needs of users.

Exercise 6

For the sixth exercise, the participants were split into the same mixed groups as had been used in Exercise 2. The aim of the exercise was to assess the current reality for Digital. The overall assessment emerging from this exercise was that the company was ready and eager to improve the way it provided user information support, and that it had the necessary talent and support from its senior management.

The participants did, however, express concern that it would be difficult to overcome inertia and resistance to change within the organisation. They also felt that it would be difficult to overcome the Digital bureaucracy and encourage more interaction between customers and those providing user information support.

The participants acknowledged that it would be difficult to introduce widespread changes while maintaining current levels of information support; after all the company still had to make a profit. It was felt that Digital would need to look again at its reward systems, and consider issues such as rewarding teamwork and improved communication with customers.

Exercise 7

The aim of this exercise was to imagine an ideal future, one that the participants would be willing to work at. The facilitator asked the participants to think back to Digital in 1972, and consider how much had changed since then. Next, he asked them to imagine themselves in the year 2012, and to describe the relationships that now existed between products, services and people. Each mixed group was to decide upon one future scenario, and then create their vision in an imaginative way to present back to the large group.

In imagining the future, participants were asked to follow these guidelines:

- Scenarios had to be feasible
- The participants had to really believe in the scenarios
- The participants had to be willing to work for the scenarios
- No consideration should be given to cost.

The scenarios resulting from this exercise were generally well thought-out and creative. Many of them seemed to relate to a more distant future than 2012, but all of them showed the growing importance of useful, accessible user information support.

After the final scenario had been presented, participants were asked to discuss the feasibility of each of the scenarios. Overall, the conference felt that there were some major barriers to achieving the scenarios. These included the lack of an overall leader who could inspire real change, the similar lack of a business model of how the change might be implemented, and the need for ethical structures to protect privacy in the new information age. Participants also expressed concern about language barriers and whether there would be enough money for continued research and development in the new company.

Exercise 8

The eighth and final exercise focused on action planning. The facilitator asked the participants to think about what had taken place during the three days of the conference, and to consider what insights had been gained.

Participants were asked to come up with two things that they would do differently, back at work, as a result of the conference. Suggestions included establishing more contact with customers; establishing links with other people in Digital outside their usual range of contacts; challenging others to take the opportunity to develop; and championing change generally within the company.

One participant reminded the group about the importance of actually taking action on the basis of these good resolutions. The facilitator pointed out that the three days were a beginning. The participants had chosen the road they would prefer to take, it was up to them to actually follow it. The conference closed with a quotation from a Buddhist text:

> *The master in the art of living makes little distinction*
> *between his work and play, his labour and his leisure,*

his mind and his body, his education and his recreation,
his love and his religion.
He hardly knows which is which.
He simply pursues his vision of excellence in whatever he does,
leaving others to decide whether he is working or playing.
To him he is always doing both.

Conclusion

Those involved in the conference felt that it had resulted in a shared view of the role of user information support amongst Digital's stakeholders, and a renewed sense of the importance of partnership.

The organisation had received a strong message about the importance of its customers and their needs. The conference had also resulted in a new definition of 'integrated' product information, which gave greater emphasis to the user's work context. Most importantly, the participants had generated a clear view of a desired future for the new, merged organisation, one that was common to them all, and which they felt able to work towards.

Using these results of the conference as a foundation, the Organisation Design Team began to develop a business strategy for the new, merged organisation. As a starting point, the team decided on a new name for the group: Information Design and Consulting. This name captured the essence of what the two separate groups were about, which was to help the users of Digital's products and services acquire the knowledge that they needed to work effectively. The new group would do this by applying their expertise in course development and documentation. By doing this they would make Digital's products more meaningful, and generate profit for both Digital and its customers. The idea of *integrated* product information, coined by the future search conference, has become the central goal of the new company.

The team decided that the structure of the new, merged company should be the last thing to be designed. The first thing to be decided upon was the organisational characteristics, as they would provide a framework for how the new organisation would operate. Only after these had been decided would the team look at the new company's people and reward systems, its information and decision-making systems, a system for organisational 'renewal', and, finally, its structure.

The team came up with six characteristics that define the new organisation:

- The organisation is to be driven by users' needs, and will make products that are meaningful in the workplace
- It will be based on extended teams, which will include customers, thus breaking down walls both inside and outside the company
- It will act strategically, and clearly envisage the path by which it can achieve its goals
- It will be based on the skill of its workforce, and value people's contribution. A wide range of skills will be equally valued in order to ensure integrated user information support
- Decisions will be made by the people closest to the source, bearing in mind the needs of the entire system
- The organisation will renew its processes based on the learnings of each member.

Next the team decided upon five values that the organisation would aim to live by:

- Collaboration
- Balance
- Openness
- Innovation
- Respect for the individual.

The new organisational structure through which these values will be achieved has done away with several layers of hierarchy, to produce a more flexible organisation, one in which information can flow more efficiently to those who need it. Teams are central to this structure and it is hoped that by 1997 each team will be self managed. To support the new way of working, peer evaluations, team rewards, and team skill development have all been built into the design.

Three overlapping goals have been set for everyone in the new organisation:

- Team goal

  To ensure that every team finds and uses some vehicle for receiving input from clients, customers, and other users
- Product goal

  To make products more 'meaningful', and to make the user's own work context more central to each product. For example, support information should focus less on 'how to use Digital's report writing package', and more on 'how to write a report for your boss every month'
- Business goal

  To move towards the consulting and intellectual property business by 1994. To do this by augmenting the skills of people in the business and changing the way they work.

The new structure, based on teams, is designed to support and facilitate the work of individuals in the new company, rather than to control it. The structure of the teams is intended to emphasise individual responsibility and empowerment. Each team is made up of the skills needed to meet particular client and customer needs.

The new organisation is starting with a decided plus: a common vision of what business they are in. But of course, introducing changes on this scale will never be easy. A new 'leadership team' was put in place in October 1992, whose responsibility is to implement the new business direction and organisation design. They expect to have the new structure in place by Spring 1993 and to be well on the way to making the design a reality. However, there are major challenges in infrastructure still be to resolved, such as developing 'libraries' of information to support sharing and reduce re-invention. And putting any group of people, however committed, through change on this scale is bound to produce a certain degree of confusion and denial.

The organisation is, to a certain extent, entering unknown territory. However, it believes that by starting from a common understanding of its preferred future, the organisation will be in a better position to exploit the increasingly competitive marketplaces of the '90s.

4 USING AND DEVELOPING INTUITION

In this chapter we look at the phenomenon often known as 'intuition'. Intuitive thinking – whether it is a flash of inspiration, creative new ideas, or the product of years of experience – is an increasingly valued part of innovative management. An intuitive approach is increasingly sought after in areas of business where old assumptions are being challenged, and new methods of working are required.

Intuition very often goes hand-in-hand with a confident approach to business problems, and a willingness to grasp the opportunities offered by change and upheaval. It is a necessary counterweight to more analytical ways of thinking about business.

We argue that intuitive thinking is something that can be learned and fostered. Much of what is often called intuition is the result of years of experience and a deep understanding of a subject. But there are also techniques that can be adopted to sharpen intuitive thinking.

In this chapter, we examine the three stages of creative or intuitive thinking. We argue that intuition needs to be given space to breathe. Often, merely taking time away from the workplace can fulfil this function, but increasingly managers are turning to other techniques, such as meditation. Finally, we argue that any intuition needs to be thoroughly evaluated and weighed up before it can form the basis of innovative action.

This term [intuition] does not denote something contrary to reason, but something outside the province of reason.
Carl Jung

We all play guessing games with life. Those who guess well are called intuitive; those who are intuitive, however, do not think they are guessing.
Philip Goldberg

The dilemma of any statesman is that he can never be certain about the probable course of events. In reaching a decision, he must inevitably act on the basis of an intuition that is inherently unprovable. If he insists on certainty, he runs the danger of becoming a prisoner of events.
Henry Kissinger

All over the world, business people are recognising the benefits of allowing their imaginations a free rein. 'Intuition' is being seen as a real plus in the fight to gain competitive advantage. By summoning up the irrational, companies hope that they may find a 'creative' solution to their problems.

Intuitive decision makers are especially valuable when new trends are emerging, and the old assumptions guiding business have to be challenged. New ideas often depend for their inspiration on 'intuitive' insights.

People often look at successful entrepreneurs who have succeeded without any formal qualifications, and feel that the secret of their success must lie in a 'gut instinct' or a 'nose for business'. Most people would agree that intuition is an important skill for business people to have. Unfortunately, when you ask them to define what they mean by 'intuition', you are likely to end up with a huge range of different answers. Even experts who have studied it in depth do not always agree on what intuition really is.

In this chapter, we will take a closer look at the concept of intuition and its importance for innovative management. We examine what is involved in the process of intuition, and how it can be used to stimulate creative solutions to business problems.

WHAT IS INTUITION?

As a starting point, let us see if we can come up with a rough definition of intuition. Most would agree that intuition is:

- A quick or ready insight or new idea, based in some way on past experience, feelings, and memories
- A kind of understanding gained without recourse to the usual processes of rational thought
- A way of arriving at conclusions on the basis of limited information
- Something you are born with, but which can be developed and extended.

One important aspect of intuition, when it is applied to business people, is surely the ability to decide what is important, in other words, to see the wood for the trees. The ability to see the big picture, and to grasp the opportunities it offers can go some way towards explaining the success of people like Steve Jobs, one of the founders of Apple Computers and founder of NeXT Computers. As an entrepreneur, he took a gamble, but one based on the intuition that people would, indeed, buy personal computers if they were offered them.

Intuitive people tend to enjoy operating in environments where change is the norm. They enjoy the challenge of thinking on their feet. The worst thing that can happen to people like this is to be put into a routine job. The great leaders in the public and private sector also stand out because of their sense of timing.

It seems that intuition cannot be had to order. It comes 'from within'. Part of the battle seems to be having the courage of your own intuition, of knowing how to value it. It is no coincidence that 'intuitive' people tend to be confident, independent individuals. These traits are necessary in order to open oneself up to unpredictable, surprising and often unconventional insights from within.

Low self-esteem, on the other hand, can lead to a mistrust of anything that comes from within oneself. Fear of change, excessive need for security, and fear of uncertainty can stifle intuition by seeking controls, or explanations and justifications for intuitive insights. Under those rules, intuition can never flourish into innovation.

A defeatist attitude, 'we will never find an answer', tells the intuitive mind not to bother. It is confident thoughts that encourage intuition and its positive insights. The person who is sure that they can manage unpredictable, changing, or ambiguous situations is more likely to act intuitively. In the current 'whitewater' of business uncertainty, the ability to look confidently for the unexpected is crucial.

Of course, intuition is not to be confused with flying by the seat of your pants, or with merely wishful thinking. The power of any intuition lies in its ability to influence one's actions. Mozart may have been able to hear the music in his head, but he still had to write it down!

The kind of awareness that enables so-called 'primitive' peoples to sense danger, when there are no physical clues to its presence, is a highly-developed form of intuition. It differs from instinct in that, while instinct remains unconscious, intuition is fully conscious, although a person may act on intuition without stopping to rationalise it. They simply know something without knowing *how* they know it.

No discussion of intuition would be complete without some mention of the 'left brain–right brain division'. This romantic theory suggests that the two hemispheres of the brain exhibit a division of labour, the 'right brain' concentrating on visual patterns and creative, non-linear thought, while the 'left brain' specialises in analytical processes and the use of language. In its most simplistic form, the theory holds that the left hemisphere carries out the day-to-day, routine work, while the right hemisphere is responsible for the creative sparks or intuition that produce works of art, scientific discovery and great management.

Unfortunately, the evidence only supports the less picturesque probability that there is *some* specialisation in each of the two hemispheres. There is no evidence that the right hemisphere is capable of problem-solving, decision-making, or discovery quite independently of the left hemisphere.

In any case, the desire to pinpoint the exact seat of intuition in the brain is perhaps less important than discovering how we can improve on what intuition we do possess.

One of the unfortunate consequences of the 'left brain–right brain' theory is the temptation to classify people as *either* 'intuitive' *or* 'analytical'. It is, of course, very unlikely that any effective manager will be able to do without a balance of *both* of these.

Of course, there may be a continuum of more and less 'intuitive' and more and less 'analytical' decision-making styles by means of which different managers can be described. And different problems may require different amounts of each. One very important managerial skill, and one which can be developed, is the ability to see whether an analytical or a more intuitive response would be more appropriate in any given situation.

A colleague and philosopher, John, is well known for his orderly, systematic and logical arguments. Yet he describes himself as being extremely intuitive, and says that his mind is always making wild leaps that turn out to be right. When reminded of his reputation as a thinker, he said, 'I've learned to construct arguments to justify my intuitions. But they always come *afterwards*.'

THE IMPORTANCE OF INTUITION

We have argued that some managers, when confronted with a problem, are likely to make more use of intuitive processes in solving it, while other managers may make relatively more use of analytical processes. Both intuitive and analytical thought-processes are important.

But there are times when it is very important to let go of a more analytical approach, and to take a 'leap of faith'. Decision-making and problem-solving are all too often seen as a series of formal steps, each one taken only after you are certain of the previous step.

Although objective setting and logical problem-solving can be important, they can be followed too mechanistically. When the problem confronting an organisation is something quite new, over-dependence on these processes can lead to what Ashley Montague, the anthropologist, has called 'psychosclerosis'. By blocking intuition and creative solutions, this can lead to frustration and a shortage of options.

Although structure and order are crucial elements of the productive process, intuition cannot be left out altogether. What is necessary is a flexibility of style, and a readiness, when appropriate, to give up some certainty and control in order to let intuition play a part. This does not mean abandoning goal setting altogether, just taking some risks.

Edward de Bono, whose teaching and many books on 'lateral thinking' have made a significant contribution to the current thinking about intuition and creativity, tells an interesting story about an office building that was built with too few lifts. The office workers complained about the delays this caused, and some were so incensed that they were prepared to resign. Many solutions were proposed, including staggering work hours, building new lifts, and replacing the existing lifts with better ones. The problem with all these proposals was that they were expensive and would involve a lot of disruption.

Finally, someone suggested a simple solution: hang mirrors near the doors of the lifts! The office workers became so engrossed in adjusting themselves or performing in front of the mirrors, or in watching each other do this, that the annoyance of waiting for the lifts was alleviated. In this example, the solution was arrived at by taking another view of the issue: the problem was not so much the lack of lifts, as the impatience of the staff.

Intuition draws on our subconscious experiences, and uses them to foster new insights. The subconscious works faster than the conscious, and is much more flexible. The theory is that the subconscious mind acts without being hampered by the need to evaluate each piece of information, as the conscious mind does.

INTUITION AND INNOVATIVE MANAGEMENT

There is increasing awareness of the importance of intuition in business. It would seem to be a particularly helpful management tool in the following, increasingly common, situations:

- When there is a high level of uncertainty
- When there is no precedent on which to base decisions
- Where 'reliable' facts are limited or completely unavailable
- Where time is limited
- Where there are several plausible options to choose from, all of which are equally well supported by reason and evidence.

A great deal of what is referred to as an experienced manager's 'intuition' is likely to involve learned behaviour. Much of it will be analogous to the way an experienced driver drives a car. Learner drivers learn to notice a red light, recognise that this means they should stop, and that this involves applying the brakes with their right foot. For an experienced driver, on the other hand, the sight of the red light 'automatically' leads them to apply the brakes.

In a doctoral thesis,[1] R. Bhasker compared the thinking processes of business school studsents and experienced business people when analysing a business case study. As expected, the experienced business people carried out the analysis very quickly, with little evidence of conscious thought, while the students took much longer, going through a fairly complex series of analytical processes.

What experienced drivers and experienced managers have in common is the ability to recognise patterns they have encountered

---

[1] Bhasker, R., (doctoral dissertation) *Problem solving in Semantically Rich Domains* (Graduate School of Industrial Administration, Carnegie Mellon University, 1978).

before, and to take the necessary action, without having to go through all the processes in between. There is, indeed, a kind of learning continuum. At one end, the learner will be in a state of *unconscious incompetence*, when he or she is unaware even of what is involved in competence. Moving to the next stage, *conscious incompetence*, may require someone else pointing out the learner's incompetence, or a flash of inspiration on the part of the learner himself or herself. Without the rather uncomfortable stage of conscious incompetence, it is impossible to move to the next stage, *conscious competence*.

The learner driver who is trying to grasp the idea of changing gear, depressing the clutch and the accelerator, looking in the mirror, and indicating, all at the same time, is in the conscious incompetence stage. Only after considerable practice will the qualified driver realise that he or she has been driving on the motorway for 10 minutes, overtaken several other cars, put a cassette on the stereo, and called someone on the mobile phone without thinking about it. It is then that the driver can be called unconsciously competent. For this driver, driving has become 'intuitive' behaviour. (Sometimes, however unconscious competence can lead us perilously close to unconscious incompetence...!)

It seems that innovative managers use intuition in several ways:

- To sense when a problem exists
- To perform well-learned behaviour patterns quickly
- To synthesise bits of information and experience into an integrated picture
- To check on the results of a rational analysis
- To bypass in-depth analysis and come up with a fast, plausible solution.

Intuition is neither the opposite of rationality, nor a matter of mere random guesswork, as we have seen. And, most importantly, 'intuitive behaviour' can be learned through experience and the acquisition of a deeper understanding of an area or subject.

HOW DOES INTUITION WORK?

Graham Wallas[2] has argued that the process of generating new ideas consists of three stages:

- Incubation
- Illumination
- Verification.

In order to exploit the potential benefits of intuitive thinking, managers need to pay attention to each of the three stages. We have already seen how 'intuitive behaviour' can, to a certain degree, be learned through experience. But there are also techniques which can be adopted to sharpen one's intuitions, and harness the power of intuitive thought.

Incubation

At this stage of the intuitive process, new ideas are brewing. This can happen while walking (Rousseau), on a bus (Poincaré), in bed (the hotel owner Conrad Hilton), or up a mountain (Nicola Phillips).

If intuition is to be set free, it needs space to breathe. Numerous accounts of innovative thinkers give the impression that great ideas are as likely as children to be conceived in bed. People often say they are going to 'sleep on an idea', and sleep, which gives a free rein to the subconscious, is certainly a major source of new ideas.

When Conrad Hilton bid for the Stevens Corporation, which was going to the highest bidder in a closed auction, he submitted a sealed bid for $165,000. When he woke up the following morning, he found that he was thinking of the number 180,000, so he changed his bid. As a result, he secured the property, and a $2 million profit (the next highest bid was $179,800).

Intuitive breakthroughs tend to occur when the creator takes a break from the work in hand. This is one of the many reasons why it is thought to be a good idea to take people away from the work-

2 Wallas, G., *The Art of Thought* (Harcourt Brace, 1929).

place in order to think strategically or to build teams (see Chapters 2 and 3). Outdoor development takes this one step further, by plunging people into a quite new and unknown environment in order to stimulate new ideas (see Chapter 7).

Our modern way of life is not conducive to creativity. Constant bombardment of the senses and distractions of all kinds, the over-powering pressure and pace of modern life, and the idea that happi-ness lies in worldly success and material possessions, all conspire to inhibit intuitive thought. Acknowledgment of this has led to the development of many 'New Age' philosophies (see Chapter 12) and techniques to improve creative thinking. Some executives have taken to meditation to clear their minds, and make room for the subconscious, although 'meditation' is a word that many business people would think twice about using in public, often preferring to describe it as 'focused concentration' instead.

Some ideas to clear the mind can sound positively cranky, but it is surely a sensible precaution for any manager to make sure that they set aside some time and space to encourage new ideas.

Illumination

This stage of the creative process is the moment when light dawns on a new idea, what Roy Rowan, the journalist, calls the 'Eureka'. Often this stage will involve a very heightened state of awareness. It is the most difficult stage of intuition to describe, but many would agree that it sharpens all the other cognitive faculties. Illumination has been described as being like standing on the top of a building, suddenly getting a quite new perspective on a familiar view.

Verification

In this, the final stage of intuition, logic and reason are brought into play to evaluate the creative thought.

Verification is a very important part of the process of intuition. Without it, there is a danger that people will simply assume that a very strong intuition *must* be correct. Intuitions are, after all, powerful things, and need to be handled with some care.

Just as intuition can be sharpened by psychological 'coaching' of various kinds, so the verification process can also be improved upon with practice. Sometimes, a person's recognition of the rightness or wrongness of an intuition can have quite physical manifestations. Many intuitive managers describe the euphoria and exhilaration of making a 'right decision', the feeling of excitement in the pit of the stomach. Others describe a sudden flash of light, or a feeling of inner calm. On the other hand, wrong decisions can be signalled by sleepless nights or an upset stomach.

It is easy to trust a false intuition when you are tired, under time pressure, anxious, bored or angry. At times like these, it is generally a bad idea doggedly to pursue that 'gut feeling'. At the other end of the scale, detachment and a failure to be honest with yourself can also lead to an unjust evaluation of intuitive judgements.

It is clear that, with careful handling, intuitive thinking can become an important tool for innovative managers. Although it is certainly not any kind of substitute for analytical thought, it should be seen as a complementary way of thinking about business problems. And, just like analytical methods, it is an approach to decision-making that every manager can practise, develop, and improve.

5 CULTIVATING THE CREATIVE WORKFORCE

The need to encourage creativity is increasingly recognised by forward-looking organisations. Effective innovation will depend more and more on creative thinking from *all* the employees in an organisation, but especially from those in 'creative' posts – the writers, designers, engineers, and scientists.

In this chapter we look at some of the methods that can be used to foster creative thinking. The first essential, we argue, is to create a climate in which creative ideas are welcomed. This country has a good deal to learn from the experience of Japan, whose companies lead the world in this field, and from other countries with a distinctive approach to nurturing creativity. We look at the use of multi-disciplinary teams, and the way in which humour can be used to foster creative thinking.

Merely encouraging a creative climate is not enough, however. Organisations wanting to capitalise on the creativity of their employees need to support innovative ideas from inception right through to completion. We look at different ways organisations have tackled this, from setting clear limits to the time allowed for innovation, to formal 'innovation programmes' allowing employees to share in the profits of their own ideas.

Reward systems offer an obvious way to foster the creativity of employees. But creative people are often not motivated by the same incentives as other employees. In particular, many lack the desire to be promoted through the ranks of management. Instead, what may be of overwhelming importance is their personal autonomy, the freedom to innovate, and their own development. We look at ways of tailoring reward systems to the needs of creative people, including the development of 'multi-track' promotion systems.

Although creativity and innovation are likely to be essential to successful organisations in the future, there is no disguising the fact that they can be difficult to manage. We round off the chapter with a consideration of some of the problems faced by managers of creative people, and some guidelines as to how these might be tackled.

Most of us will never achieve great imaginative insights; we might at least be tolerant of those offered us by others.
R.W. Gerard

"There is no use trying," said Alice. "One can't believe impossible things."
"I dare say you haven't had much practice," said the Queen. "When I was your age, I always did it for half an hour a day. Why, sometimes I've believed as many as six impossible things before breakfast."
Lewis Carroll

Works of the mind exist only in action.
Paul Valery

Everyone is capable of having a good idea. But not every organisation is capable of taking advantage of these ideas. There are frequently barriers between individuals, and bureaucracies and other unhelpful structures that prevent ideas from being effectively explored, debated, communicated, and nurtured. Breaking down these barriers can be difficult, but it is probably the most productive and at the same time the most radical thing an organisation can do. After all, employees' ideas are the intellectual capital of the organisation. Without them, it might as well be run by computers.

It makes no commercial sense to stifle creativity. But business managers are often too concerned about protecting short-term earnings to innovate themselves, or even to nurture other innovators. The best companies, however, see creativity and innovation as something that needs managing. The means used to manage it can include giving workers incentives for successful innovation, and refusing to punish those whose gambles don't pay off. Good ideas do not go very far unless they are tended and nourished, and that means nurturing, developing and rewarding those people who can think creatively.

Managing those people whose jobs particularly require them to be creative, whether they are writers, designers, researchers, scientists, or engineers, is an important part of innovative management. It is very often through harnessing the creativity of these people that an organisation can produce real innovation and change. In this chapter we shall look at some of the techniques used by forward-thinking organisations to make the most of the creativity of their workforces.

AN ENCOURAGING CLIMATE

It is increasingly accepted that the first thing organisations need to do, in order to maximise the benefit from their creative workers, is to create a culture where new ideas are welcomed and encouraged. And just as important as the creative person who comes up with innovative ideas is the manager who knows how to harness the creative process and come up with concrete results.

On a recent trip to Japan, Peter Drucker, consultant and author, noted that many Japanese companies are reorganising their research and development functions so that a single team of engineers, scientists, marketers and production people can work together on a particular project. He identified three levels of innovation that could be fostered by this approach. At the simplest level, these teams seek to make gradual improvements to an existing product. At a slightly higher level, they aim for a significant imaginative leap, such as Sony's move from a micro-tape recorder to the Walkman. At the third and highest level these teams aim to produce quite new ideas from scratch. By working at all three levels simultaneously, these teams are much more likely to produce a new product which can become a market leader.

One mechanical engineering manufacturer sent a very clear message to its engineers about the value of innovation. One of its teams of engineers thought it could save time and money by using an experimental moulding technique on some equipment. However, once the technique was integrated into the assembly line, the team found that it did not work well at high production levels. The result was a serious loss of sales.

When the members of the team were summoned to the chief executive's office, they felt sure they were about to be dismissed. However, they were greeted with balloons and a cake. The chief executive congratulated them on their decision to take a risk. In the end, the gamble was not a complete failure, either, as the company has found it can use the moulding process on other products where it works better.

There is a good deal of evidence that if people's creative ideas fail the first time, the worst thing to do is to berate them for it. This will only lead them to give up trying, and the company will get nothing, or, worse, demotivated workers. If they are encouraged, on the other hand, creative thinkers will tend to work even harder towards a solution. As a Japanese proverb puts it, failure is the threshold of success.

William McKnight, one of the founders of 3M, the American corporation that covers many industries from mining to pharmaceuticals, is one of those who has argued strongly that criticising mistakes kills initiative. But if a company is to continue to grow, people with initiative are one of the first essentials.

In the whitewater of global change, understanding and facilitating the creative process and its instigators becomes a crucial tool for the innovative and forward-looking manager. Frequently, organisations will regard the creative person as an eccentric or misfit. They can, indeed, sometimes be difficult to deal with, but it is important for those who have to manage creative people to understand a little of the creative process.

Creativity typically begins with a vague, even confused excitement; some form of yearning, or hunch. Sometimes a new idea will appear spontaneously, but ideas rarely appear fully formed. Creative people will often have an inordinate appetite for discovery, but they often also have the irritating habit of ignoring anyone who gets in their way or who does not understand what they want to do.

Unfortunately for everyone, creative people are usually at their most impatient with outsiders just at the stage when they need the most support from the outside, when their idea is growing. A certain amount of patience is necessary on both sides. It requires courage to be creative, to move away from the norm and towards uncertainties. This applies just as much to those responsible for managing creative workers as to the creative people themselves.

ENCOURAGING CREATIVITY THROUGH HUMOUR

Some companies are starting to recognise that humour is one of the most effective ways to promote creativity at work. Here are a few examples:

- Sun Microsystems encourages annual April Fools Day pranks targeting upper management.
- Kodak has created a 'humour room' at its Rochester, New York, business campus where its employees can go for a 'fun break'.
- Price Waterhouse holds humour programmes in conjunction with its annual continuing education seminar.
- Ben and Jerry's Ice Cream has a 'joy gang' charged with distributing joy grants, worth up to $500 each, to work units that come up with creative ideas for bringing 'long-term joy' to the workplace.

Whilst humour is a good energiser for creativity, so too is conflict. If conflicts in an organisation can be aired and talked through, then this will often release dams of feeling once the tensions are over. This is usually a very good time for creative thinking.

TAKING IDEAS A STEP FURTHER

Achieving successful innovation means more than just encouraging the innovators, however. It is also important to have a system which supports the idea from the conceptual stage right through to production. This is an area where the Japanese lead the world. It has been found that most Japanese companies spend around 40 per cent of their time planning, compared to 25 per cent in the US and 20 per cent in the UK. As a result, they experience far fewer interruptions during the development of new products, and fewer problems after the products are launched.

Japanese car manufacturers, for example, settle on the specifications for each new product as late as possible. In this way, people in the company can spend more time planning and debating the best specifications. Once they have been agreed, however, these companies are very reluctant to allow late changes to the specifications. Setting a fixed boundary to the amount of discussion and revision that can take place sharpens people's approach and enhances their commitment.

One American software company uses a similarly rigorously scheduled process, which has enabled it to develop and launch most of its breakthrough products in less than 18 months. The company 'closes down' each project the second it is finished, forbidding further revision, and goes on to the next. In this way, the design engineers are kept on their mettle. Because they don't have to fiddle with details, they are able to keep coming up with more creative ideas. The company has succeeded in a market where getting your ideas out before the competition is crucial to success.

By setting fixed boundaries to creative thinking, the company has reduced the tendency, evident in some British firms, to tinker with a design indefinitely. This tendency often means that by the time a new product gets to market, it bears little resemblance to the original idea which inspired it. This can diminish the uplifting effect of a successful product on company morale.

LEARNING FROM OTHER CULTURES

Different countries tend to take quite widely diverging approaches to the management of creative people. A good example of this divergence is drawn from a real-life training programme recently organised for a multinational corporation.

The participants were divided into four groups: a British group, a French group, a Dutch group, and an international group, composed of a mixture of Belgians, Americans and a Swede. The groups were positioned in a large square in which chocolate eggs of different colours were scattered about. Each group was given some bamboo canes, some string and a funnel, and told to devise a way of collecting one egg of each colour without touching the eggs with their hands, using all the equipment they had been given.

Within two minutes the British group shouted to the others, 'We've got it, we know how this thing works'. The other groups all listened patiently and then went about building their own devices for collecting the eggs. The results of the exercise were quite striking. The French had produced a device to collect the eggs that was very neat, aesthetically pleasing, and worked like a dream. Using the British group's idea, they had divided tasks among each other, and came up with a product that worked. The international team, on the other hand, had trouble working together at all. They ended up throwing their eggs.

The Dutch model worked, but only just. It was seen as a testament to their strong desire to get the job done, and to worry about the quality later. The British contraption, although it worked, was messy, with bits added on here and there. Coming up with the solution was the most important thing to this group, but it fell down on execution.

The attitude of the British team in this example is very revealing. Although the team members came up with a solution to the problem at an early stage, the idea fell down when it came to production. It is this lack of self confidence and an inability to manage an idea right through to completion that often loses British firms the market edge in product development.

British companies could perhaps learn something from the American experience. Several US organisations reward employees who propose good ideas by granting them paid leave to receive training in skills such as writing business plans and development schedules. In one company, employees can invest up to 10 per cent of their salary in the new product or service, and receive up to five per cent of the revenues if the product gets to market. The scheme has generated two patents, with eleven more pending, since the inception of the programme in 1989. The idea behind this system is to provide a challenge to the creative person, providing opportunities for limited risk taking whilst maintaining the support of the company.

A special innovation programme at 3M provides start-up funds for new ideas and projects other than those being developed by the company's own research and development function. One million dollars a year is available to support these projects. All 3M employees are eligible to submit proposals, and awards are announced twice a year. The key considerations on which ideas are judged are the uniqueness of the idea, its potential for success, the commitment of the person proposing the idea, and the potential benefits. Innovation that crosses functional and unit boundaries within the company is especially encouraged.

To ensure a steady stream of new products, 3M says that each business unit must ensure that 25 per cent of its sales come from products introduced within the last five years. Although this goal is inflexible, the means to achieve it are left up to the units' own managers.

Another means of ensuring an innovative approach at 3M is its 'bootleg' policy. This states that anyone can devote up to 15 per cent of the working week to their own 'pet' projects. Many of the ideas worked out in these projects do not come to anything, of course, but the company feels that 'bootlegging' is a fruitful breeding ground, and it has led to some real successes.

REWARDING INNOVATION

In this chapter so far we have looked at some of the ways being used to encourage people to think creatively, and to support creative ideas from inception right through to final production.

Another very important method of encouraging innovation is, of course, to reward those who come up with new ideas.

Appropriate rewards do more to communicate the company's commitment to creativity and innovation than almost anything else. But motivating creative people requires a different approach from that used for salespeople or accountants or assembly line workers. Perhaps this is one reason why communication between research and design departments and salespeople, for example, is often very poor: neither side really understands or respects the other.

One of the crucial differences between creative workers and others is their seeming lack of corporate ambition. This in itself takes away one of the most commonly-used tools for motivating people in employing organisations, namely promotion.

In many organisations, promotion can only mean promotion into management. But this frequently creates a two-fold problem when it comes to the promotion of creative people. Firstly, the creative person's technical or other expertise is lost in the job of managing, and often, he or she will make a poor manager, lacking the necessary interpersonal skills and the desire to manage others.

The managing director of one company, promoted out of a technical role in which he excelled, described the experience as being like walking through a forest of koala bears, who were all clinging to his legs! He was terribly frustrated by the fact that having to manage his staff's problems got in the way of what he really wanted to do, and was best at.

In some cases, this problem can be dealt with by moving a highly-valued creative person back into a role where they no longer have to manage people. But in organisations where there are large numbers of creative people, careful thought needs to be given to creating systems of reward which don't rely on promoting these people into inappropriate management roles.

One company decided to try a new method of promotion for the creative people working in its information systems division. Instead of being automatically promoted to team managers after a certain point, creative people in the division were given the choice of three promotion routes:

- **Technical**

  By taking this route, employees were able to gain a higher grade while continuing to do technical work.

- **Project management**

  This route was designed for those who did want to go into management. Employees taking this route were given increasing exposure to resource management, problem-solving, team building and communication across the company.

- **Systems development**

  Treading a middle path between the other two, this route emphasised technical skills, but required employees to take on more responsibility for product design. This involved more communication and liaison with other people, though it rarely meant managing a team.

This three-track system was very much welcomed by the company's employees. But, although it was seen as a very good idea, it has proved only partially successful, largely due to the ease with which it could be manipulated to suit individuals' personal interests.

For many creative people, motivation depends upon three things:

- **Autonomy**

  Creative people often want to work on their own, without someone looking over their shoulder, and telling them what to do, and how and when to do it.

- **Innovation**

  These people frequently feel the need to innovate, to make changes, and to put a personal mark on something.

- **Personal development and growth**

  Creative people often need to be doing something new. They dislike routine, wanting instead something that will stretch them, and enable their constantly-questioning minds to keep learning.

Any reward system for creative people will need to take all three factors into account if it is effectively to motivate these people to produce their best work. A magazine called *Machine Design* once carried this provocative checklist:

How to kill creativity
- Always pretend to know more than everyone around you.
- Police your employees by every procedural means you can devise.
- Run daily checks on the progress of everyone's work.
- Erect the highest possible barrier between commercial decision makers and your technical staff.
- Be sure that your professionally-trained staff do technician's work for long periods of time.
- Be certain not to speak to employees on a personal level, except when announcing rises.
- Try to be the exclusive spokesperson for everything for which you are responsible.
- Say yes to new ideas but do nothing about them.
- Call lots of meetings.
- Put every idea through the appropriate channels.
- Stick to protocol.

PROBLEMS FOR MANAGERS OF CREATIVE PEOPLE

Most of those who have studied creative people agree that one of their most notable characteristics is independence. They are much more influenced by their own, inner standards, than those of the organisation or profession to which they belong. In a study of architects, the individuals who were judged the most creative were concerned primarily with meeting their own artistic standards of excellence. The least creative were concerned with conforming to the norms and standards of the profession.

Indeed, it is debatable whether the most highly creative people are suited to a corporate environment at all. The highly original person is likely to be impatient with less gifted colleagues. And he or she is less likely to be in need of the support and reassurance which an employing organisation can offer.

Many software designers, for instance, find the structure of large companies too stifling or encumbering, and so either work on their own or in small organisations. In recent years, the recession has created a dearth of jobs even in the once huge software market. This has brought many software people into companies they would not normally consider working for, with sometimes frustrating consequences for both the individual and the organisation.

Also, it has to be remembered that new ideas are sensitive plants, easily damaged by premature criticism. The reluctance of creative people to share their ideas before they are completely formulated is probably well founded. However, this lack of communication can make managing these people very difficult. It is important that the manager should understand when a creative person is being uncommunicative because they fear that their ideas will be rejected. In these cases, it is very helpful if the manager can respond in a nurturing rather than a dismissive way. All too often, managers tend to view 'secretive' behaviour as a personal threat, and their defence mechanisms are aroused. Thus a cycle of fear, rejection, and misunderstanding is set up.

It is sometimes helpful for people working in very technical areas to have access to a 'translator', when communicating their ideas to others. Sometimes, very innovative people may lack the interpersonal skills needed to put their ideas across, without the help of such a translator. This is particularly so for those working in information technology, and enlightened organisations are increasingly providing these employees with a translator who can help them when dealing with clients.

Psychometric tests have shown that creative people often have a preference for complexity, asymmetry and incompleteness. It may be, as the psychoanalyst Antony Storr suggests, that creative people prefer the incomplete because it stimulates them to provide an order of their own. The creative person's tendency to be very independent is also likely to make him or her dissatisfied with things that have been completed by someone else.

This can cause problems for those trying to manage creative people, especially in areas like product selection. For one thing, it may lead creative people into conflict with others on the team, such as economists and market predictors, who are likely to have very different preferences.

Although it is a common complaint from creative people that they only want to be left alone to complete their work, many find it all to difficult to complete one project before starting on the next. Creative people tend to be happiest when faced by the challenges of a new problem; when the problem is nearly solved, they may easily lose interest. Managers of such people will need to find ways of ensuring that they are encouraged to complete the project in hand before starting on another.

To many organisations, the flexible approach to dealing with creative people can sometimes look like chaos. Companies like Apple or Microsoft, where people go to work in jeans or even shorts, may raise a shudder with those who wonder whether people can really do business in that way. The success of both these companies would seem to indicate that they *can*, but it is worth remembering that even in these organisations, people still need some sense of structure and discipline. If they didn't, they would probably be working for themselves.

CREATIVITY FOR THE FUTURE

There is an increasing awareness of the need to encourage the creativity of all an organisation's employees. One sign of this is that the research and development function is being seen less and less as a drain on a company's resources, and more and more as an essential part of a company's competitive strategy.

Whether managers understand their technical and creative people or not, they have to learn to manage them successfully, or risk losing their competitive edge. Many creative scientific people, particularly in the field of information technology, have successfully crossed over from research into management.

One physicist, who is vice-chairman of one of the world's biggest corporations, feels he now approaches business problems in very much the same way as he approached scientific problems in the past. He is only too happy to encourage other creative scientists in his organisation, arguing that a very strong work ethic, and the desire to see something through to the end, are common features of all true scientists. Indeed, extending the intellectual curiosity and tenacity shown by creative technical and scientific people more widely through business life could show tremendous benefits.

To be truly successful in business, after all, requires taking creative risks to achieve a long-term goal or vision. There are clear similarities with research and other creative endeavours. The most successful scientists and designers are those who are able to develop a long-term vision of the future, and who have the courage to stick to that vision through thick and thin.

In the future, business people will be presented with complex problems not just involving their own organisations, but also having an impact on society as a whole. They will increasingly need to take a creative, innovative approach. They might do worse than to take a leaf out of the scientist's book.

6 TRANSFORMING TEAMS

'Teamworking' is one of those buzz words that seems to have gained almost universal currency in business life. In this chapter, we look at the reality behind this popular concept, examining its potential as a means of innovation, and considering some of the potential pitfalls for organisations that adopt this way of working.

Many of the flatter, more democratic companies of the 1990s are adapting to their changing environment by moving to ways of working based on teams. We examine how teams are being used to support innovation, and adapt to change, and look at the growth of cross-functional approaches to teamworking. A case study describes how one car firm has used teamworking as a lever for a radical overhaul of its manufacturing processes.

In the second half of this chapter, we turn to a closer examination of the workings of a team. We argue that there is much more to teambuilding than just deciding to call a group of people a 'team'.

One of the crucial features of an effective team is respect for the different skills, backgrounds, and attitudes of its members. Honesty and openness are also vital, as are the establishment of clear ground rules of acceptable behaviour, and working for consensus.

The chapter concludes with two case studies of organisations which have experienced difficulties in teamworking. It examines the way that special teambuilding events can be used to tackle these problems, and to restore effective teamworking in an organisation.

Certainly a strong strain of individualism is alive in all of us nurtured in the spirit of democracy. However, the complexity of the environment and the goal structure of the enterprise create a situation in which it is no longer possible to comprehend or conduct the operation of the enterprise without some form of teamwork and teambuilding.

Douglas McGregor, *The Professional Manager* (1967).

Teamwork and teambuilding have received a great deal of attention of late. Every grouping of people at work seems to be called a 'team', even if the members rarely see each other, and certainly never work co-operatively together. In fact, 'team' is one of the most overworked clichés in business today.

Sometimes the undoubted benefits of flexible teamworking can blind an organisation's senior management to the potential pitfalls. Many make the mistake of announcing a move to teamworking without effectively communicating what this means. Some may not even have a clear understanding themselves of how a team-based workplace operates.

Some managers think that simply calling a group of people a team is enough to promote effective team behaviour. But this is no more likely to succeed than simply calling someone a manager, and expecting him or her to behave like one with no help or support.

Nevertheless, in the 'flatter', more democratic corporate structures of the 1990s, teamworking has to be seen as one of the keys to success. In the face of almost any large-scale change, teambuilding is likely to be a necessary part of the process of adaptation. Motivating, supporting, and developing people in changing organisations is more likely to be done on a team basis in the organisation of the future.

In this chapter, we shall examine some of the ways in which teams can be used to support innovation and change. We also look at ways of building and maintaining effective teams.

TEAMS FOR INNOVATION

One of the major uses of teambuilding in innovative management is its role in introducing major change. Large-scale innovation requires constant communication, both for the sharing of ideas, and the co-ordination of activities. This in turn demands closer relationships between employees. Such relationships cannot develop amongst those who are working in isolation, whether entirely on their own, or in insular departments. It is only in the context of teams that these relationships, and the improved communication that comes with them, can be cultivated.

By focusing on groups of people, rather than individuals, many organisations are finding that they can implement change more quickly, and with a greater sense of commitment. Teams, with all their potential for co-operation, and the harnessing of diversity, can often be a crucial factor in making the breakthrough to a new way of working.

One company, Polaroid, is currently redesigning all of its work sites, to enable the work to be carried out by teams of employees, each of which is responsible for an entire work process. Each team will handle work scheduling and organisation, quality control, problem solving, and other issues previously handled only by supervisors. The redesign involves building meeting rooms where the teams can come together to carry out their work.

Changing the physical space within which people work can, in fact, improve or damage team performance quite dramatically, and sometimes quite minor changes will have a disproportionately great effect. At one insurance company, one team's performance was dramatically changed for the better simply by knocking out a pillar in the middle of the room that was preventing members of the team from seeing each other.

Many of the issues that need to be addressed when an organisation is undertaking major change cannot be tackled within a function, because they cut across traditional organisational boundaries. Many of the more innovative companies are starting to build cross-functional teams. Issues like safety, quality, the environment, and so on can often be most effectively addressed by cross-functional teams. Some of these teams are being even widened to include representatives from the organisation's customers or suppliers.

When building cross-functional teams, special care is needed to ensure clear communication. The members may have quite different interests, and be used to using quite different kinds of language. For example, a cross-functional team that included information technology specialists, people from the finance department, and personnel experts would need to steer clear of the technical language commonly used by all three groups when talking to their peers. The second example, described later in this chapter, illustrates the importance of taking care over the design of cross-functional teams, and the problems that can arise when this is not done properly.

The following description of Volvo, the Swedish car maker, illustrates the way in which teamworking can be used as a lever for real innovation and change.

Volvo is currently conducting an experiment in teamworking at one of its sites. The assembly line has been dismantled. Instead, cars are built by employees working in small, decentralised teams of between eight and 10 people. Instead of working on a moving assembly line, the workers now make the cars in a fixed spot. Workers at the plant's materials centre supply these assembly teams with materials on a 'just-in-time' basis, using automatic carriers moving on magnetic floor tracks. A computer controls the flow of materials, but workers are able to vary this flow to match the working rhythms of their teams.

Workers at this plant now have a high degree of autonomy and responsibility. They set their own break times and holiday schedules, and allocate tasks to cover absence. They participate in policy making and are responsible for a variety of tasks including quality control, production planning, and floor layout, and also for developing work procedures, servicing equipment and ordering supplies. In addition to basic wages, these employees earn bonuses for maintaining quality and productivity, and for meeting delivery targets.

The new assembly teams have no supervisors or foremen. The

only 'chiefs' are the managers. Each manager is responsible for between 80 and 100 employees. Each assembly team has a leader, called a 'co-ordinator', who is chosen from among the workers on a rotating basis. This role is crucial to the new way of working, as the co-ordinator forms the main link between the team and its manager.

All the members of these new-style teams receive training in teamwork. Without such training, there is a real danger that the teams would feel lost. As with most organisations that choose to devolve power in this way, Volvo has also discovered that effective communication is crucial to this way of working.

The company provides employees with abundant information, to ensure that they have a good understanding of the company's strategy, its history and traditions. Of course, communication is a two-way process, and the company also encourages the employees to air their views on everything from process innovations to new product ideas.

The new way of working has been sufficiently successful for Volvo to extend it to another plant. However, it has not been quite the rousing success its sponsors had hoped for. Although morale has been boosted, and absenteeism reduced, the rate of productivity at the site where the new methods have been adopted is much lower than at other plants. Nevertheless, some in the organisation remain convinced that teams are the way forward, pointing out that any radically new way of working puts heavy demands on people, and cannot always produce results immediately.

BUILDING A TEAM

We have been looking at some of the ways in which teams can be used as a catalyst for change. But, as we argued at the beginning of this chapter, there is more to moving to a team approach than simply deciding that a group of people is to be called a 'team'.

Adopting a truly team-based approach to work can often mean a complete transformation in an organisation. It can involve unlearning deeply-ingrained beliefs about authority, responsibility and individualism. It involves the development, not only of team behaviour, but also of the ability to look beyond the immediate team to more extended worker networks. Like all major transformations, teambuilding requires effort, commitment, and, most of all, communication.

Moreover, teambuilding is not just something to be done when a new team is first brought together. Rather, it is something that needs to be carried out continuously to ensure the proper maintenance of effective teamworking.

In the rest of this chapter, we will examine the fundamentals of effective teambuilding, and examine their application in practice.

There are many different methods of building a team. Different methods may be appropriate for different situations. Teambuilding techniques can be used to address conflicts in a department, to set goals, or to facilitate major change.

Teambuilding is designed to lead to more openness, greater trust and co-operation between the members of a team, and more effective working. However, there are certain conditions that need to be met if any teambuilding exercise is to be a success:

- There must be a clear incentive for each member of the team to work together, and each should have an interest in resolving any difficulties. Teamwork needs to be seen as an essential part of resolving a problem, rather than just a philosophical outlook.
- All the members of the team have to agree to participate in teambuilding, and they should each have an equal opportunity to influence the agenda.
- The team's manager must want to improve performance enough to warrant taking some risks.

The key to building a team lies in the balance between two factors: the team's external focus, that is, the operational demands of the business, and its internal focus, that is, the interactions between the members of the team.

Any attempt to build and maintain a team needs to focus on four major factors:

- An appreciation of and respect for the differences within the team
- Honesty
- Team structures and roles
- Agreed decision-making processes.

Let us look at each of these factors in detail.

Respect for differences

Most people need to belong, to feel part of something, to be valued and respected. An effective team is one where all the members have tasks that are recognised as important, and are accepted as true members of the team. No matter how disparate the team members are in terms of their background, skills, and motivation, each needs to be able to accept that the others have something to contribute. Differences between team members should, in fact, be welcomed. 'Homogenised' teams, which are made up of people with very similar characteristics, rarely produce innovative results.

By acknowledging its diverse skills, a team can maximise the resources it has to draw on. Of course, for some tasks, not all the skills available will be required, or some skills will be more important than others. However, it is still important that each team member should know that his or her contribution will be valued.

Narrow assumptions about who can and should do what can prevent a team from tapping all its available resources. The fact that a technician has a scientific background does not mean that he or she is incapable of making a business decision. Far from it; they may in fact be able to provide a different perspective to a problem.

Honesty

The second essential for effective teamworking is openness. The members of a team need to be honest, both about what is going on in the team, and about what is happening in the organisation as a whole. Only in this way can a team respond to the needs of its own members, and the needs of the organisation.

Openness, and the knowledge that all contributions will be welcome, are fundamental to teamwork that achieves results. Team members need to feel they have some 'safe space' where they can talk through problems and examine issues. They need to be able to express both delight and anxiety, to admit to uncertainty, and to express differences of opinion constructively. Quite often, openness on these matters can help to show people that they are not alone in their fears and concerns.

Consideration of openness and honesty leads directly to the question of trust. Teams do not function for very long without commitment, and commitment is built on trust. Trusting team members is, in fact, one of the best ways to manage through difficult times. To be effective, any attempts at teambuilding must look at issues of trust between team members. It is often necessary to expose a lack of trust before any progress can be made.

Team structures and roles

Everyone needs boundaries within which to work. Contrary to popular belief, boundaries do not inevitably result in inflexible behaviour. Indeed, appropriate boundaries are necessary for even the most creative work. It is only when people know how far they can go, and what is expected of them, that they feel free enough to think constructively.

Although teamworking can be used to break down inappropriate hierarchies and barriers to co-operative working, it still needs to operate within carefully-set boundaries. For example, team meetings are often made more productive when structured into agenda items. Each agenda item should be carefully defined. As well as allowing the team members to focus precisely on the matter in hand, this also enables them to make checks on their progress. An agenda item like the following, for example, is vague. It sets no time limits to the discussion, and gives no idea of the outcomes expected:

Agenda item: car parking

Compare this with the following agenda item:

Agenda item: car parking (15 minutes)
During this item, the team will put forward proposals for deciding how spaces will be allocated.

In the latter example, time limits have been set to the discussion,
and a desired outcome described.

Another important kind of boundary for effective teambuilding
is boundaries to acceptable behaviour. Clear and explicit ground
rules governing behaviour are essential for the functioning of any
team. It is astonishing how much difference they can make.

For example, one manager had an annoying habit of leaving
team meetings whenever she got bored. This was usually when the
team was discussing operational detail. By doing this, the manager
belittled the team's activity, and also excluded herself from the
team. The team was initially unwilling to challenge her about this
directly. However, at a special teambuilding workshop, to the sur-
prise of the team members, she confessed quite happily to this failing. As a result the team decided that, if in future they felt any
member of the group was undermining another member, then they
all had a responsibility to address this directly.

Boundaries are particularly important when it comes to defining
team roles. Sometimes, teams decide to negotiate on individual
members' roles within the team. In this case, there should be no
final 'deal' until all the members of the team are happy. Rules of
this kind become crucial when it comes to deciding who should
lead the group. Ground rules for behaviour within a group should
also cover which issues need full consultation with, and approval
from the group, and which just require the group to be kept
informed.

Of course, there is all the difference in the world between
ground rules that are agreed by the team, and those that are
imposed on the team by the leader or by the organisation. These

latter kind of rules are not helpful or enabling. To be of real value, boundaries and ground rules need to be fully discussed and agreed on by all the members of the team.

Agreed decision-making processes

The final aspect of any effective team is to agree on decision-making processes. This aspect is closely linked to the team structures and roles considered above. Faced with boundaries, ground rules, or roles they cannot influence, team members will feel disempowered and lose self-esteem. This happens at all levels of an organisation, from the clerk in a team of 40, to a board member overruled by an autocratic chief executive.

People who feel powerless have a habit of being disruptive in order to gain some kind of control within a team, albeit a destructive one. Decision-making on the basis of consensus is one of the least understood but most useful techniques of teamworking.

Of course, consensus decision-making is not always appropriate. When the fire alarm goes, that is not the time for the team leader to ask for an opinion about what to do. There will always be times when there is no opportunity for team discussion, and managers simply have to implement a senior management decision. This does not have to demotivate a team, provided it was not expecting to have a say in that particular area.

The problems arise when a team expects to be consulted, and is presented with a *fait accompli* by the boss. This can set up a parent–child relationship between managers and their team members: 'She treats us like children, and never gives us the opportunity to try things for ourselves.' Of course, the boss may feel that,'They act like children, and always pass the buck to me.' Sometimes it is hard to see where this circle of mistrust begins and ends. But for a team to function effectively, the circle has to be broken somehow. It is often a question of striking a balance between democracy and active leadership.

True consensus means that each member of the team should feel that he or she is being heard and understood. This task is made easier, as we saw above, if each member feels free to speak openly. It is also helpful if teams' bosses can share their own dilemmas with the team. To maintain team cohesiveness, everyone should be satisfied that they had at least an opportunity to influence the eventual decision, and feel able to support it.

The two case studies that follow provide an illustration of some of the problems that can arise for teams, and how teambuilding techniques can be used to address these problems.

CASE STUDY 1

In this manufacturing company, the buying teams were recently reorganised cross-functionally. The idea was for creative, technical, and finance people to work together to achieve product sales and development. In reality, however, people from each discipline rarely listened to people from another, and there was a great deal of hostility. The main problem for these teams was that they were composed of people who were all at a similar level of seniority, working in a very competitive environment, and chasing a very small number of promotions. This was hardly calculated to foster trusting, co-operative relationships.

The organisation's personnel manager was very conscious of these problems, and invited in a consultant who was familiar with the organisation. Together, they designed a one-and-a-half-day intensive teambuilding workshop called 'Valuing the difference'.

The workshop looked at practical ways of building and developing teams in a changing environment. The aim was to create more versatile and cohesive teams, that were able to recognise opportunities and to create quick, workable and appropriate solutions. The aim was to harness the enormous range of talent within the teams, and to encourage them to pull together, rather than competing.

The workshop started off with a large-group outdoor exercise to identify some of the problems being faced by the teams. This vividly illustrated members' lack of respect for each other's skills, and the lack of communication within the teams, which resulted in duplication of effort, and unproductive use of resources.

In the next exercise, the participants were grouped into their usual work teams to discuss some of the problems they faced. The process was painful for some, but most saw it as an opportunity to say things they had wanted to say for some time.

As a result of the workshop, the teams were able to:

- Identify areas for change in the business, and ways of both instigating and managing these changes.

- Recognise cross-functional issues in their work teams, and identify ways of dealing with them.
- Identify ways to value the difference in their skills, rather than seeing it as an obstacle.
- Examine ways of maximising their negotiating power as a team, rather than as individuals.
- Identify individual, team and organisational barriers to productivity, and ways of breaking down the barriers.

Six months later, the prognosis is good, and the company feels that the move to cross-functional teams may, after all, prove to be a success.

CASE STUDY 2

In the following case study, we look at the way teambuilding techniques were used in one particular organisation to tackle some major operational problems.

A retail outlet had recently lost some of its best people, had poor sales results, and, on top of all this had been asked to take control of several smaller units nearby. The manager of the outlet enjoyed running the show her own way. Although very successful in the past, her performance was starting to deteriorate, but she seemed to be unaware of this. The shop's second-in-command was very capable, and took most of the company flack for the poor performance of the unit. She was happy to do so as she was very ambitious, and saw it as an opportunity to put herself forward.

The staff in the shops were not working as a team. Partly because of the manager's hands-off style, and partly because of the recent changes, they were becoming more and more demotivated. The crunch came when a series of major commercial disasters focused corporate headquarters' attention on the team.

As a result, the whole team agreed, albeit grudgingly, to go away from the workplace for a day to try to work out their problems. An external facilitator was brought in, as it was felt that the team would get nowhere on their own. This was partly because habits had become too entrenched, and partly because the other members of the team were too scared of the manager. As well as being frightened of her, though, they were also very protective towards her, seeming to feel that she was not capable of acting differently.

The event involved some preparation prior to the day. Each member of the team was asked to complete a questionnaire which which described various aspects of the team and its place in the organisation. For example, it asked questions about how the person felt about changes in the company, and their unit, and how the change had been communicated; it asked about what were the particular problems they perceived their team to have, and what they might do to improve team working. They were also asked to complete an inventory which asked about their preferred role in a team, and also to mark on a continuum where they saw their team in various aspects: for example, leadership, decision-making etc. All this data was sent to the external consultant to collate. From it, she developed an agenda for the event, focusing on issues which each individual had expressed, in confidence. Most of their issues were around the same areas: lack of honesty and open communication, lack of overt leadership. The results of the team inventory were collated in graph form; one for each member which showed their individual way of working, and one for the group.

The consultant showed them their collated views and her proposed agenda, and then handed the responsibility over to them to manage the process, only intervening at appropriate moments, for example when she thought the team were avoiding difficult issues. They decided to take it in turns to manage each agenda item, and developed norms of behaviour for expressing views and decision-making. The review of the results of the team inventory probably was the turning point for their development. This was one of their biggest eye-openers, as it quite clearly showed that the nominal leader had no desire to lead, but their second in command had an extraordinarily high need to control and push things through. When the team saw this, it was a graphic representation of what they felt, but could not express. It opened the door to some very honest and frank discussions about the way they operated, and the way they wanted to operate in the future.

On reviewing the event, the members of the team felt that they had been more honest with each other than they could have hoped. They were relieved to find that this honesty had no adverse effect on their personal relationships back at work; in fact it had enriched them.

As a result of the day, some individuals felt much more confident of their ability to influence the team's direction in the future. There was also felt to be some unprecedented progress on issues affecting the everyday work of the shops.

During the weeks that followed the event, the team became increasingly aware that some of the new ways of behaving they had agreed on on the day were quite difficult to maintain in the workplace. But when they were adhered to, they were extremely effective.

For example, the manager had admitted to some fairly adolescent behaviour, which the team had agreed they colluded with, by merely complaining amongst themselves. When they got back to work, for the first few days, the manager's behaviour was exemplary. After a week, she began to revert to her old ways, and other team members went back to to complaining amongst themselves. This continued until one member of the team pointed out that, during the course of the one-day event, the manager had specifically asked that the team should tell her if her behaviour was unacceptable.

This was a real turning-point for the team. Eventually the other members decided to challenge the manager as a group at one of their meetings. They felt they had nothing to lose, but everything to gain.

The manager's initial reaction was quite frosty, but the group's timing was good. They had begun to work together as a team, and this was starting to be visible in the shop's performance. Levels of motivation and subsequent effectiveness had dramatically increased. The individual members felt strong enough as a team to challenge a non-performing member, even if that person was their boss. In the end, the boss apologised to the team.

This team still has a long way to go, but the overall feeling of its members is that it has made a good start on the way to becoming an effective team, and maximising its precious resources.

7 MANAGEMENT DEVELOPMENT USING THE OUTDOORS

Management development in the outdoors is a technique that is very much on the increase. It is, indeed, in danger of being seen as a panacea for a whole range of management development issues.

The central idea behind outdoor development is that by taking managers away from their familiar environments, it is possible to enhance their awareness of their own behaviour and interaction with other people. By removing the familiar paraphernalia of job titles, hierarchy, and company politics, this kind of development event can lay bare the fundamental principles involved in the management of individuals, groups, and resources.

In this chapter, we take a closer look at the issues that can be effectively dealt with by this development method, and examine some of the rules of good practice that should be observed by those offering such events.

Outdoor development should certainly not be seen as a panacea. At best, we argue, it will complement more traditional management development carried out indoors.

One key to successful management development in the outdoors is undoubtedly an effective tutor. A good tutor is someone who is both skilled in particular outdoor activities, and, more importantly, able to relate these activities to everyday management issues back at the workplace. The client organisation also has an important role to play, however. It is crucial that an organisation using outdoor development should clearly define realistic targets for these development programmes, and continue the process of relating the lessons learned in the outdoors to real work issues.

Another issue examined here is the fear felt by many participants at the prospect of outdoor development. We look at ways of minimising this, but argue that overcoming apprehension is a major benefit of the outdoor approach.

The chapter ends with a checklist summarising the main requirements for a successful outdoor development programme.

Managers apply their skills to a range of tasks which are quite dif-
ferent to those they face at work, but which are challenging and
real. The results of their actions are immediately apparent, provid-
ing clear evidence of their performance. ... Although the outdoor
tasks are not 'normal' they are inescapably 'real'. Managing an
outdoor situation is like managing life ... the underlying manage-
ment processes are laid bare.
Chris Creswick and Roy Williams, Food, Drink, and Tobacco Industry Training
Board internal paper

More and more managers are being sent on outdoor programmes as
part of their development. But all too often neither the participants
nor those who send them have any idea of what management development is really about, or what it is designed to achieve.

Some providers of management development in the outdoors
appear to claim it as a universal panacea. And this idea may appeal
to some managers, who are encouraged to see it as a short cut to
solving their problems. Given the inflated claims of some
providers, it is hardly surprising that people are misinformed about
what outdoor management development is really for.

So what is outdoor development all about, and when should you
use it? The heart of management development in the outdoors is
the idea that, in order to become more effective as an individual or
as a team member, people need to develop an awareness of themselves and the way they operate. But in any training and development programme, there is only a very limited period of time in
which to increase this self-awareness. One of the major advantages
of outdoor development is its immediate impact. The mental and
physical stimulation involved in outdoor activities provoke
thought, while the fact that the development takes place in a different environment helps to heighten awareness.

The objectives for an outdoor development programme can be
diverse, and can operate at one or more of the following levels:

- **At the individual level**

  Here, management development in the outdoors involves under-standing one's own behaviour, improving self-awareness and gaining insights into one's own personal style.
- **At the team level**

  Here, the development activity aims to develop effective team-work, and to provide a greater understanding of how teams work and the roles individuals take in teams.
- **At the inter-team level**

  At this level, outdoors development looks at issues concerning how to manage effectively between groups, and aims to improve understanding of competitive and collaborative behaviour.
- **At the organisational level**

  Finally, management development in the outdoors at this level examines how to create effective strategies and to manage change.

The most common issues this management development technique is used to examine are:

- Communication and interpersonal relationships
- Assessing individual strengths and weaknesses
- Personal development
- Confidence building
- Self-awareness
- Teambuilding
- Maximising team potential
- Leadership
- Decision-making
- Problem-solving
- Resource and information management.

Management development in the outdoors is also sometimes used as a kind of incentive event, an enjoyable group experience which is provided as a reward for employees.

WHAT TO EXPECT

Many myths and misconceptions have sprung up regarding the activities used in outdoor training programmes. Most of these are based on second-hand knowledge or hearsay about dawn swims in icy mountain lakes, and other masochistic exercises.

Many of these myths date back to the early days of outdoor training, when it was chiefly used by the army. Development in the outdoors was, and is, used by the military to develop 'character' and leadership skills, and to build teams. The first outdoor training centres and organisations were set up and staffed by ex-army personnel.

But the kind of outdoor development offered by today's specialist training providers is rather different. Perhaps the main difference lies in the increased emphasis on teamwork. While the more military-style organisations believe in an authoritarian, leader-centred approach, the newer training providers favour a greater emphasis on teams.

The actual activities offered by outdoor training providers are now extremely wide ranging. They include mountaineering, abseiling, canoeing, orienteering, construction of bridges and other large structures, and various activities using ropes. They are usually, but not always, put into the context of a major task, usually a quest of some kind, which will involve them in these activities.

At an informed estimate, there are probably well over a hundred providers of outdoor programmes now operating in the UK . Some are specialist outdoor organisations, diversifying into management development in search of a wider customer base. Others are experienced management trainers who choose to use the outdoors as their medium.

Exercises can range from twenty-minute, simple problem-solving exercises, to more complex exercises and to projects lasting several days. The exercises may involve both indoor and outdoor components. Normally, planning will take place indoors, while the activities take place out-of-doors.

SOME RULES OF GOOD PRACTICE

Any outdoor training should aim to offer a programme which provides a whole range of new situations and experiences for the participants. And, obviously, the activities should be carefully tailored to the participants' own standards of fitness.

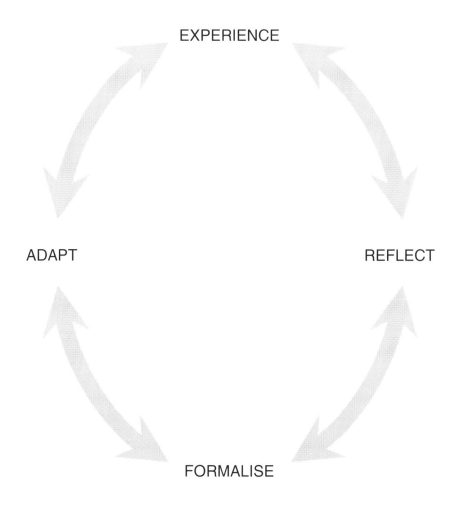

EXPERIENCE

ADAPT

REFLECT

FORMALISE

Figure 7.1 Standard approach to learning in the outdoors

In any management development, but especially that in the outdoors, the role of the tutor is the key to success. Those who offer training in the outdoors need to possess both the technical skills needed for the outdoor exercises, and the facilitation and management development skills needed to make sense of them in a development context. If training organisations cannot provide an individual with both kinds of skill, then they need to ensure that they can provide two or more trainers who have both between them.

The standard approach to learning in the outdoors, adapted from Kolb's learning cycle[1] is shown in Figure 7.1.

In management development in the outdoors, participants are typically given a task to complete. Once they have completed the task, they are asked to reflect on what happened and how it happened. The tutor's role is to facilitate this process, to provide formal theoretical input, and to help the participant to understand why things happened in a certain way.

This demands a broad range of skills from outdoors management tutors, but above all it demands the ability to achieve a balance. The tutors have to make sure, on the one hand, that they are not allowing the group to flounder in unfamiliar situations, but that, on the other hand, that they are not taking over the decision-making process for the group.

This process of reflection can take place at the end of an activity, or it can be done 'on the hoof', in the middle of an exercise. At the end of this review process, the group should be ready to move on, and start to adapt their behaviour, either in readiness for the next exercise, or back at the workplace.

In the outdoors, no amount of rationalising can alter the fact that a group of people are standing amidst the ruins of a task that has failed because of their own behaviour. It is reflection upon the failures and successes of the outdoor exercises that provides the core of any good outdoor programme. The tasks and activities that people are asked to perform, whilst essential to the learning experience, are only a means to an end.

---

[1] Kolb, D, *Organisational Psychology: An Experimental Approach* (Prentice Hall, 1971).

A CAUTIONARY TALE

The following extract is a first-hand account of the early experiences of the director of one British outdoor development centre.

'My own first involvement with this aspect of education came in the mid sixties, when I was asked to run adventure, teambuilding, and leadership courses for junior managers. I was employed, along with colleagues, for my mountaineering expertise. We met our groups in Snowdonia, following a fairly minimal exchange of correspondence from which words and phrases such as 'aims' and 'objectives', and 'transfer to work', were noticeably absent.

'There then followed two days of frantic rock climbing and peak bagging interspersed with regular soakings in local lakes and rivers, punctuated by totally indifferent dehydrated food. Occasionally a junior manager destined for greatness would say, 'Look, we're not doing this right', and be completely ignored.

'The group would leave North Wales extremely tired and exhilarated, having learned very little about anything other than mountaineering skills, but feeling that the weekend was tremendous stuff. Throughout their stay, any work-related learning would have occurred only by chance. "Aims", even though none had been set, they would unanimously agree had been achieved. I would return home and tell anyone who'd listen that I had just run a really good course for managers!'

This extract highlights one of the major problems with management development in the outdoors. Because the environment is so different from the average workplace, the experience can cloud the very issues that participants were there to investigate.

It is very difficult to have a 'mediocre' experience on an outdoor course. Generally, participants refer to them as the best courses they have ever done, largely because they are so 'different'. In some cases, this assessment is due to the participants' pleasure in what they have achieved, or to their sheer relief that they have not made fools of themselves! This in itself is not a bad thing, but nor is it the primary aim of a good management development programme, and it may have been achieved at the cost of the main objectives.

What is crucial is the participants' ability to transfer their experience on the programme back to the workplace. One of the first questions that anyone investigating this kind of training should ask, is how the provider intends to relate the activities to what goes on in the participants' real place of work.

If the facilitators of management development in the outdoors are doing their job properly, they will be constantly asking participants to evaluate their experience, and to assess its relevance to their working lives.

Client organisations, too, have an important role to play in ensuring the transfer of learning. Arrival back at the workplace after an outdoor programme is a crucial time for further evaluation and assessment, if the programme is not to be seen as just a junket. Individuals should, at the least, be debriefed by their line managers, preferably against objectives set before their departure for the course.

Some training providers will send their tutors back to the client organisation after about three months to talk further to the participants. The transition back to work is often a lot easier, in fact, if a whole work team has been involved in the programme. The shared memory of such an event can lead to remarkably strong teams.

Outdoor programmes are *not*, however, a panacea that will guarantee improved performance in the workplace. Outdoor training should never be perceived as a replacement for other types of management development carried out indoors. Rather, the two types of development should be seen as complementary.

Perhaps the most distinctive feature that the outdoors can add to a management development programme is the fact that it is a great leveller. It is very difficult to pull rank on your fellow managers when you are all dressed in the same rain gear, soaking wet, and a long way from achieving your target.

Management development in the outdoors can be an invaluable means of getting away from the hindrance of job titles, company hierarchy, and company politics. Handled well, it can lay bare the more fundamental principles involved in the management of individuals, groups, and resources. At a time when an organisation wants to introduce major change, management development in the outdoors can be a valuable medium for dealing with the unknown.

SOME IMPORTANT ISSUES

To finish this chapter, let us look at some of the important issues that should be borne in mind by anyone considering management development in the outdoors:

- The skills of the provider
- The organisation's expectations
- The participant's expectations.

The skills of the provider

Some organisations conduct a great deal of research into the different providers of outdoor training before they select one. For many, the fundamental criteria are the provider's standards of safety and hygiene. Quite sensibly, they take the view that any organisation that could not conform to these rudimentary requirements would be unlikely to provide them with a good programme of management development in the outdoors.

However, it is also crucial, as we have seen, to find an organisation that will concentrate on the developmental process, and on the transfer of learning to the workplace, rather than on the outdoor activities alone. It is also important, of course, for the provider to establish a rapport with the client, and to develop a good understanding of its needs.

As we have already seen, the skills of individual tutors are one of the decisive factors in the success of any programme. The most creative, exciting and well-planned exercises can fall apart if the tutor lacks the appropriate skills to relate the tasks that have been achieved to the processes and problems of management.

Tutors will need the skills to help the group to deal with conflict, and to face up to the implications of their actions, when all they want to do is to complete the task in hand. They need to be able to spot when the group has reached the limits of its ability, and adjust the exercise accordingly, without intervening too soon or too often.

The organisation's expectations

In order to run a successful outdoor training programme, the client organisation must be very clear about what it wants to achieve, and have discussed this thoroughly with both the training provider and the participants. Without clarity of objectives, it is impossible to know what has been achieved when the programme is over.

Organisations need to take a realistic view of what can be achieved through a management development programme in the outdoors. As we have seen, this kind of development technique is far from being a panacea.

The participant's expectations

Many reluctant participants in outdoor development often feel a great deal of apprehension about what will be expected of them before the course. They may assume that there will be over-demanding physical challenges, and worry about being fit enough, or being the wrong size or shape. Many participants fear that they will not be able to complete the tasks required of them. The often unfamiliar environment of outdoor programmes can further add to their fears.

In order to calm these fears, participants need to be thoroughly briefed on the activities involved, and, most importantly, on the purpose of the whole programme. They need to understand the connection between outdoor activities and everyday work issues.

However, it will never be possible to quieten all the apprehension aroused by an outdoor development programme. Expecting to do so is a bit like saying, 'trust me', and expecting trust to be immediate. The realisation that they will be all right does not usually dawn on participants until after the first one or two exercises.

Indeed, a certain degree of apprehension is a desirable part of an outdoor programme. Learning to deal with individual and group apprehension can be one of the most positive results of an outdoor event. It has clear parallels with change management, for apprehension is is often a large part of the resistance to change.

One woman described her experience on an outdoor course as being like the period leading up to her divorce. She was terrified by the thought of what she had to do, and was never at ease as the programme progressed. But when it was over, she felt empowered. By doing something new by herself, and putting herself in a position of risk, she felt a tremendous sense of freedom and achievement.

A CHECKLIST FOR RUNNING MANAGEMENT DEVELOPMENT IN THE OUTDOORS

Observance of the following criteria appear to be crucial to the success of any programme of development in the outdoors:

- The programme should have very clear objectives
- The programme must be designed as part of an overall training programme
- Careful checks need to be made on the training providers' safety standards
- The provider should be familiar with the client organisation
- The programme must be tailored to individual client needs and objectives
- The course should have a high tutor-to-participant ratio
- The programme and the tutors must relate each activity back to the workplace

- The emphasis should be on reviewing the process, not on the outdoor activity itself, from day one
- The tutors must be capable of conducting continuous reviews
- The course should be followed up with evaluation sessions in the workplace.

CASE STUDY

'Visioning on the island'

This case study looks at one group's experience of management development in the outdoors. The group in question consisted of district sales managers working for the UK division of a European multinational.

This organisation – Firm A – had recently agreed to joint ventures with a well-known British engineering group. Its market had become very competitive, and it was seen as the successful leader in this market. Success had in large part been due to the efforts of an aggressive and highly-paid salesforce.

However, it was becoming increasingly apparent that the management style of the company had emphasised securing immediate sales at the expense of long-term strategy and customer satisfaction. The climate within the company was, in fact, starting to encourage deception. There was a lack of trust within the salesforce, and it was becoming common practice for the salespeople to lie to their managers, to each other, and to their customers, in order to secure business and the high commission this earned.

A crisis was reached when the current recession began to bite, and the company started to experience severe problems with dissatisfied customers. At the same time, a major competitor started to change the way it operated, emphasising quality and customer care.

The problem

Firm A's recently-appointed UK marketing director was increasingly aware of the need for change. He saw that, if disaster was to be averted, the organisation's business practices and the more fundamental values, attitudes and beliefs of the people in the organisation needed to be shaken up. So he arranged a meeting with an external consultancy group that had worked with the firm before. Between them, the marketing director and the external consultants put together a plan for change.

Implementation of this strategy relied on the willingness of the company's district managers and their staff to undergo major changes in their working practices. Those responsible for the strategy felt that if it was to be successful, the district managers needed to be consulted, and involved in the solution to the company's problems. In the past, policy decisions of this magnitude had only ever been made at board level, and line managers were rarely, if ever, consulted.

In the general climate of mistrust, it was assumed that the district managers would be sceptical of the motives of senior management. But the success of the plan depended on the district managers being able to sell the idea of change and new attitudes to the wider salesforce, many of whom would suffer financially as a result of the new policies.

First steps to a solution

As a first step towards a solution to this problem, the marketing director commissioned the consultants to design a learning event for the district managers, designed to allow them to explore their current situation, and the problems they were facing. These managers were to be encouraged to approach the problems with a completely clean sheet, not ruling out any solutions providing they were practicable.

The idea behind this learning event was for the district managers themselves to see the need for a new company culture of honesty and openness, and to formulate ways of achieving this. In this way it was hoped that the managers would feel some ownership of the solutions proposed, and a commitment to ensure their success.

The proposed learning event had to ensure that each participant:

- Endorsed a new philosophy of quality, commitment, and creativity, and was personally committed to it
- Had acquired the skills to inspire his or her team with this philosophy
- Had formulated an action plan to implement the philosophy.

It was agreed that the programme for the learning event should consist of a pre-event consultation day between the participants and the UK senior management team. The core of the programme was to be a four-and-a-half-day residential programme for district managers, who would be joined by senior management for a final day's consultation and reporting back. This was to be followed up by a further one-day event to ensure transfer of learning to the workplace.

Using the outdoors

The consultants were under a great deal of pressure to deliver a workable solution. They only had one opportunity to succeed in what would be a high risk venture. If they missed the mark, the scepticism of the district managers would make it very unlikely that they would receive any more work from Firm A.

In the circumstances, the temptation for the consultants to start prescribing solutions was considerable. In a way, their dilemma echoed the organisation's own – both had to choose between a 'quick fix', and a potentially more rewarding, but more risky strategy of long-term investment.

The consultants resisted the attractions of the quick fix, however, and went instead for an undoubtedly risky solution: they decided to hold the event for the district managers in the outdoors, but chose their location with care, as the participants had already had a 'standard' experience.

The thinking behind this decision was to allow the natural world to serve both as a metaphor and as a catalyst for beneficial change in a competitive environment.

The participants were flown up to Inverness and bussed out to a remote activity centre on the west coast of Scotland. Here, preparations were made before taking the group out to an uninhabited Inner Hebridean island. The plan was for the district managers to return to the mainland for the final day's meeting with the senior management team.

The experience

Day 1

The participants arrived at the mainland centre, as expected, in a high state of excitement, due partly to the genuine thrill of doing something different, but also partly to a certain fear about the unknown.

The first thing was for them to become familiar with their new environment and the tutorial team. After a meal prepared by one of the tutors, they all took a short walk along the coast. This was a chance for people to meet on informal and equal terms, and to see that, although remote, the centre was comfortable and not too daunting. It was also the tutors' intention, however, that the power of the spectacular scenery would work its magic and suggest that something serious was about to be encountered.

After this initial introduction, the participants began to relax. They had the added bonus of seeing two porpoises swim past, and on their return to base, they were eager to start the task in hand.

In the days ahead, the participants would be encouraged to examine their behaviour, and take some risks. At this early stage, therefore, the group needed to be allowed to explore ways of doing this for themselves, rather than being 'told' how.

What was necessary first of all was a process that allowed the participants to look at course objectives, while at the same time alerting them to the fact that this was no ordinary course and that some unusual things might happen. To this end, the group were given a brief to design a collage, with pictures taken from magazines, depicting the company and the main 'people issues' facing it. These issues were to include relationships with customers.

The participants' immediate reaction that this was just like going back to primary school prompted some input on creative thinking from the tutors. The resulting increased enthusiasm for the task gave rise to some surprising insights. Lots of pictures of windows, junctions, and doors clearly indicated that the participants felt the company to be at a crossroads. They felt, too, that it was the quality of the relationships formed by the company that would make the difference required to succeed. This exercise also revealed a recognition that environmental issues needed to play a key part in corporate policy.

The participants themselves were surprised at how much could be gained from an ostensibly facile exercise, and at how differently they were already thinking.

Following the collage exercise, the participants were asked to carry out their first tasks in the outdoors. Two related tasks were set: to design and construct a catapult, and to untangle a continuous loop of rope to form a target which met certain specifications. The participants were familiar with this way of working, and set about their tasks with great enthusiasm.

But the resulting behaviour accurately reflected many of the problems facing their company. The participants all acted selfishly, blaming each other, cheating, bending the rules, and ignoring required standards and norms. They failed miserably, but claimed success, defending their own achievements.

This kind of behaviour, where participants deny their failure to complete the task as instructed by blaming their materials or other participants, but never themselves, is very common at his stage of outdoor courses. In the debrief that followed the exercise, the tutors used the Kolb learning cycle to make connections between the participants' behaviour and their work, and to future exercises.

The group began to realise that denial behaviour was not going to help them respond positively, or to change the situation at work. This was probably the most crucial insight delivered by the programme.

At this point in the programme, they knew in 'headline' terms the issues that had to be addressed, but the detailed content of the course was still a mystery to them. After a short period for reflection, preparations began for the transfer to the island which was their next destination.

At this point the tutors adopted a more directive style, instructing them in the skills needed for the next phase of the programme.

This provided some much-needed structure and support for participants still coming to terms with their new-found realisation of the need to change their behaviour. During the next few hours, each member of the group learned new physical skills. Gentle reminders of the need for quality, commitment and support for each other, rather than just looking out for number one, were liberally sprinkled in the tutors' briefings. The evening meal prepared by the participants, which rounded off the first day, reflected their good intentions for personal change.

Day 2

As experienced managers, the participants took control of the timing, scheduling and sequencing of the transfer to the island, using the tutors as the kind of technical support function they would use at work. This encouraged a feeling of ownership and empowerment. At eight the following morning, they were all in a chartered fishing boat on their way to the uninhabited island of Rona.

Once they had arrived at the island, the participants all worked hard to establish a camp, after which they were briefed on the next exercise, called 'Solo'. Here, the participants were given half an hour to explore the island and their thoughts. At the end of half an hour, all the group members had returned except for one, who was still missing. This was the first unplanned event in the programme. The tutors were not unduly concerned, as they felt it would throw up plenty of material for the group to work with. The safety factor was also well covered, as the island was in fact a fairly benign environment, and the tutors had the wherewithal to cover most eventualities (including radio links to the mainland and emergency services).

The other members of the group became very concerned about their colleague, however. Although there appeared to be a genuine concern for his safety, this was not the issue uppermost in the minds of the participants. The individual in question had a history of taking unilateral action at work which was not supportive of group aims. The group seemed to see in his non-appearance an opportunity to 'nail this once and for all'. This diverted attention from more legitimate concerns and gave a focus for collective displacement of the issues at hand – in fact, a mirror of standard behaviour within the organisation.

Intervention by the tutors managed, however, to redirect the participants' energy into two organised search parties co-ordinated by radio. After some puffing over hills and through wooded gullies, the parties were informed that the individual had returned to camp.

At this point, the tutors needed to put in some work both with the group and with the individual before they got back together again, to help each party to understand how the other was feeling. If this behaviour was indeed a mirror of the organisation, what implications did it have?

When the whole party was eventually reunited, a frank, open and sometimes raw discussion ensued about the organisation and its politics, and about personal responsibility. It was generally felt that some progress had been made.

The next exercise involved negotiation between two teams. Each team was set the goal of achieving a positive score. In this particular exercise, it is only possible for both teams to achieve such a score if they both trust each other and agree to 'play fair'. Otherwise, one team must win, and another lose.

The exercise was designed to model 'old' corporate behaviour vying with 'new thinking' behaviour. In the end, corporate behaviour won out. However, the implications of this fact were not lost on the participants, who were starting to realise how hard it was going to be to change their behaviour, and how easy to be distracted from one's objectives.

The next exercise was a very simple, but stimulating one, designed to mirror ever-increasing demands for higher standards and greater productivity at work. The participants stood in a circle and were given a football. They were told to throw the ball in a random sequence, but ensuring that everyone could catch it once, and then return it to where it started. The group was asked to repeat the sequence, and then to set and meet a target time within which they could complete the cycle.

After a few cycles, the group was feeling quite pleased with its target time. The tutor then told the group that its competitors said they could do it in half the time, so the group had to improve its standard or lose to the competition. As a result, the participants started to throw the ball harder, in an attempt to improve their time. Although this led to all sorts of frustrations and anger within the group, it did achieve a faster time.

The tutor made further interventions, giving all sorts of different reasons why the group had to improve further. The group eventually halved its target time, by setting up a standard pattern for throwing the ball. At this point, the tutor said that the Japanese had done it in half this final target time, and the group had to beat that or go under.

The group members felt they could not improve any more, but at this point someone in the group finally thought that there might be another way of solving the problem. This participant saw that to cut its time further, the group would have to let go of some old habits and familiar tactics. It had to think laterally, and indeed, following this insight, the group did come up with the solution.

The major learning point of this exercise is that most organisations reach a point where no further improvement is possible simply by doing something faster and harder. Once this limit is reached, only radical rethinking of perceived wisdom allows movement through the 'change barrier'. This inevitably involves restructuring the way information is managed, creativity and risk taking. Substantial learning from a 'ball game'!

Day 3

The time had now come for the group to let go of old patterns of behaviour and to start the real process of change. At this stage of any programme, despite a certain commitment to change, uncertainty abounds. The tutor's skill is crucial, as it is very difficult for the group to make progress by itself. However, too much direct intervention will take away the group's sense of ownership and achievement.

To get through this stage, these particular tutors decided on an unusual style of working. They felt that it was important for each individual to concentrate on his or her own behaviour and attitudes for a while. Using a process of guided thinking and visualisation, participants were encouraged to create a picture that they would be able to draw on later, either during the rest of the programme or back at work.

The participants were asked to create a picture in their minds of how they would ideally like their company to be. Using the island as background, the tutors asked the participants how they would run this ideal organisation if it were based in one of the coves on the island!

There was a great deal of initial resistance to this exercise. However, the fact that the tutors could even propose such an idea to these hard-bitten managers could be seen as a testament to the effects of the unfamiliar environment on them. They were far more open to this unconventional approach than they might have been had they been at work or on a programme in a management conference centre.

This opportunity to share experiences, feelings and insights acted, in effect, like the release of a pressure valve. The participants' language changed, becoming more optimistic and dealing more frequently with the future. The participants became visibly more relaxed. Volume levels dropped, and people started to listen to each other for the first time. That evening the participants spent their time relaxing, going fishing, collecting mussels, and enjoying each other's company as they watched the sun set over Skye and the Outer Hebrides. The tutors felt that their gamble had worked.

Although there were signs that many in the group had turned a personal corner during this exercise, not everyone had achieved the same level of insight or understanding. The important role for the tutors at this stage was to try to ensure that everyone in the group could gain an improved understanding of the issues being addressed.

Day 4

The task for the fourth day was to formulate a new foundation for the company. The aim was to look at the strategic issues from an operational manager's point of view, and to identify solutions which could be discussed further with senior management.

The participants surprised the tutors by requesting a second opportunity for focused thinking and visualisation to get into the right frame of mind for the day ahead. With the group's permission, a tutor taped the proceedings. The clarity with which the participants were starting to see problems and solutions was, in fact, quite astounding. (Indeed, when the tape was played back to the senior management team, they found it hard to recognise their own district managers in the voices they heard.)

One of the major exercises for the day was to consider the strategic issues in syndicate groups. These groups were self-regulating, in that they set their own agendas, and liaised with each other at will.

The participants functioned well in these groups, planning, organising, directing and controlling activities with considerable clarity and focus. Much discussion centred on finding common ground between individual perspectives. The participants took great pains over one individual, whose views seemed to be at odds with the rest of the group. This behaviour was markedly different from that displayed three days earlier, when participants would probably have metaphorically 'shot and disposed' of this individual. During this period, the tutors remained in the background, operating as sounding boards for thoughts, and as suppliers of equipment, such as tape recorders, flip charts, planning boards, and copious amounts of tea and coffee.

Team confidence was growing, as was a sense of interdependence among the group members. One of the outcomes of the day was an agreed value system which participants thought they could recommend for adoption by the company. Participants agreed on eight 'core values' to underpin the company culture.

The final activity of this, the last day on the island, was designed to test these proposed values and to draw together much of what had been learned during the course of the programme. Each member of the group was assigned the role of 'custodian' of one of the core values. Each was asked to note how well the other participants respected this particular value during the exercise, and to report back to the group afterwards.

The task, to construct a rope bridge, was designed to provide a test of the group's new-found ways of managing personal relationships in an atmosphere of perceived risk. Having spent much of the day in mental activity, participants also found this very physical task a welcome break.

In carrying out the exercise, the team could be seen to be working consciously to uphold the new company values. When reviewing the exercise, participants displayed a high level of honesty about their respect or otherwise for each of the core values. Most importantly, participants were able to see that they had actually managed to devise a workable system which upheld these core values.

This was a high point on which to end their stay on the island. Participants felt that they had achieved, not just some new ideas, but some practical and workable solutions to the problems facing them at work.

Epilogue

It had always been the intention for the participants on this outdoor programme to meet with their senior managers to report back on their conclusions and proposals for action. On the evening of the fourth day, around the camp fire, the tutors made an announcement. They told the participants that the report back to the senior management team would take place, not at headquarters, as the participants had assumed, but the very next day. The senior managers would be arriving at the mainland base soon after the group's return.

Not surprisingly, this news was not well received. A discussion ensued as to what form the participants' presentation should take, based on 'political' considerations. Regression back to the 'old' style of thinking was perhaps inevitable. Although some members of the team appreciated that this was happening, others did not. Two factions emerged, and people stopped listening. A good deal of criticism of the tutors' 'dishonesty' was also voiced. By the end of the evening, campfire revelry had returned sufficiently to ensure a level of cordiality, but one that masked doubts and reservations all round.

Although it was done in good faith, this action was seen ultimately to reflect the kind of secretive organisational culture that the programme had been supposed to change. However, it did give the participants a live opportunity to deal honestly with the issues that created conflict in the workplace.

Nevertheless, the participants made a confident presentation on the final day to their senior managers. During the presentation they covered many of the learning points gained during the outdoor programme, and outlined their proposed company core values. A very constructive discussion ensued, during which the district managers and their bosses were able to agree some future actions for change.

Although these plans are only just beginning to be implemented, there is a feeling that progress is being made. Overall, the participants' judgement of the four-and-a-half-day programme was that it represented a successful beginning.

The event was followed up by two one-day events, with the district managers and their direct reports, to follow up the changes that had been started on the island. It was agreed that the learning event had involved some very enlightening experiences for the participants, both personally and in their role as managers. And, indeed, it is very unlikely that the same level of awareness could have been reached as quickly without the special stimulus afforded by holding the event in the outdoors. All in all, the event has been seen as helping Firm A to undertake a more far-reaching investigation into its own practices, and to make more radical changes as a result, than would otherwise have been possible.

PROVIDERS OF MANAGEMENT DEVELOPMENT IN THE OUTDOORS

The following organisations provide management development in the outdoors, and some of their work has featured in this chapter.

DRYLL MANAGEMENT DEVELOPMENT (residential centre)
Deiniolen, Gwynedd, North Wales
0286 870369
0286 871487 (fax)
Director: Chas Sewell

EXECUTIVE AND STAFF TRAINING (**EAST**)
4, Mornington Terrace, Harrogate, North Yorkshire, HG1 5GH
0423 531083
0423 521073 (fax)
Director: John Campbell

HORIZON DEVELOPMENT TRAINING
14, Springbank Road, Chesterfield, S40 1NL
0433 631662 (telephone/fax)
Director: Derek Furze

8 NEW STRUCTURES FOR A CHANGING ENVIRONMENT

In this chapter, we take a look at some of the radical changes now taking place in many forward-looking organisations. These include changes in their way of working and in their management styles, both of which are increasingly being reflected in changing organisational structures.

We look at some of the wide variety of structural and other changes taking place in organisations, and argue that, despite the diversity, some common themes can be discerned. One of the most important of these is the empowerment of the workforce.

Empowerment cannot, however, be achieved merely by introducing new techniques piecemeal. What is required, very often, is a more radical overhaul of an organisation's approach to its working practices and decision-making structures.

We examine the notion of empowerment, and argue that, paradoxically, it requires strong leadership in order to be successful. Strong messages, and effective decision-making at the top are still required in empowering organisations. Empowerment certainly *does not* mean abdication of management responsibility, although it may require a change in management styles. Equally, however, an empowering organisation needs its employees to accept responsibility for their own actions. This may take time, and considerable investment in training.

Finally, the chapter turns to the process of change itself, in an attempt to understand the underlying reasons for the resistance to change so often experienced by organisations. We argue that organisations and individuals need to accept denial, confusion, and resistance as uncomfortable, but necessary, parts of the cycle of change and renewal.

Experience is not what happens to a man. It is what a man does with what happens to him.
Aldous Huxley

There is nothing more difficult to carry out, nor more doubtful of success, nor more dangerous to handle, than to initiate a new order of things.
Niccolo Machiavelli

Perhaps one of the most telling signs of the changes now taking place in the business community is the extent to and rate at which organisations are making radical changes to the way decisions are made. New structures – often flatter, and more democratic – are emerging in place of the rigid hierarchies that have dominated corporations in the past. And other structural changes are becoming increasingly necessary in response to quite radical new ways of working, and different styles of management.

This chapter looks at some of these new ways of working, and at the new structures and new management styles which are making these radical approaches possible. It also examines the process of change itself, arguing that the resistance, difficulties and confusion often encountered during periods of organisational change are, in fact, a necessary and productive part of the process of renewal.

NEW STRUCTURES FOR NEW APPROACHES

Let us start by taking a look at some of the new management structures and working methods now being adopted by some companies in the UK and America.

In March 1992, Unipart ended recognition of trade unions in its workplaces, and now pays salaries rather than hourly wages to all of its 4,000 employees: blue-collar workers, office staff, and managers alike. De-recognition of the unions was not, however, an isolated action; rather, it represented another milestone in a process that had begun in a corner of the company's Oxford factory in 1987, and gradually expanded to transform the whole organisation.

Back in 1987, production in part of the Oxford factory had been organised into 'cells' in which small, flexible teams of employees carried out a variety of tasks. As this new method was adopted throughout the factory, more radical changes in the structure of the organisation took place in its wake. The existing seven layers of management were cut to three; traditional 'piecework' pay rates were replaced by salaries based on ability; the posts of foreman and supervisor were eliminated; and 'contribution circles' of management and employees were formed to work on special cost-cutting projects .

Saturn Corporation, General Motor's innovative start-up car plant, is another example of an organisation which has adopted a radically new way of organising the way it works:

- At each managerial level from the President down, and within each staff function, a union counterpart shares decision-making equally with company managers.
- All employees are part of at least one team, where decisions are made by consensus.
- Employees can expect to spend at least five per cent of their time annually in training. This is tied to the company's 'risk and reward' compensation system, so that the company guarantees 95 per cent of each employee's base wages but only pays the remaining 5 per cent when *everyone* in the company has met their training goals.
- Half the training time allotted to production workers is devoted to interpersonal skills such as conflict resolution, problem solving, presentation skills, and communication.
- There are no time clocks, no privileged parking spots, no private dining rooms and no job titles.
- Everyone's dress is casual.

Pitney Bowes has reorganised its people into self-directed teams whose members are self-selected and set their own production goals and holiday schedules. Remuneration is now based on competence rather than seniority.

At Suma foods, Britain's largest democratic co-operative, employees do all the hiring and firing, and decide on policy. All staff members are paid the same wage regardless of tenure, functions or responsibilities.

After three employees left, the remaining 29 members of a Hoechst Celanese plant decided not to replace them – and management was not involved in this decision. More than 70 per cent of the plant's production employees have now been involved in team decision-making through work design teams. Members of these teams are selected by their peers, usually on the basis of how much they know about a particular job. Teams examine the internal and external factors affecting their jobs, decide their work and holiday schedules, and seek peer performance review.

EMPOWERMENT

The new structures and working practices adopted by forward-looking organisations are varied and diverse, as the handful of examples given above illustrates. Nevertheless, there are some common themes which run through many of the new approaches currently being adopted by such organisations. We might summarise some of these themes as follows:

- De-layering of supervisory management
- A meritocratic approach to reward
- Creation of self-managing teams.

The feature of many of the new approaches that stands out most clearly of all, however, is the fact that they act to *empower* the people working for the company.

Most empowerment programmes in organisations are based on the principle that people are generally willing to commit themselves to things that they have *agreed* to. Only by gaining a high level of employee commitment is an organisation likely to achieve the improvements in quality, productivity and service that such programmes aim for, as well as the other potential benefits, such as personal growth and development for individuals and the company as a whole.

The idea behind the empowerment of employees, also known as *power sharing*, is to move resources and decisions as close as possible to where the action to implement the decisions is actually taken. Organisations that have adopted such an approach often find that the resulting decisions are cleaner and can be implemented more quickly, so more work can be done. In comparison, the traditional model of management, where the managers' prime role is to keep a check on everyone else's work, seems to be an unfocused way of achieving productivity.

Kurt Lewin, the social psychologist, suggested that in order to effect change in any organisation, an experiment in genuine participation is required. Similarly, W Edwards Deming, the statistical guru who was involved in introducing Quality Circles in Japan, showed that by emphasising quality instead of setting production targets, organisations could achieve higher output.

It is this startling insight which has been partly responsible for the growth of Total Quality Programmes. The ostensible purpose of these programmes is to raise the quality of products by encouraging worker participation, support and accountability. However, in some organisations they have also led to a major rethink of the way things are done, by encouraging employees to set their own goals, to choose their methods of working, and to take decisions.

We are going to look at the idea of empowerment in more detail in a moment. But first, it is important to emphasise that empowerment means much more than just 'participation by the book'. If managers try to raise productivity and morale by introducing group decision-making alone, they are very likely to fail. Allocating places for workers on the board and worker ownership cannot in themselves increase output or motivate workers, so long as traditional styles of supervision and hierarchical structures are still intact. What is required is, rather, an entire restructuring of an organisation's systems, attitudes, and ways of working. It is only through this kind of radical change that organisations are likely to gain the potential benefits of employee empowerment.

The principle of participation, of empowering the majority of employees, is a difficult one to master, particularly if an organisation's leaders have come to think of themselves as the 'experts' in their organisation. However, empowerment cannot be achieved simply by an organisation's managers abdicating responsibility. There is evidence that effective empowerment depends on effective leadership. Warren Bennis, the professor and author, suggests that in organisations with effective leaders, empowerment is achieved in the following ways:

- **People feel significant**
  In organisations which are well-led, everyone feels that he or she makes a difference to the success of the organisation, however small that might be.
- **Learning and competence are seen to matter**
  Effective leaders value learning and mastery of a subject, and encourage the people who work for them to do so too. This kind of leader makes it clear that there is no such thing as failure, only learning and feedback from errors that tell you what to do next.
- **People feel themselves to be part of a community**
  Where there is effective leadership, people feel they belong to a team, a 'family', or a unity of some kind. Even those who do not like each other feel a sense of community.
- **Work is thought of as exciting**
  Where there are effective leaders, work is regarded as stimulating, challenging and fun. This is an indication that people have been 'pulled' rather than 'pushed'. In this kind of environment, people are very self-motivated, usually through identification with the goals of the organisation rather than through punishment or specific reward. Employees and management in such organisations tend to have a clear, agreed idea of the goals and ideals which the organisation is striving towards.

When they hear the word 'empowerment', many managers fear anarchy. This resistance is likely to be more emotional than logical, however. Their sense of worry usually comes less from any real business risk than from their own fears of being 'out of control'. Traditional management practices give the illusion of safety, both for the manager and the managed. The manager feels in control, while the managed employee feels 'looked after'. However, this feeling of safety only lasts for as long as the managed employees want no more than the manager is prepared to give them, or for as long as they agree with the manager's way of doing things. Problems arise when the managed person wants something different.

One of the things traditional management styles often miss is the fact that delegation is an extremely forceful use of power. As power works best when it is invisible, empowerment can, paradoxically, give a lot of power to the person doing the empowering. John Kotter, a Harvard professor, said in a recent article in *Fortune* magazine, 'When you decentralise in a management sense, it does take power from the corner office. But decentralising leadership is different. The more power in the whole organisation, the more you can influence and change.'

As we have seen, organisations that empower their workers still need leadership. The role of the leaders, however, does need to change from the traditional one of watching others do the work and checking on how it is going, to providing vision and direction, and a more facilitative approach. Empowerment does not mean that management no longer manages. On the contrary, management still has to make decisions at the corporate level. Giving employees the power to make decisions about areas where they know nothing can be frustrating for everyone and disempowering for the workers. Strong messages from an organisation's leaders are also very important, especially in a time of rapid change and adjustment. This does not mean that employees should have *no* input into corporate decisions; rather, employees should to be given their say, but some final decisions still need to be made by management.

But it is not only managers who can stand in the way of employee empowerment. It is very easy for employees themselves to get caught in the trap of rationalising why they cannot take responsibility for themselves at work. It is easy to say, 'I want to take responsibility, but *they* won't let me'. Empowerment offers employees more choice and greater control, but the price tag is accountability; taking responsibility, in some cases, may result in failure.

Of course, if an organisation chooses empowerment through the introduction of self-regulating teams and other new approaches, it is very important to train the workers in the new ways of working. If your people have been trained for years to follow orders and not to question authority, then, of course, it is very likely that some of them will not know how to take responsibility.

And, of course, there is a limit to how much can be achieved in this area, even by the best training. Though many may be coachable, some employees will simply not want to take on the responsibility involved in these new ways of working, while others will be unable to cope with this responsibility, and will crack if put under pressure. Management of the situation for these employees needs to be handled carefully, so that it does not alienate or demotivate those who have chosen to go forward. It may, indeed, involve some very hard-nosed selection decisions.

INTRODUCING CHANGE – A NATURAL CYCLE

New technology, new structures, new methods of working, in fact anything new, threatens people's security. When trying to introduce new approaches to doing things, managers constantly face resistance from their workforces. In the rest of this chapter, we are going to take a look at the process of change itself, and at some of the underlying reasons for people's negative reactions to change. For it is only by understanding the change process that managers can begin to understand how best to tackle the problems it may bring.

Claes Janssen, the Swedish social psychologist, has suggested that the people's reactions to change involve moving through something akin to a 'four room apartment'(see Figure 8.1).

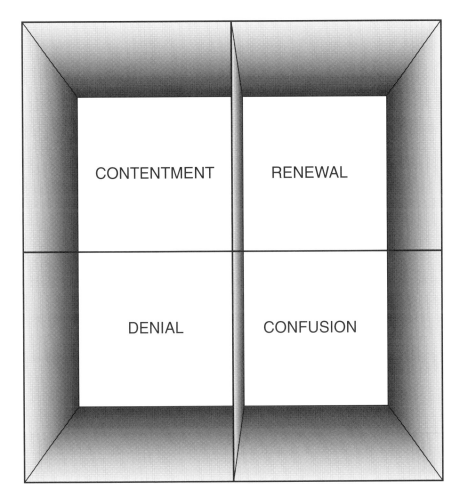

Figure 8.1 Reactions to change: the four room apartment

Individuals, groups, and organisations going through a process of change can be seen as moving through the sequence of 'rooms' one by one.

The four rooms represent cyclical phases, which are not unlike the phases of the grieving process. This is not surprising, since every change that people undergo can be seen as a loss of some kind. The extent of the loss, and the circumstances surrounding it, will determine how long it takes for an individual or an organisation to walk through all the rooms. For example, commuters whose train is cancelled will go through the rooms far more quickly than someone dealing with, say, redundancy. Nevertheless, in both cases all four rooms are visited, however briefly.

In Janssen's model, we can never leave the apartment itself, only move through the rooms one by one. This reflects the idea that change is not a downward spiral, but a perpetual circle. Once it is accepted that change is part of the natural order of things, and that, in fact, rebuilding or renewal cannot take place without change, then the negative or uncomfortable effects of change can be seen as an inevitable part of the whole process of renewal.

Let us look in more detail at the four rooms in Janssen's model. He describes people in the **contentment** room as being comfortable with what is happening around them. They are calm, satisfied and able to keep things in perspective.

Of course, people should not be moved out of the contentment room unless it is absolutely necessary. Change for change's sake is both destructive and unproductive. Any personal or professional change, such as a job threat or reorganisation at work, is likely to send people into the **denial** room. In this room, people do not accept their situation, but appear, instead, to be oblivious to it. The reason for this is that the first reaction of the human mind to what it perceives to be a loss of any kind is to pretend that it is not happening. Since they are pretending that nothing is happening, people in this room do not have to do anything about the changes confronting them. Some people find it extremely difficult to get out of this room, and, indeed, most of the problems encountered in dealing with change come from the process of denial.

There is no chance of moving out of the denial room until an individual is able to own up to his or her fears, anxieties, and anger about the changes taking place. By staying in this room and denying any feeling, people avoid having to deal with their feelings and fears of something new. To get past the resistance that comes with any change, these feelings have to be 'owned up to' and expressed openly.

Letting go of the past is essential for moving on, but, of course, this often requires time, and support. The desire to hold onto the past, to familiar patterns and structures, is common to all of humankind. When people are in the denial room, it is often helpful to ask questions and 'give permission' for them to have negative feelings. It is extremely unhelpful and indeed counterproductive to offer advice. If you offer advice to someone who has not yet admitted that they have a problem, then they are likely either to reject the advice, or to find reasons for not doing it, or to do it without commitment.

When we finally own up to our fears, we are able to walk into the **confusion** room. In this room, everything we have been frightened of actually happens, we feel unsafe and insecure, and feel that we are wandering in thick fog without a clear sense of direction.

It is this unpleasant state that people are trying to avoid when they seek to deny change. Hence the discomfort managers have when delivering 'bad news' to other people. However, far from being a room to be avoided, the confusion room is in reality the place where we are probably most ready to learn. In this state, anxiety is an energy source to be harnessed and used. Every major change requires a degree of anxiety if it is to be successful. However, too much anxiety and we become paralysed; too little and we become demotivated and apathetic.

The key to moving out of the confusion room lies in accepting that confusion is the only way to get into the renewal room. Individuals and organisations that can see confusion as something that is positive in the long term, although initially uncomfortable, are well on the way to accepting change.

When people are stuck in the confusion room, the most helpful kinds of behaviour are similar to those recommended for the denial room. Encouragement to talk is essential, but by attempting to take control of the conversation you may send people back into the denial room. People need to 'let go' in their own way and in their own time.

Through the experiences of the confusion room, people and organisations can begin to see the door to the **renewal** room, where they are able to accept the new, and begin to experience the excitement of positive change. Once we have attained the renewal room, we have let go of the past, and can build for the future. Here, our acceptance of what is happening allows us to develop plans and ways of dealing with the changes.

Once people have moved into the renewal room, they may, of course, need support to help them implement any ideas they may have, and encouragement to see them through. Once this process is complete, people are able to move back into the contentment room once again, and there they stay until the next change arrives, and the process begins again.

ACCEPTING RESISTANCE

What does Janssen's model have to teach managers trying to introduce new ways of working, and the structures that go with them? Clearly, the major lesson that needs to be learned is that anyone who offers the chance of renewal without accepting the need for a period of denial and confusion is likely to be a false prophet. Quite apart from the fact that no-one has a sure-fire solution to every problem likely to be encountered during a process of radical change, there is no chance of empowering employees, of giving them a sense of achievement, if someone else has all the answers.

Organisations attempting to introduce major change need to accept that there is no magic cure for anxiety and chaos. Indeed, these conditions are necessary in order to breed creativity, excitement and commitment. Resistance is a natural process, and one that is essential to effective change. By understanding the processes involved in change, you may be helped to get through some of the unpleasant side-effects, but it is never possible to avoid them altogether.

Marvin Weisbord, the writer and consultant, compares people's attitude to organisational change to people's reactions in 1915 to the motor car: 'many people have heard of them, few have actually seen one, not everybody wants one, and those who do are more interested in cost and speed than quality. Those people who do own one find it both stimulating and frustrating, threatening and inspiring, unpredictable and hard to describe!'

CASE STUDY

Restructuring for change

In this case study we examine how one large brewing organisation has restructured its operation in response to radical changes taking place in its market.

Bass Brewers is part of Bass Plc, one of the biggest companies in the UK. Since 1777, it has been one of the major players in this most traditional of industries.

Bass Brewers is the largest brewing company in the UK, with a market share estimated to be about 22 per cent. In 1989, in a response to a reference by the Director General of Fair Trading, the Monopolies and Mergers Commission (MMC), published a report on the supply of beer. The Commission was concerned that the vertically integrated nature of the UK brewing industry, through which brewers controlled varying proportions of the production, wholesaling and retailing layers of the business, operated against the public interest. Their suggestion was that this structure resulted in higher prices and reduced consumer choice.

The MMC thus recommended that the brewers should be allowed to control no more than 2,000 pubs each. Lord Young subsequently moderated this decision, and the Department of Trade and Industry published orders requiring brewers who owned more than 2,000 pubs to sell, or lease free of tie, their outlets. This was in order to reduce the number of pubs owned to 2,000, plus half the number in excess of 2,000 they had originally owned. For example, Bass, which had owned about 7,000 pubs, had to reduce to 2,000 plus half of 5,000, a final total of 4,500, and subsequently sold 2,500 pubs. The Department of Trade Orders also imposed additional regulatory constraints upon brewers in respect of their ability to tie non-owned outlets and introduced new concepts, such as that of 'guest beers'.

The Orders had a major impact upon Bass, upon other major brewers, and indeed, upon the whole industry. In addition to these imposed changes, beer consumption in the UK, which had been slowly falling in the UK, was hit by the recession and volumes declined significantly.

The need for change

Prior to October 1989, Bass was a vertically integrated company structured on a regional basis. Its brewing and pub interests were essentially a collection of local businesses, including Tennants in Scotland, Bass North in the North of England, Bass Mitchells and Butlers in the Midlands, Welsh Brewers in Wales, and Charrington and Co. in the South East. Each business had its own board and managing director, and its own supporting functional structure, including finance, production, local distribution, and sales.

In the past, this structure had served Bass well, allowing it to capture the biggest share of the beer market. However, there were disadvantages. Economies of scale and synergies between the businesses were not optimised. Irrational examples of autonomous regional approaches existed, businesses operated differently because they always had, rather than for any rational business reasons. Information technology was tailored to accommodate regional differences, and was effectively an automated version of historic means for normal collection and processing of information. Differences would lead to difficulties in consolidation. Moreover the vertically integrated structure had not allowed sufficient focus on the establishment of specialist business skills; for example, in hospitality retailing.

It was the shake up of the industry brought on by the Commission's inquiry, however, that provided the real impetus to change Bass' traditional structure. The company found it increasingly difficult to react effectively to the national changes taking place through the medium of a loose conglomeration of different businesses, each with their own way of doing things.

Bass Plc then restructured into five divisions:

Holiday Inn worldwide
The largest hotel company in the world had recently been acquired. Based in Atlanta, USA. The only non-UK based company.

Britvic
This is the only non-wholly owned company. Bass Plc have management control and half the equity. (The other half is owned by Allied, Whitbread and Pepsico.)

Bass Leisure
This covers companies such as Coral Racing, social clubs (Gala), Bingo halls, and Amusement With Prizes (slot machines).

Bass Taverns
The Retailing division, which owns and runs the pubs and includes Toby restaurants.

Bass Brewers
Brewing, wholesaling, distribution and brand marketing.

All of the divisions faced up to the changes in differing ways. This case study looks at the way Bass Brewers tackled the new order.

Even in the face of these major changes in its environment, though, it was difficult for Bass Brewers to accept the need to change its own way of working. It had always been a paternalistic organisation, strong on tradition. Until very recently, the skills that served a brewer well were what its Chief Executive called 'custodial skills'. In other words, each person had simply to learn to do their job in the same way as their predecessor. The company was strong on technical and financial skills, less strong on reacting to change.

In the end, however, the results of the Commission's inquiry, coupled with the threat of increasing competition from the other brewers, forced a major re-think, and finally, in 1989, the company took the decision to restructure.

Before taking a decision about a new structure for the company, Bass Brewers decided to undertake a major study of the beer market, its future development, the nature of the competition, and how the company could best succeed in these new conditions.

The company felt that nothing less than a top-to-bottom strategic review would do. With support from a leading consultancy firm, it established a series of task forces to look at every aspect of the business, from brands to the organisation of Bass Brewers itself.

The task forces were composed of groups of senior managers plus one or two consultants. This gave the senior managers a chance to take part in the new strategic decision-making, hitherto done only by the board.

To show the level of its commitment, the company took these managers off their usual jobs to work full time on the task forces. This was certainly good from the point of view of the managers and their own development, but it also put a tremendous amount of pressure on the business, as performance had to be maintained in their absence.

This risky strategy was seen as the start of a continuing process of change. To date, the company reckons it is 90 per cent of the way through the task of reviewing its business, and 70 per cent through the process of implementing its new strategy. Altogether, 153 new initiatives have been generated by the task forces; of these, 35 are in human resources areas.

Restructuring

The business review undertaken by the task forces provided a sound basis for decisions about how to restructure the company. A major finding was that the structure of the local businesses making up the Bass Brewers conglomerate was not getting the best out of the workforce. The business was structured into a series of functions, or 'chimneys', such as sales, finance, marketing production and distribution. Each 'chimney' had its own hierarchical structure. Communication between the functions was poor, and employees frequently felt that the hierarchy prevented them from working effectively. Teamwork, especially between functions, was limited.

It was decided to restructure the organisation, superimposing 'lateral' processes on the 'vertical' functions. On the basis of the fundamental review of its business, the company came up with six processes that are at the heart of what it does:

- Customer service and sales
- Brands portfolio management
- New product development
- Integrated logistics
- Funds flow
- Information management.

Each of these processes is the primary responsibility of one designated director of the Company, and each function's responsibility is now defined in terms of servicing these processes.

By placing the main emphasis on the 'lateral' core processes, rather than on functional 'chimneys', Bass Brewers has found that it can prevent some of the blockages to effective working identified by the task forces. For example, it is now easier to control production and distribution costs by using 'just-in-time' methods. This would not have been possible under the old 'chimney' system.

As a result of the restructuring, Bass Brewers' workforce has been reduced from 9,500 to 7,200, and its 13 national breweries have been reduced to 10.

Despite the changes, the structure of the company is still fairly conventional. There are no plans to abolish the functions entirely, as the company believes that focused sources of professional expertise are key requirements to drive the core processes. A less defined hierarchy still exists in that technical experts and managers within each function still have a good deal of authority. However, the principle is now that all functions are service functions: that is, they are there to service the core processes, not the other way round.

The company believes that it is making significant progress. A major step forward is the fact that information management has been defined as one of the processes central to the company's success. This move recognises the fact that the business has always needed information, and that the new structure is even more heavily dependent on information flow, hence on information technology.

Bass Brewers is spending £70 million on new information systems over the next few years. Unlike the old days, when the local businesses making up Bass operated their own information technology systems, the new system is being centralised The company's new facility at the Burton headquarters will have the largest IBM 400 conglomeration in Europe. And Bass Brewers was the first division of Bass Plc to have an Information Services Director on the board.

Changing the way people work

Identifying and defining the core processes crucial to success was, though, just the first step in adapting the company to its new environment. With the restructuring came an urgent need to change the way people in the company worked. And crucial to a new way of working, was for people to learn to work more productively together in their new, tougher, more competitive environment.

Another issue vital to successful management in the new, competitive environment was communication. The Chief Executive of the company likened its situation to a football match. Each player had on a different jersey, which denoted the function this person worked for. Each player was coached within his function, but the team was not trained as a whole. Some players communicated with each other, others did not communicate with anyone. Some of the players had poor vision and could not see the ball, if it was any distance away; some had been told that they could not kick the ball without permission from their boss. The result of all this was that it was extremely difficult for them to play as a team.

Only by ensuring that each team member communicated with the others, that they took off their different jerseys, that when necessary they were fitted with contact lenses, and that they were each allowed to decide whether and when to kick the ball, could a dynamic and efficient team be organised.

It was recognised that achieving improved teamwork and better communication in the company was no easy task. Bass Brewers has always had a strongly traditional, paternalistic culture. It was accepted that, in order to achieve the required changes, a new, equally strong company culture would need to be created in its stead.

Identifying competences

The Board of Bass Brewers saw clearly that the new culture would need to be more flexible, and meritocratic. To achieve this, the company has identified a set of core competences they believe to be crucial to the company's future.

These core competences are:

- Putting the customer first
- Teamwork
- Dedication to quality
- Bias to action
- Commercial focus
- Fairness and decency.

For each core competence, behaviours that are 'unacceptable', those which are 'on target', and those which are 'outstanding', have been defined.

For example, when it comes to putting the customer first, 'unacceptable' behaviour includes not visiting, or losing customers, perceiving customers as a nuisance to smooth operations, or providing customers with a service that is not needed. 'On target' behaviour includes regarding colleagues in other functions as internal customers, and acting as a single point of contact with customers, reaching out to involve other appropriate Bass resources. Proposing initiatives to improve customer service, and anticipating customers' needs before being asked are examples of 'outstanding' behaviour.

A new approach to reward

One of the major implications of the company's new focus is the need for a changed approach to reward systems, especially for managers. One of the main purposes of a reward policy is, of course, to encourage the kind of behaviour valued by an organisation. After identifying the core competences they wanted to encourage, Bass Brewers felt that some changes were required. Although they were familiar with the Hay method of job evaluation and grading in the organisation, they wanted to change the way it was applied.

It was felt that managers in the organisation put too much emphasis on status and grading, and that this deflected attention away from what really mattered, namely an individual's performance and potential. Over the next year, Bass intends to introduce a new grading structure with fewer grades, which extends to both management and staff. This will result in a 'flatter', less hierarchical organisational structure. The aim is to ease organisational change by shifting the focus from job evaluation and grading to individuals' output and performance.

The new system will be based on the idea that an individual's progress in the company is based on his or her talent, potential and performance, and on nothing else. Under this system, it is intended that an employee working in a brewery who has no formal qualifications should have the same opportunities to progress as technical and graduate staff.

Responsibility for financial reward will increasingly be given to line managers, rather than policy makers. This will give managers more control and flexibility, but also greater accountability for their decisions, which will need to be backed up with evidence.

The new system will mean that base pay makes up a smaller proportion of an individual's total salary than in the past, with incentives taking a more significant role. While base pay is seen as rewarding the skills people bring to their jobs, incentives are seen as rewarding what they actually do with that mix of skills. They refer to the skills as 'inputs', and the achievements as 'outputs'. The base pay will reflect 'inputs', and the incentive related pay will reflect 'outputs', how you meet your accountabilities, and use your 'inputs'. Individuals' performance will be measured by 'key performance indicators'. These indicators have been set at different levels for different grades within the organisation, from the board downwards.

The new reward system involves regular appraisal of an individual's personal competences. The idea is to stress the fact that the company values its individuals and their skills. Although appraisal had been used for some time in the company, the old system had been seen as bureaucratic and over-complex. Many managers did not understand it. Because old-style appraisals focused on functional objectives, emphasising the value of an individual's technical knowledge and grade rather than their personal competences, it was felt to be unsuited to the new ways of doing things.

The new approach will include appraising the way people work in teams *across functions*. In this way, the company aims to reward the behaviours it wants to see more of, for example, teamwork. This is seen as a way of emphasising the value and driving the core processes.

Commitment from the top

Bass Brewers has committed itself to major changes in the way the company works. It is clear that changes on this scale could not have taken place without the backing of the company's Chief Executive. A scientist by training, he viewed the changes in the business and the external environment as a normal evolutionary process, subject to the laws of natural selection. Rather than see if their current model would survive in the new environment, he felt he had to make the environment work for them. In fact, his personal commitment has been enormous, and he has done a great deal of the work of 'selling' the need for radical new measures throughout the organisation, describing himself as an 'evangelist for change'.

The company's recognition of the need for improved internal communications has resulted in its recruiting a new director of communications with a brief to continue the process of change in the organisation. Senior managers are now briefed regularly on the company's strategy, progress in its implementation, and on the results of the changes undertaken so far.

Bass Brewers has broken new ground by getting all its shop floor production supervisors together for briefings on the company's new strategy. Its briefing groups are invariably cross-functional. Communications within discrete functions are discouraged. The aim is to explain the company's objectives to each employee over the next year. A first step in this direction has been the development of a mission statement, distributed to every employee. This is seen as a guide to the company's changing direction, and is intended to help each employee to understand what he or she needs to do to support its new objectives. It not only describes what direction the company is heading in, but also what that will mean for employees.

Channels of communication have in all these ways been dramatically improved; the test will be whether this improvement can be maintained. Training and coaching are also seen as a priority in the organisation's drive for change following the restructuring process, and change management programmes are now being introduced for all levels of staff.

People adapting to change

But how has the restructuring, and the initiatives to support it, been received by those who really matter – Bass Brewers' employees? The company reckons that between 20 and 30 per cent of the staff have adapted easily to the changes. Others, the majority, are adapting with coaching, training and support. A minority exists which feels that the new way of doing things is not for them, and some of these have now left the company.

There is evidence that those at senior levels see the benefits from the changes more clearly than those on the shop floor. Perhaps the most difficult group to enthuse are junior middle managers, who have suffered the most from the restructuring of the company into a flatter, less hierarchical organisation. Their role has become increasingly more difficult to define. With devolution of responsibility, their role has been reduced. Attempts are being made to redress the balance in favour of those at less senior levels. For example, the company intends to give salaried status to all its staff currently paid on an hourly basis. Executive dining rooms, and most of the chauffeured cars will also be abolished in the interests of a more meritocratic approach, where people are paid on performance, rather than rank.

The changes described in this case study are recent, and the company is still in the process of carrying out some of the initiatives described. Some would argue that positive results can already be seen in the company's market share and in the improvement of its performance during a recession.

Evaluating progress is difficult, of course, and Bass has commissioned an independent organisation to carry out a confidential survey to gauge the reactions of its employees. This will investigate:

- The amount and quality of information received by employees
- Communication with line managers
- Employees' views on their line managers
- Employees views on senior managers.

Perhaps the biggest challenge the company faces is getting used to the idea of change itself. Its senior management has realised that there is little point in sitting back and looking forward to the time when all the change stops, because that time is unlikely ever to arrive. For the past two decades, Bass Brewers remained relatively unchanged. But the company can now see that this period was atypical, and that this fact needs to be communicated to the whole company. In the future, change will be the norm, and 'routine' the exception.

It remains to be seen whether Bass Brewers can make a success of its new approach. It has, though, received a good deal of admiration from other companies for its response to a changing environment. There is, of course, also some cynicism about the solidity of these foundations for change. However, the company believes very strongly that the way forward must be through the increasing empowerment of individuals. Here, the need for openness and honesty in the organisation is crucial. If the previous foundations of the company were status and grade, the new foundations have to be built on trust.

9 MOTIVATING THROUGH CHANGE

Some of the major changes currently being experienced by organisations can have unpleasant results in the form of redundancies and other restructuring. Unless they are sensitively handled, these issues can lead to severe problems of poor employee morale. No programme of innovation can afford to ignore the human costs of change.

Even those organisations which have avoided redundancies may find that they can no longer reward performance with automatic promotion or extra financial benefits. Increasingly, innovative managers are having to turn to alternative ways of motivating their staff.

In this chapter, we look at ways in which organisations can improve employee motivation in times of upheaval and radical change. We examine, first of all, the contribution that sensitive personnel policies can make to staff morale. Effective selection and induction methods can play their part. And innovative approaches to promotion can also be very effective in improving motivation.

It is, however, the issue of communication that can perhaps most strongly affect the success or otherwise of a programme of restructuring or other change. Unfortunately, effective communication is frequently one of the first casualties of such an upheaval. We look at what is involved in the effective communication of change, and how it can help to restore morale.

Organisations need, first of all, to commit themselves to minimising the adverse affects of radical change, and to make sure that this message is understood by their employees. As well as a programme of communication to explain the what, why, and when of restructuring, an organisation's senior managers need constantly to 'take the temperature' of the organisation to assess the impact of any changes. Action to minimise the stress on individuals can include introducing measures like mentoring.

The chapter ends with a case study. This examines how one organisation has tackled the problem of motivating its staff during a period of prolonged and radical change.

Knowledge is a function of being. When there is a change in the being of the knower, there is a corresponding change in the nature and the amount of knowledge.
Aldous Huxley

The current business climate has resulted in some unpleasant changes for many organisations. Redundancies and other kinds of restructuring are the almost inevitable result of worldwide recession, the introduction of new technology, and changes in the business environment. These changes can often result in poor morale and reduced levels of performance amongst an organisation's employees.

Even when redundancies are avoided, many organisations have to respond to external changes in ways that mean they are no longer able to provide the frequent and speedy promotions many employees have come to expect. People have to stay in the same post for a great deal longer, with fewer opportunities even for sideways movement. The danger of this situation, of course, is that it can lead to a severely demotivated workforce.

Increasingly, senior managers are having to find ways of motivating their staff other than through money or promotion. In this chapter, we examine some of the problems organisations can face in motivating their employees in these changing times, and look at some of the alternative ways of motivating their staff that are available to innovative managers. We look at the positive impact that sensitive personnel policies, and an effective communication strategy, can make on organisations going through the upheaval of major change.

DEMOTIVATING ORGANISATIONS

As long ago as 1960, Donald McGregor[1] described two competing theories about people's behaviour in organisations. Theory Y sug-

[1] McGregor, D., *The Human Side of Enterprise*, McGraw Hill, New York, 1960.

gests that most people will take responsibility, care a good deal about their jobs, wish to achieve, and, if given a chance, will do excellent work. What actually prevents people from achieving this is that many of their managers believe a different theory, theory X. This theory holds that people are lazy, irresponsible, passive, and dependent. They must have their work broken into easily-understood pieces, and need to be tightly controlled and supervised in case they make a mess of things.

Theory X can be seen at work throughout many organisations. Some of its manifestations are the all-too-familiar time clocks, strict work rules, and demarcation. In these organisations, employees are treated like children, never consulted on management decisions, and given little information of any consequence about the business, its direction, or even about their own work.

Organisations which base their assumptions on McGregor's theory X expect their employees to work for them without reasoning why, in return for a raise once a year, and the chance of promotion to management, sometime. Once they achieve the title of manager, the same people who have up to now been treated like children are suddenly given the license to make decisions for other people. They instinctively understand that they are required to pretend to know how, because, after all, that is what their own bosses did.

In times of change, determination is necessary to push through restructuring, introduce new technology, and implement the new policies that the situation demands. What more and more organisations are learning the hard way is that just as much energy needs to be put into the organisation's care of its staff as into the mechanics of change. Organisations that ignore this fundamental principle are likely to squander many of the potential benefits of their carefully-formulated new policies.

IMPROVING PERSONNEL POLICIES

Many of the potential difficulties in achieving dynamic change without damaging an organisation's morale can be avoided by good personnel management. For instance, careful selection, placement and promotion can do much to avert the strains resulting both from inappropriate appointments and also from vague job descriptions. Job descriptions which are accurate enough to provide a basis for a person specification will also serve to reduce role ambiguities and the conflicts they can provoke. Skilful induction can do much to ensure that newcomers become as happy and useful as possible in the shortest possible time, as well as reducing wastage.

Marks and Spencer, for example, reduced wastage of trainees on its graduate training schemes by the simple process of seeking selection interviewers' advice as to the type of store which would best suit each candidate. The initially shy benefited from a time in a small, quiet store, while the over-confident discovered the size of their task in stores in central London.

Promotion also demands care if it is to serve as the powerful boost to motivation it ought to be. It is no longer a question simply of rewarding those who have shown the most diligence or served the longest. Such a policy today can result in turning a highly competent and satisfied computer programmer into an ineffective and unhappy systems analyst, or a first-class salesman into a poor sales manager, with consequent distress for everyone involved. These posts need to be filled by those with the appropriate abilities, and alternative ways have to be found of recognising and rewarding the achievements of the programmer and the salesman.

The Exploration Division of British Petroleum has replaced its employees' job descriptions with 'skill matrices'. These are used to specify the roles involved and the levels of performance required in whole 'job families'. Each matrix describes steps in the career ladder within a particular job family along the vertical axis. The skills and competences required for each step in the ladder are described along the horizontal axis.

Employees are now rewarded for gaining the skills and competences described along the horizontal axis. As a result, it is no longer necessary for an employee to be promoted into a new position to receive a higher salary.

Different matrices have been created for those who want to go into management, and for individual contributors whose talent and expertise lie elsewhere. While the management matrix is common to all job families, the individual contributor path is unique to each job family. This means that those who excel in their own jobs, but are not interested in management, can continue to be rewarded by developing their own specialist roles.

MINIMISING STRESS

Major organisational change will almost inevitably lead to stress of one kind or another. However, there are several steps the senior management of an organisation can take to minimise the stress felt by individual employees. These include the following:

- Giving as much priority to plans to reduce the impact of change on staff as to financial plans
- Regularly forecasting possible sources of stress and devising plans to mitigate this
- Encouraging a culture in which individuals accept responsibility for their own mental and physical health and are helped to maintain it
- Planning to tackle particular problems, such as the loss of team members, team restructuring, or the loss of career paths, as they arise.

COMMUNICATION FOR CHANGE

Many of the changes currently facing businesses offer great opportunities, as well as the potential for disturbance. Although they may lead to stress for individuals, and some consequent debilitation of the organisation as a whole, they also offer opportunities for maximising the potential of the company's human resources.

Whether or not those opportunities are realised depends largely on how the organisation's senior management responds to some of the adverse effects that are likely to follow any major organisational change.

In most organisations, the major casualty in times of upheaval is communication. This is particularly unfortunate, since sensitive communication is perhaps the single most important factor in adapting to change. Effective communication can make all the difference between ensuring an enthusiastic response from the workforce and thorough disenchantment.

An effective communication strategy at a time of increased stress due to organisational change is likely to involve some or all of the following elements:

- Communicating policy
- Taking the temperature
- A communication programme
- Mentoring.

Let us look at each of these elements in detail.

Communicating policy

A company determined to reduce the adverse impact of major change should begin by making a public commitment to that effect.

Many corporate statements about merger or closure now frequently include a commitment to avoid involuntary redundancy. Fewer organisations think to make a similar commitment to reduce the other adverse effects of change, such as stress, excessive overwork, and the potential damage to health this can cause. Such a statement should indicate that, in accepting responsibility for introducing change, the organisation also accepts responsibility for mitigating its effects.

Taking the temperature

When undertaking major change, an enlightened organisation will make sure that it can continually monitor the effects of that change on its people. What is more, it will ensure that these effects are understood at the highest levels.

Of course, it is hard for bosses to give a welcome to someone who has nothing but trouble to report, especially when they are under pressure themselves. It is sometimes a brave manager who will feel able to report the demotivating effects of a new policy. However, the following cautionary tale should serve to illustrate the dangers of ignoring danger signals of this kind.

One large organisation decided, for good reasons, to relocate several scattered units in one large office building. The pressures of moving on time led top management to skimp on explanations and consultation with those affected. Failure to explain why the move was decided upon, how the employees would benefit, and on what terms people would be employed in the new premises led to widespread dissatisfaction. Line managers' early warnings were ignored, or dismissed with the comment that things would settle down soon. But long before things had a chance to settle down, absenteeism and sickness rose and nearly half of the key staff affected found other jobs.

This is a classic case of an important message being underplayed by overworked senior managers, who were too preoccupied with the mechanics of change to give due attention to the danger signals.

There are several ways in which organisations can gather objective information about staff attitudes to a new situation. Attitude surveys are one, well-established method. Another method is to employ an independent consultant to conduct structured interviews with a sample of staff.

Questionnaires may also be used to yield objective and anonymous evidence of attitudes at different levels. Some organisations use an 'organisation climate questionnaire' which measures individuals' subjective experience of working in the organisation in terms of their perceptions of the following:

- The degree of formal control exercised in the organisation
- The amount of initiative permitted
- The extent to which good work is recognised
- The ease with which communication flows
- The quality of contact between individuals
- The extent to which they feel they belong to a supportive team
- The clarity of the organisation's goals
- The organisation's expectations of work standards.

In the course of a period of restructuring, Bass Brewers is 'taking the company temperature' every few months, with a company survey designed to look at the way the company is managing the changes.

Subordinate surveys are another means by which an organisation can 'take the temperature'. Such surveys might require a subordinate to rate his or her boss in terms of the ability to give a clear direction, to supply useful information, to enhance team spirit, to listen and encourage, and so on. A number of ratings by different subordinates are required to ensure the anonymity of the individual rater. Scores are aggregated by an independent scorer and given to the manager. IBM is one organisation that uses both peer and subordinate assessments to help pinpoint strengths and weaknesses in the organisation.

Upward appraisals are company protocol at Rosenbluth Travel, a medium-sized, Philadelphia-based company. Managers are reviewed by their subordinates at least once a year. The company encourages openness, but also provides a free telephone number directly to the Chief Executive's office for those who wish to offer their appraisals anonymously.

British Petroleum, Eastman Kodak, and Arthur Andersen are just some of the companies now relying on continuous employee feedback to transform their organisations and improve their effectiveness.

A communication programme

The most important contribution to staff morale during a period of major organisational change is likely to be a thorough and well-planned programme of communication. This should be designed to ensure that everyone receives written and verbal explanations of the changes, why and when they are occurring, and how they will be affected.

Any such programme needs to be timetabled and planned to release accurate information ahead of the grapevine. Special care must be taken to include those at junior levels in the organisation where the impact of change is least often explained. Managers must have the information to enable them to brief their own staff and to answer individual queries.

Information clinics, run by senior and respected people, can do much to supplement normal channels of communication or to allay any worries that staff may have. When morale dropped at Ford Finance, the Chief Executive decided to conduct a 'canteen clinic' once a month. For an hour during the lunch break he visited the canteen, with a promise to answer truthfully whatever questions were put to him. The hostility and fear revealed by the questions at early meetings gradually gave way to greater acceptance and a more constructive approach.

Taking the human factor into account from the outset must also involve retraining plans. A problem encountered by many firms on introducing computers has been the long delay between the arrival of the system and any realisation of its full potential. Too often it has been assumed that once the new machines are in, all systems will be simplified, all controls perfected, and much-needed information will be instantly available. In practice, very few benefits are realised until all the staff, from the managers downwards, understand the equipment's possibilities and are to some extent competent in operating it. Retraining staff not only ensures that the equipment is properly used as quickly as possible but also reaffirms the value the organisation places on its employees.

Since major change gives rise to feelings of great insecurity it is important for an organisation to provide as much security as possible when it comes to those policies and practices that are unaffected by change. Issues of health and safety, such as the hygiene standards in canteen services and other areas need to be specially protected, and the continuing importance given to these issues clearly communicated.

As we have already seen, good personnel policies and practices can help to maintain motivation during difficult times. The changes which British industry has seen over the past decade would certainly have been even more traumatic without effective approaches to redundancy pay and redundancy counselling. But these policies need to be complemented by planned, comprehensive programmes of communication. Without effective communication, the most well-thought-out personnel policies in the world are unlikely to avert widespread demotivation at times of organisational upheaval.

Mentoring

Mentoring, a familiar technique of employee development, can also play an important role in a communication strategy. In this context, it can offer a way of helping individuals to gain a clearer perspective on their situation during a time of upheaval.

Mentoring provides a forum in which individuals can raise professional and personal issues without jeopardising their appraisal or promotion prospects. Through mentoring, individuals can be helped to an understanding of their circumstances, and regain the motivation to achieve their full potential within the organisation.

However, like any development tool, mentoring needs careful, systematic introduction.

Early consultation can help to ensure that the mentoring service would be welcomed and will be appropriately used. Early consultation also constitutes the first stage in explaining the service and dispelling any doubts and fears to which it may give rise.

A written statement of intent about the mentoring system should be issued and well publicised. It should include statements of support from top management and other influential groups such as trade unions and those involved in health and safety. It should make clear the purpose of mentoring and what it can and cannot achieve. It should include a guarantee of absolute confidentiality, and present mentoring as a service that is valuable for both the individual and the organisation.

Training programmes and explanatory meetings should be planned for all who may be involved, whether as mentors or as clients. Everyone should be briefed before they take part in the mentoring system, to ensure that they have realistic expectations about what can and cannot be achieved.

A facilitator of sufficient seniority should be appointed with responsibility for the publicity and training programmes mentioned above, and for the implementation of the service and the monitoring of its effectiveness.

Questions about the conditions for mentoring need to be decided in advance. Issues which need addressing include:

- Will the individual have a choice of mentor? If there is to be a free choice of mentor, how will a manager select who they take on and how many they take on? Who will train and mentor the mentors?

- What are the constraints on mentoring? How much time can an individual client spend with a mentor? How will the benefits of mentoring be made known? How will the service be monitored? What measures are planned to ascertain whether the cost of time spent in mentoring is being offset by improved performance?

- On many counts, it may be wise to limit the mentoring service initially to a particular group of staff while skills and experience are built up. There must be good reasons for choosing a particular group and there must be expressed commitment to extend the service if it proves useful.

CASE STUDY

Bass taverns

To conclude this chapter, we take a close look at the way one organisation – Bass Taverns – has tackled the problem of motivating its staff during a period of prolonged and radical organisational change.

In 1992, Bass Taverns, the retailing division of Bass Plc, had already experienced two major restructurings in as many years. When a third reorganisation was announced, the Personnel department felt that this time it had to take a more pro-active approach. The department identified three key problems with the organisation's previous approach to restructuring:

- Communication about the changes had been carefully
  planned, but in operation had been ad hoc and poorly co-ordinated during both the previous restructurings
- The speed at which the business imperative had forced changes meant that little thought had been given to either the consequences of breaking up teams during the process of restructuring, or to the difficulties of the managers responsible for managing the process of restructuring.
- Questions of how to manage those 'left behind' after the redundancies involved in the restructuring had not been fully addressed, and little progress had been achieved in dealing with the inevitable low morale and demotivation that followed.

The Personnel specialists were determined to tackle these problems, to ensure that the least damage was done both to those individuals who would be made redundant, and to those individuals who would be 'left behind'.

Two sections of the organisation that were particularly badly hit by the third restructuring exercise were the Finance group and the Property group. The Finance function would suffer major job losses following the introduction of a new computer system which vastly cut down on the paperwork involved in administration and clerical work. The Monopolies and Mergers Commission report into the brewing industry had resulted in the company having to sell off thousands of pubs. This too potentially reduced the future volume of work for both the estates and finance groups.

The senior managers of both departments, like the Personnel department, were very keen to do something to improve the situation. For a start, they were very apprehensive about having to serve redundancy notices on their staff, and felt that they needed training and other support to do this. The senior managers also wanted to improve their handling of the people who would be left behind after the redundancies.

The company's situation was complicated by the fact that the restructuring had to take place over an extended and open-ended period of time. This was due to the fact that the impact of the new technology was expected to be a gradual one. The danger was that this state of flux would increase the pressure on managers, who were certain to be on the receiving end of a great deal of flak from their staff.

As a first step, and early on in the process, the company ensured that those managers who would be most affected were all trained in managing difficult situations, and given training in how to assess whether staff needed counselling, and how to manage that process. As a result, many of these managers expressed their gratitude that the company recognised their position and were prepared to help.

The second major step was to set up a task force to manage the restructuring process. This task force was made up of key members of the Personnel department. The positive results of what became known as the 'Garibaldi project' could be summarised as follows:

- A standardised approach was developed for redundancy decisions. This approach, which covered selection for redundancy, policy issues, and outplacement, is being used throughout the restructuring exercise.
- A guidance manual for those responsible for redundancies was prepared with the help of an outside consultant and the comp-

any's own managers. Most of the managers involved in the restructuring were given training in:
– How to appropriately deliver bad news;
– Motivating a restructured workforce;
– Counselling skills.
- Personnel staff were given training in specialist counselling skills.
- A range of in-house outplacement initiatives was developed, for different levels of staff, with training for those staff involved in delivering it. External outplacement was also organised. Both in-house and external outplacement was made available to all levels of staff. A self-help manual on outplacement was also developed.

There were also some negative results from the project. The taskforce was unsuccessful in securing widespread communication about the project throughout the company, and this led to avoidable communication breakdowns and misunderstandings. On some occasions, too, the fact that decisions had to be taken jointly by the taskforce hindered fast decision-making.

However, the project did have an empowering effect on middle managers within the Personnel department . They were entrusted with a very delicate operation, and allowed to make their own decisions regarding the best interests of individuals.

The decision to provide training on how to deliver bad news was also a brave one, as this issue is all too often pushed under the carpet. Most of the staff involved in delivering redundancy notices were trained in preparing to deliver the bad news, the actual delivery, managing the reactions of the individuals, and also managing their own feelings. The accompanying manual covered all the issues they were likely to encounter, including when to discuss issues directly with the individuals concerned, and when to refer them to other sources of guidance.

When it came to dealing with the people, and the teams that were left behind, the project also made considerable progress. This is an area which is rarely dealt with by organisations undergoing restructuring of this kind. The approach adopted by the taskforce was to work with the managers of the disrupted teams in order to give them a deeper understanding of the change process, its effect on their teams, and some techniques for managing the process. These managers were also given access to an external counsellor at any time, either to discuss issues relating to their teams or themselves.

Overall, the result of the project is seen as a greater acknowledgement by staff that the company really wishes to take care of its employees. This has, in itself, proved to be a source of motivation during a difficult time. The Personnel department, in particular, has gained an improved profile and been enabled to take a much more pro-active role, in managing and motivating at a time of upheaval and major change.

10 STRESS: CAUSE AND EFFECT IN A CHANGING ENVIRONMENT

In this chapter we examine a very important aspect of innovative management, namely how to deal with stress in organisations which are undergoing a rapid process of change.

We examine the phenomenon of stress. While different individuals find different things stressful and respond differently to stressful situations, there are a number of common physical and psychological symptoms associated with stress. We look in particular at the way 'burn out' can lead to feelings of futility and personal failure.

It is important to realise that almost any kind of change – good or bad – is stressful to some degree. We examine the major sources of stress at work, many of which are exacerbated by periods of radical organisational change. The responsibility for managing other people makes managers' jobs particularly stressful. We look at some of the pressures on managers, from dealing with the stresses affecting their own staff, to the all-too-common problem of overwork.

In the second part of the chapter, we look at the ways in which both organisations and individuals can minimise the stresses associated with organisational change. We argue that both organisations and individuals need first to recognise the signs of stress, and secondly to face up to the problem. We look at ways of measuring the stress levels of organisations, and ways in which managers can set about tackling stress amongst their staff. We argue that employee counselling, far from being a luxury, is a necessity of enlightened business practice.

Finally, we look at how individuals – both managers and workers alike – can tackle their own stress levels. More important than the choice of methods of relaxation is to develop a sense of perspective. This can be achieved by developing a scheme of personal values which can help individuals to determine their actions and evaluate their own circumstances.

Stressful occasions are those in which environmental or internal demands (or both) tax or exceed the adaptive resources of an individual.

Lazarus and Launier

Stress – both individual and organisational – is one of the most obvious results of the kind of radical organisational and environmental change which forms much of the subject-matter of this book. And one of the most important techniques that innovative managers in changing organisations need to learn is how to deal with this stress.

A great deal of attention has been paid to the new circumstances facing organisations, and the way in which the changing demographic, technological, and sociological features of the business environment have affected the way they operate. But rather less attention has been paid to the impact of these changes on individuals in organisations. We have some idea of what we should be doing about training and retraining. Companies have accepted some responsibility for easing the pains of redundancy. But we have paid less attention to the stresses and strains which these changes are imposing on those remaining in employment.

In this chapter, we are going to look in some detail at the phenomenon of stress. We will be investigating the links between organisational change and stress, and examining ways in which organisations and their managers can help to reduce the stress involved in major change.

RECOGNISING STRESS

Modern life, and modern management in particular, is beset by stressful events, from production deadlines to managing a meeting in a foreign language, or pulling together a team which seems intent on pulling itself apart.

However, the point at which our normal coping mechanisms

cease to be effective on these occasions and we start to suffer from stress differs for each one of us. At one end of the scale are the highly nervous, anxious types who have difficulty in coping even with a quiet domestic life and may not be capable of holding down any sort of a job. At the other are the people capable of handling worldwide responsibilities, or stepping into a capsule to be fired off into outer space. However, whatever our own personal capacity for adjustment, once that capacity is over-stretched, each of us begins to suffer the mental and physical symptoms of stress.

The lifestyles of the Western world ensure that certain periods of life are stressful for most of us. Our early years are taken up with learning ways of relating to others which will powerfully affect our future. It is also likely that we will face particular challenges in adolescence and mid-life, and on retirement.

It is when life's daily challenges become excessive that stress begins to manifest itself. One of the most revealing symptoms of stress is a distorted sense of time, often caused by the desire to do things faster. Some doctors and counsellors diagnose stress by asking an individual to sit in a chair and say when they think a minute has elapsed. One doctor recalled a manager who thought a minute had elapsed after just nine seconds!

Stress becomes apparent through both physical and psychological symptoms. It can manifest itself in feelings of dissatisfaction and a continuing feeling of being overburdened, as well as by physiological measures such as blood pressure, cholesterol levels, heart rate, and adrenalin excretion. It is also apparent in the incidence of ulcers, heart attacks, and other stress-related illnesses, and by changes in health-related behaviour such as smoking and drinking.

Stress can, in fact, contribute to or trigger off a whole host of physical illnesses: high blood pressure, heart disease, chronic backache, bronchial asthma, dermatitis and eczema, diabetes, migraines, peptic ulcers, and alcohol or drug dependence. Moreover, people under stress often adopt health-damaging behaviours such as reducing sleep, smoking and drinking excessively, and eating poorly-balanced diets.

Long before illness is established, however, individuals under stress will experience psychological reactions. They may become aware of increased irritability with others, or else become indecisive if too many important matters suddenly have to be decided in a hurry. Under prolonged strain, individuals may begin to wonder if anything is worthwhile. Boredom and depression increase and so does a general dislike of other people. Social skills deteriorate; responses become clumsier and more offensive; the will to communicate with anyone at all is weakened.

A sense of stress easily translates into a feeling of being persecuted and unable to cope. An individual may suffer feelings of futility and failure and lose their sense of personal worth. 'Burn out', sometimes called the disease of modern life, is a particular form of stress, typified by emotional exhaustion and the inability to respond to others as human beings or to carry out work of a normal standard. Burn out has three main dimensions:

• Physical and mental exhaustion, a loss of feeling and concern, and a loss of interest and spirit
• Negative or inappropriate reactions to other people, loss of idealism, and irritability
• Negative perceptions of oneself, low morale, depression, and reduced productivity or capability.

Most of all, someone with burn out experiences personal dissatisfaction, and a sense of failure to achieve the goals that are important to him or her.

THE STRESSES OF CHANGE

Almost any kind of change, 'good' or 'bad', creates stress. One scale of 'stress value', developed by Holmes and Rahe[1], ranks marriage as the seventh most stressful of the 43 'life happenings'.

[1] Holmes, T.H., and Rahe, R.H., 'Rahe's Social Readjustment Scale', *Journal of Psychosomatic Research* (Vol 11, 1967).

Marital reconciliation comes ninth, pregnancy twelfth, and outstanding personal achievement around mid-way on the list.

Holmes and Rahe also looked at the stress caused by changes at work. On a scale of 1 to 100, on which the death of a spouse scores 100, they gave the following scores to work and work-related changes:

Business readjustments	39
Change to a different line of work	36
Change in responsibilities at work	29
Change in living conditions	25
Change in work hours or conditions	20
Change in residence	20
Change in social activities	18.

Some well-defined sources of stress at work are:

- Working conditions
- Poor job definitions
- Relationships
- Changing roles
- Responsibility for other people
- Value conflicts.

And each of these potential sources of stress can become more pronounced in times of organisational change.

Some kinds of work appear to be particularly stressful for some types of people, while some kinds of work appear to be stressful to many people. Stress can be minimised by careful matching of the needs of the worker to the requirements of the job. How well-suited an individual is to a particular job is more than a matter of resilience to stress, of course. It involves all aspects of his or her temperament, ability and motivation. For instance, people who perform best when they are guided by rules, receive strong leadership, and know exactly what they have to do, will suffer particularly badly if put into ambiguous or fluctuating conditions. And great stress can be caused to individuals who are given a job which requires them to work much faster or slower than their 'natural' pace.

A job which superficially seems to suit an individual well may still contain elements which they cannot master and which are therefore major sources of stress. Those high on logic but low on creativity, for instance, can impose great burdens upon themselves and others if they are put into a job where new solutions are regularly required.

Particularly stressful change is characterised by:

- Being unpredictable and unfamiliar
- Being involuntarily imposed
- Demanding a high *degree* of change
- Demanding *very rapid* change
- Denying individuals any feedback on whether their attempts to cope with events are succeeding
- Denying individuals the warmth and support of their colleagues.

There is potential for much misunderstanding, waste of effort, sense of unfairness and general anxiety when members of staff are left uncertain about their work objectives and responsibilities as a result of major organisational change. There may be differences with bosses and with colleagues over the tasks to be done, and disagreement about the extent of responsibility to be exercised in carrying out a task effectively. Interference from above may seem excessive; on the other hand, a superior's support may seem quite inadequate.

Discrepancies between employees' responsibility and their authority as a result of restructuring can seriously reduce their capacity to carry out the job. Again, in a restructured team where the manager is not on site, and lines of responsibility and authority are not clearly defined, the manager may be subject to conflicting loyalties to the home office and to the team, which will have adverse effects on the team's performance.

In times of change, if structures are not provided to help employees to cope with new ways of working, and people start to feel unsafe, stress takes over. Whatever their level of resilience, everyone shares the need for equilibrium, to make sense of their experiences and the events around them, and to feel that they have some degree of control over them. If this equilibrium becomes damaged, people will start to feel stressed.

THE STRESSES OF MANAGEMENT

One of the most important sources of stress, as we have seen, is responsibility for other people. The jobs that have been found to carry the highest levels of stress – miners, policemen, construction workers, doctors, dentists, and managers – all involve a high degree of responsibility for the safety and well-being of others.

As well as coping with the stress of their staff, managers working in organisations that are undergoing major change will also face undoubted stresses in their own role. They have to sustain relationships, to cope with pressures from above and below and from outside the organisation, to deal with frictions, accept blame for subordinates' limitations, confront outsiders on behalf of the department, confront subordinates where necessary, and to attend often demanding and seemingly unproductive meetings.

Conventional wisdom paints a picture of the 1990s as being less obsessed with careers than the previous decade. Nevertheless, many managers are still struggling with overwork. Those who have survived downsizing and restructuring are often so concerned about keeping their place in the organisation that they feel pressure to be seen to be doing more. Many companies change their working practices and structures without thinking about how to reshape the resulting workload.

Because every individual reacts differently, it is hard to generalise what overwork really is. One manager's exhilarating schedule is another's impossible grind. In Japan, the phenomenon of *karoshi*, death by overwork, usually means death from a heart attack. But this phenomenon is not generally caused so much by long working hours as by the mental attitude of Japanese workers.

However, while there are some managers who may thrive on a 13-hour day, most people do not. The ones who do are usually those who love what they are doing and feel fulfilled by their work. The health risks of hating your job have been known to medical researchers in the US since 1972, when a Massachusetts study showed that dissatisfaction with your job was a strong predictor of heart disease. Over the past 20 years, many other research projects have confirmed this finding.

However, many medical practitioners, while happy to say 'eat more healthily', or 'give up smoking', would be very unwilling to say 'leave your job'. Of course, leaving the job is not the only alternative. It may be just as helpful for an individual to accept his or her situation and put work in perspective.

It is important to remember that longer hours do not necessarily result in higher productivity, but frequently have the opposite effect, as people become too tired to think clearly and act effectively. Of course, it is difficult to prove that a company would make better decisions, and be more innovative if their managers were less busy, and less tired. However, there is undoubtedly a danger that successful, senior people in an organisation reach the point where they can only feel they are doing their job properly if they are running on water. Very soon, this idea filters through the organisation until it affects all the workers.

In one British organisation undergoing a major restructuring exercise, managers were badly prepared to deal with the inevitable conflicts and demands arising from the new emphasis on devolution of responsibility. Caught in the middle, between the executives who wanted to push change through, and the workers given the job of implementing it, the managers tried to please everybody. Their way of 'coping' was to formulate vague and often ambiguous objectives.

Because the managers in this organisation had very little sense of control, they increasingly relied on bureaucratic mechanisms to get things done, creating more paperwork. Some of their staff became increasingly resistant to change and the pressure on the managers intensified. Many could not cope and 'burnt out', thus putting even more pressure on their staff.

In stressful situations, managers are often their own worst enemies. Henry Mintzberg, the American writer and professor, comments that the pressures of many managers' jobs drive them to be superficial in their actions. He suggests that they tend to overload themselves with work, encourage interruption, respond quickly to every stimulus, seek the tangible and avoid the abstract, make decisions in small increments, and do everything abruptly. As well as increasing the stress on themselves, these tendencies reduce managers' efficiency at work.

DEALING WITH STRESS IN AN ORGANISATION

As we have seen, organisational change is a potential source of major stress for workers and managers alike. Let us now examine the steps managers and their organisations can take to minimise the harmful effects of stress.

The first thing to be done, of course, is to recognise the signs of stress in an organisation. Although individuals are likely to be the first to experience the mental or physical signs of stress, these private warnings are likely, sooner or later, to be translated into behaviours which others can observe. For instance, a good time-keeper might start coming in late; someone who always meets deadlines begin to miss them; or a constructive member of a team might become an irritable nit-picker who makes untypical attacks on others.

Some of the following groups of behaviour should also signal to a manager that a member of staff is suffering from stress:

- The individual is eager to please, wants to help rather than to take responsibility, is looking for a friend, cannot accept success, constantly worries about failure, is dependent on others, is indecisive, is always taking on new work, never completes to deadlines, is constantly at meetings.
- The individual is aggressive, talks 'at' you, doesn't listen, bosses others, is obstinate, has fixed views and opinions, is autocratic, unwilling to delegate, critical, and contemptuous of others, is

unreasoned and envious, and cannot take criticism.
- The individual cannot organise his or her own work properly, blames others constantly, finds it difficult to finish jobs, is defensive and secretive, has few friends, is irrational and prone to panic, avoids personal contact, is unco-operative and sometimes deprecating about the organisation, uses memos too often, puts off work, is anxious.

Behaviour at meetings is also a very useful indicator of stress in an organisation. In a 'healthy' meeting, everyone contributes, problems are shared, and members show a recognition of each other's values and a determination to resolve difficulties together. Meetings of people who are under stress are markedly different. Discussion will tend to be aggressive, and some members will attack while others withdraw into passivity. There is much searching for scapegoats, and plenty of non-verbal behaviour indicating withdrawal, lack of interest, and hostility. The behaviour of key players in any team is crucial. Once they demonstrate disaffection, poor morale will quickly spread through the whole group.

There are a number of ways in which an organisation can measure the levels of stress amongst its managers and staff. Standardised measures of stress have been developed, and a range of products based on these measures are available to organisations. NFER-Nelson, for instance, offers an 'occupational stress indicator' for use in a team or on training courses.

An organisation concerned about levels of stress amongst its employees may, on the other hand, choose to design its own survey. For example, a simple questionnaire might list work elements which are known to be a source of stress, such as work overload, time pressures and deadlines, travel, poor consultation, attending meetings, office politics, and so on, and ask staff to tick the five they find most stressful. A section for any additional sources of stress experienced can provide useful additional information.

Once the signs of stress have been recognised, managers need to face up to the problems it poses the organisation. During a period of radical organisational change, it is very important that managers should be able to help their staff to cope with the stress they may experience. The process of adjustment required is too often damaged by a manager's evasions and platitudes ('You'll soon get over it') or by putting off discussion ('I'll see you about it next week'). Some managers escape from the need to address the issue by pulling rank ('Sorry, but I really am pressed. The show must go on. Personnel will see you.') Others offer palliatives which may or may not alleviate but which amount to evasion ('Take the afternoon off').

Ignoring or evading the signs of stress runs the danger of lowered productivity, and poor team morale, as well as damage to the wellbeing of individuals. Enlightened self-interest, at least, requires that organisations undergoing major change or other stressful experiences should investigate ways of relieving the strains these can cause.

Among the measures organisations could consider, employee counselling must surely come high on the list. Whether or not the wider circumstances of the organisation can be changed, counselling can help individuals to make constructive moves to ease their own situation, or at least to accept what must be accepted. It can speed the process of coming to terms with change, and check the development of damaging reactions which rebound upon other staff. For many organisations in the current climate of change, counselling is not a luxury service, nor even an integral part of a humane personnel programme, but simply sound business practice.

Managers need to be able to recognise patterns of stressed behaviour in their staff which can be dealt with by counselling. Counselling can perhaps offer the greatest benefits as a preventative measure, when the early signs of stress have been recognised, or even before. Although it is not possible to predict people's behaviour with certainty, there are some situations which will create stress for most people, most of the time. At times of change, in particular, managers should consider introducing counselling programmes well before any overt signs of stress have become apparent.

DEALING WITH STRESS AS AN INDIVIDUAL

We have been looking at the ways in which organisations can act to minimise the effects of stress. But, of course, there are a number of ways in which individuals can reduce their own stress levels.

As with organisations, the first step for any individual is to recognise that he or she is suffering from stress. There is a strong temptation either to deny that it exists or to give up altogether and go under. However, the effective management of stress involves, first, an awareness of the stress experienced by yourself and others, and secondly an awareness of the options available to reduce it. Without an awareness of your own experience of stress, you are very unlikely to find an appropriate remedy.

A positive approach to managing stress very often involves deciding what is important in your life, and measuring everything else against those values.

Sometimes very traumatic experiences, such as the early death of a friend, or a child's sickness, lead people to put their lives in perspective. For one manager, this was exactly what happened. He had been working extremely hard, immersed in what he was doing, to the extent that he was unable to see what his work priorities were, let alone his personal values. His company was pushing all its employees very hard, but his reaction, like many others in the company, had simply been to work harder and harder. He became irritable with his family and colleagues, shouted at his secretary, and missed deadlines.

However, at this point his youngest child was found to have a potentially life-threatening disease. The manager dropped everything at work, spent three days at his son's hospital bed, and then returned to work to await further medical tests. He arrived at his desk, looked at the mounds of paper which had accumulated over three days, and suddenly realised that the paper 'did not amount to a hill of beans' in comparison to the health of his son. It was as if someone had opened a window for him. With a wider perspective, and able to see the wood for the trees, he was able to get through his mound of paper in no time. He felt calmer and more able to cope. When the medical tests gave his son a clean bill of health, he did not lose his new-found perspective, and has felt himself to be far more efficient as a result.

There are a wide range of different ways of reducing stress. It doesn't matter whether you decide to meditate once a day, or diet, or work out twice a week. Recharging the batteries can take many forms depending on individual taste, including walking, watching films, playing with your children, or bunjee jumping!

Whatever form of relaxation you decide to adopt, the really important thing is to decide what things make life worth living for you. It could be always leaving work on time, never taking work home, reading, watching football, or climbing mountains. And actually doing these things should be the physical manifestation of a deeper, internal decision to put life into perspective.

For some people, there comes a point when they realise that they are working 70 hours a week, and they don't know why. These people, who are unlikely to have given much previous thought to their life priorities, may finally decide they have to get off the overwork treadmill, take better care of themselves, and give more time to their personal life. The interesting thing is that those who do decide what is important to them, and take action accordingly, are often able to work more productively.

People with a clear sense of their own priorities are generally also better able to cope with change. Not only are they likely to be more successful as individuals, but their employer is more likely to benefit from their motivation, and from the improved morale of the people around them. Their internal 'stability' will often have a knock-on effect on the people they work with, making them calmer too. Stressed managers tend to produce stressed teams or departments, but the reverse is also true: self-aware, calm, and focused managers can produce a healthy department, able to respond positively and innovatively to change.

11 PROBLEM MANAGEMENT

In this chapter we examine another important technique for managers in organisations which are responding to change: the technique of problem management.

Problem management is more than just problem-solving. There is a natural temptation for managers to want to take decisions quickly, especially when confronted by major organisational change. But effective problem management depends on a careful consideration of the real nature of the problem in hand, and its wider organisational context, before a final decision is reached.

We look at ways in which a creative, lateral approach to the definition of a problem can help in the development of workable solutions, and at some of the techniques for putting a problem into context in order to arrive at effective solutions. These include 'reframing' the problem from someone else's perspective, breaking down the problem into smaller ones, working backwards from an intended goal, and 'force-field analysis'.

We argue that when it comes to making a final decision, managers need to ensure that ideas are gathered from as wide a range of sources as possible. We examine the classic, but much misunderstood technique of brainstorming, and other methods such as the use of hypothetical situations and alternative scenarios. These techniques can be beneficial in helping an organisation to arrive at truly innovative solutions.

The chapter concludes with a look at the ways in which managers tend to block effective problem management by their own behaviour, and an analysis of the kind of helpful behaviour which managers can adopt to encourage wider staff participation in the management of problems.

It isn't that they can't see the solution. It is that they can't see the problem.
G K Chesterton

I know quite certainly that I myself have no special gift. Curiosity, obsession and dogged endurance combined with self critique have brought me my ideas.
Albert Einstein

In developing innovative ways to survive and compete in the current turbulent business climate, there will be many occasions when managers are faced with problematic situations. This chapter looks at the issue of how such problems can be tackled to ensure innovative solutions. It examines the technique of problem management, and investigates the ways in which a manager's own behaviour can maximise the effectiveness of problem-solving in his or her team or department.

New systems, new environments, new products, new strategies are all essential for growth. Whenever something new is sought, the hardest part is knowing where and when to look for it. The 'something new' is often referred to in business circles as a 'problem'.

What is a problem? For the purposes of this chapter, let us define a problem as being in a situation which differs from the situation you would like to be in. In trying to develop innovative ways of management to survive and compete in 'whitewater', there will be many occasions when management finds itself in a situation that it did not want to be in.

Problem *management*, as distinct from problem *solving*, is not just about finding a solution. Finding a solution to a problem is only half the story. In problem management, the focus shifts to emphasise asking the right questions, seeing how the problem fits into the bigger picture or context, and only then managing the dynamics of the problem in hand.

Problem management is about understanding what the problem means to you and to those around you; and what its implications are. Any workplace counsellor will tell you that nine times out of 10 there is no 'solution' to his or her clients' problems. Much of the time, one of the main aims of problem management is to encourage people to come to terms with a situation. All the techniques in the world will not provide a way of dealing with a problem, unless the individuals concerned will admit they have one, and understand what this means.

Problem management can be seen as consisting of three stages:

- Problem definition
- Putting the problem into context
- Managing the solution

Let us look at each of these stages in turn.

PROBLEM DEFINITION

The first stage of problem management demands acute observation skills, and the ability to take a very wide view. Nothing can be achieved without a clear, objective picture of the problem, who is involved, and what they are saying. It is also important at this stage to establish what is *not* the problem, which in itself can be illuminating. Understanding the limits of what can be achieved is also important. At this stage, it is useful to ask the following questions:

- 'How would we like the situation to be?'
- 'How is the present situation different from that?'

This first stage of problem management is the one that matters most. If too little attention is given to this stage, then all the energy that follows could well be misdirected.

Very often, the apparent problem in hand is not the real issue that needs to be tackled. In their haste to get a result, managers will often address side issues, the symptoms not the causes of their

182 Innovative Management

problems, just to feel they have done something positive. The danger here, of course, is that the underlying problems will usually reoccur at a later date, so that more energy has to be expended on the same problem.

The temptation to avoid the real issue can also result in the 'corset' effect. That is, by containing problems in one area, you may push out problems in another.

Once the real, underlying problem has been identified, it must be precisely defined. People can agree that a problem exists, yet differ on how they describe it. But different definitions are likely to lead to different strategies for its solution. An appropriate definition of a problem can also be of major help in thinking through and solving problems.

There are many examples of scientists who were successful largely because their definition of the problem to be solved was more appropriate than their predecessors'. The American scientist Carl Sagan[1] points to one example in the case of the astronomer Copernicus. Although astronomers before Copernicus had collected vast amounts of data on the movements of the planets, no one could account for them. In order to explain and predict the movement of the planets, Copernicus completely redefined the problem, by asking another question. Instead of asking why the sun and the planets moved around the earth in a particular way, he asked why the earth and the planets moved around the sun.

Often a creative person will redefine a problem in a way that suggests simpler and more workable strategies. J.L.Adams[2] reports the experience of a group of engineers who were trying to design an improved method of picking tomatoes without bruising them. The implicit definition of the problem was how to design a mechanical picker that would not bruise the tomatoes. On the basis of this definition, suggestions for strategies included putting more padding on the picking arms, slowing down the speed of the picking arms, and so on. However, one of the more creative team mem-

---

[1] Sagan, C., *Broca's Brain* (Ballantine, 1980).
[2] Adams, J.L., *Conceptual Blockbusting* (Norton, 1979).

bers suggested another definition, namely how can we keep tomatoes from getting bruised while they are being picked mechanical-
ly? This different perspective led to completely different strategies
including developing a new strain of tomatoes with tougher skins,
which grew further out on the tomato vine.

Most managers define problems in terms of how easy or difficult
they are to solve. Almost as soon as they realise a problem exists,
they will run a subconscious feasibility check to determine
whether they think they can solve it. Only if they get a positive
answer will they invest any time or energy in understanding the
problem's causes and ramifications. But taking such an approach
will often limit an individual's perspectives on the problem and its
possible solutions.

By limiting themselves to a cursory inspection of all but the
most obviously soluble problems, managers run the risk of limiting
the number of strategies open to them. By taking the time to develop alternative ways of defining or interpreting a problem, they are
likely to increase the number and quality of their options.

PUTTING THE PROBLEM INTO CONTEXT

Once a problem has been clearly and imaginatively defined, managers next need to put it into its organisational context. This stage
of problem management requires questioning skills to collect
information, and to establish as broad a context as possible.

One technique that is useful at this stage is 'reframing' in order
to get a picture of how the problem appears to others, and how it
fits into a bigger context, or 'frame', than your own. For example,
it is sometimes helpful simply to put yourself in someone else's
shoes and to 'reframe' the problem from their perspective. It may
help to start with the perspective of someone unthreatening, such
as a colleague, and then move through other perspectives such as
those of your competitors, customers, chief executive, and so on.

One strategy often adopted by effective problem managers is to break down complex problems into smaller, more manageable issues. Those who fail to do this, frequently conclude, wrongly, that complex problems are impossible to solve.

Another technique for putting a problem into context in order to arrive at more effective solutions can be illustrated by the following example, taken from Bransford and Stein[3].

It is 4.00 pm and you have just received notification that you are expected at an important company meeting in Chicago at 8.00 am tomorrow morning. There are two flights available to you. One is a dinner flight that leaves at 6.00 pm tonight and arrives in Chicago at 6.00 am tomorrow. The other flight departs at 7.30 pm tonight and arrives in Chicago at 7.30 am tomorrow. When you arrive in Chicago, you will need to wait 20 minutes for your baggage, and it will take you another 20 minutes by taxi to get to your meeting. Which flight should you take?

Obviously, the quickest way to solve this problem is to work backwards from your goal, which is to be in Chicago at 8.00 am tomorrow morning. If you do this, it quickly becomes obvious what you should do.

Here is another illustration of the technique of addressing problems by working backwards from an intended goal. In tests of reading comprehension, students are usually presented with a passage to read, and then asked to answer questions about the passage. An effective strategy when presented with one of these tests is to work backwards by *first* reading the questions and only *then* reading the text, with the questions in mind.

Addressing the difference between what we want to achieve and what we have now is one of the principles behind the 'force-field analysis' pioneered by social psychologist Kurt Lewin. This technique of contextualising problems is based on the idea that the behaviour of any individual or situation is the result of a combination of restraining and driving forces.

Force-field analysis involves describing what the problem situation would be like if everything fell apart: the worst case scenario.

[3] Bransford, J.D., and Stein, B., S.,*The IDEAL Problem Solver* (W.H.Freeman, 1984).

Then, one has to describe the ideal situation. The 'centre line' between these two extremes represents the current situation. The next stage of the analysis is to list the forces that are acting in the situation to make it better or worse. What are the driving and restricting forces? Which forces make the situation more ideal, and which are threatening to take it into the realms of catastrophe? In this way, a picture of the 'force-field' affecting the problem situation is built up.

By building up such a picture, one can see how to take action on the problem on three fronts:

- By strengthening an already-present positive force
- By weakening an already-present negative force
- By adding a new positive force.

This is an easy-to-remember approach to putting a problem in context, and actively encourages flexibility. One of its major benefits is that it identifies the strong points in a situation which may provide a launching-pad for solutions, as well as the problem areas.

There are thousands of similar techniques available for putting a problem into context in order to arrive at a better solution, and we will not attempt to address them all here. A good compendium can be found in Simon Majaro's *The Creative Gap*[4]. The important thing to remember is that these are just what they are called, tools or techniques, and are only useful in the right hands, and in the right circumstances. No problem-solving technique can replace a manager's responsibility for managing problems.

MANAGING A SOLUTION

This, the final stage of problem management, requires managers to let go of the past in order to develop the future. Once the problem has been defined and placed in context, and the time comes to attempt to devise a solution, it is essential to gather all ideas with-

[4] Majaro, S., *The Creative Gap* (Longman, 1988).

out criticism or judgement, and to take as broad an approach as possible to the evaluation of the options.

Two possible ways of exploring possibilities for the future are called 'hypothetical situations' and 'alternative scenarios'. Both methods generate new approaches by breaking managers' habitual ways of perceiving their environment. Both involve imagining future situations and hypothetical ways of managing them. For example, one might ask, 'If in 10 years' time the Eastern European market was to be competitive, what would we do? What conditions would render our organisation vulnerable in that market? How could we protect and mange this vulnerability?'

Since the early 1970s companies have used alternative scenarios to make decisions that would position them to take advantage of unlooked-for trends and to innovate. Many Japanese and European companies are now using alternative scenarios in this way, although American companies appear to think that planning more than three to five years ahead is impractical.

Probably the best known, and certainly the most abused, method of generating ideas for solutions is brainstorming. Many managers use this technique without understanding the ground rules. There is also a misconception that brainstorming only takes place in groups, but it is also an extremely effective private ideas generator for individuals. The idea of brainstorming is to produce as many ideas as possible, without evaluating them.

Here are some guidelines for brainstorming:

- Keep the problem definition broad, so as not to limit imagination
- Suspend all judgment until all ideas have emerged
- Aim for quantity: in the case of brainstorming, it is the way to quality
- Accept all ideas
- Write the ideas up so they are visible to all concerned
- Encourage building on ideas
- When you think you have enough, try one more round of really outrageous suggestions.

The idea behind brainstorming is that by not evaluating ideas it makes it easier for the more inhibited and under-confident to contribute. If it is played according to the rules given above, brainstorming forbids people from making fun of, or dismissing anyone else's ideas.

Brainstorming should also keep at bay what the American consultant and author William Miller calls 'idea killers'. These are the knee-jerk reactions we all have, and which are sometimes very difficult to get rid of, unless someone points them out to us. Idea killers include the following: 'Oh, we've tried that before', 'We've managed very well without it up to now', 'Ah, but our business is different', and 'Well, I'm not sure it's our responsibility'. It is quite an interesting exercise to ask yourself what idea killers you use yourself, and what are the prevailing idea killers in your organisation. It may help you to understand why innovation and change can never quite get off the ground in your organisation.

Of course, brainstorming on its own provides no guidance about how to take ideas forward, but it may offer a starting point for innovative solutions.

Particularly in the current climate, it is all too easy for managers to feel that they have to get on and produce a result quickly. But even once a solution has been arrived at, this is by no means the end of the problem management process. It is very important to plan the implementation of the solution, deciding who is responsible for what and by when. Ensuring that each individual has authority commensurate with responsibility is an important part of this process, as is identifying how the organisation will recognise success when it comes, and deciding how to gain and maintain support.

MANAGING THE PROCESS

When managers are trying to get to grips with problems, they tend to block participation from their staff by talking too much. They find it very difficult to be non-judgmental, and hard to share decision-making power. As a result, their staff very often end up with little responsibility or commitment to the solutions decided upon.

We have been looking at the major stages of problem management, seeing how problems need first to be defined and set in a context, before effective solutions can be arrived at. In conclusion, let us focus briefly on the question of how managers can ensure that problems are effectively managed, by adapting their own behaviour to the need for greater participation and involvement from their staff.

Some of the most common blocks to successful problem management are as follows:

- Believing that there can be only one way to do anything
- Failing to investigate new ideas
- Looking for 'quick fixes'
- Being afraid of making mistakes
- Being unwilling to question others
- Being unwilling to accept others
- Feeling stressed.

To ensure effective problem management in a team or a department, managers need to be able to combine two quite different approaches to management. These have been termed the 'task' role and the 'maintenance' role. Let us look at each of these roles in turn.

The task role is concerned primarily with completion of the team's work. Typically, a manager who adopts a task role will:

- Initiate activity
- Be concerned with structure and procedure
- Give and (sometimes) seek opinions
- Give and (sometimes) seek information
- Clarify
- Elaborate
- Co-ordinate

- Summarise
- Test for (or, more usually, insist on) consensus
- Watch the clock.

From what has been said about task management earlier in this chapter, it is clear that these behaviours are very useful in the first stage of problem management, but could be very restrictive in the second two stages.

The maintenance role is primarily concerned with maintaining the communication flows within the group, and keeping the group together. A manager who adopts a maintenance role will:

- Set the climate
- Seek and (sometimes) give opinions
- Seek and (sometimes) give information
- Seek to resolve conflict
- Compromise and encourage
- Set and test standards or codes of behaviour
- Diagnose
- Seek ways of making decisions (rather than seeking decisions).

It is generally most helpful if managers adopt this kind of role in the later stages of problem management, when it is crucial to get commitment to solutions.

The key to effective problem management can be seen in a shifting emphasis between task and maintenance roles at different stages of the process. Too much task management, and the people involved in implementing solutions may feel disempowered; too much maintenance management and nothing will get done at all! Successful problem management requires managers to adapt their behaviour so that they are able to use just the right amounts of both, at the appropriate time.

CHECKLIST: PRACTICAL PROBLEM MANAGEMENT

Tactics	Outcomes
DEFINE THE PROBLEM: 1. Describe 2. Differentiate 3. Reconstruct 4. Separate	DEFINE THE PROBLEM – A list of significant data or events, each labelled as either 'fact' or 'assumption' – A statement of 'most probable cause', framed as a cause and effect hypothesis – Differentiate symptoms from cause
DEFINE OBJECTIVES: 1. Seek 2. Avoid 3. Build 4. Restore	DEFINE OBJECTIVES – A list of short-term and problem orientated objectives – A list of long-term, global, strategy orientated objectives – An explicit statement of your own personal objectives related to this problem or decision – How the situation fits into the organisational context
GENERATE ALTERNATIVES: 1. Brainstorm 2. Copy 3. Adapt 4. Combine	GENERATE ALTERNATIVES – A list of as many situations as possible and practical. Those which were used before in 'similar' circumstances should be labelled as such
DEVELOP ACTION PLAN: 1. Compare 2. Force Field Analysis 3. Prioritise	DEVELOP ACTION PLAN – A list of prioritised criteria used to evaluate all the available alternatives

Tactics	Outcomes
4. Subjective Evaluation	– A rationale explaining the final choice which is relevant to the criteria listed – A 'game plan' for implementing the alternative chosen: when, how, in what order?
TROUBLESHOOT: 1. Exemplify 2. Test 3. Exaggerate 4. Predict	TROUBLESHOOT – A list of potential future problems with the Action Plan, based on a benefits/pitfalls analysis of the solution chosen. – For each potential problem, a mechanism to modify the Action Plan so that the problem can be addressed or avoided – Keep the definition in mind, so that measurement of achievement is possible
COMMUNICATE: 1. Verbalise 2. Write 3. Promote 4. Symbolise	COMMUNICATE – A list of persons likely to be affected by the Action Plan, and who should be informed of the Plan and their role in it – A list of peripheral others who may influence or be influenced by the implementation of the Action Plan – Specific methods for informing the relevant persons involved
IMPLEMENT: 1. Do It Yourself 2. Delegate	IMPLEMENT – Each activity in the Action Plan should have a designated

Tactics	Outcomes
3. Phase In 4. Systemise	person responsible for accom plishing the activity by a certain time – If systemising or phasing in a solution, then a timetable for doing so (a plan for the Action Plan) – Keep troubleshooting and referring back to the original def inition and objectives

12 NEW AGE, NEW WAYS

In this chapter we examine some of the main components of what is now sometimes called 'New Age management'. While the more bizarre manifestations of New Age thinking have become notorious in some circles, there is also a serious side to some of these ideas.

One of the common strands behind many New Age management ideas is that popular human values, and perhaps especially our attitudes to work, are changing at an unprecedented rate. These changing values, it is argued, necessitate a quite different approach to management than that adopted in the past.

In this chapter, we examine some of the new popular values that are gaining increasing recognition, and look at the ways in which some innovative organisations are responding to these changes.

It is becoming apparent that the current economic gloom, along with other factors, is leading to a questioning of the widespread materialism of the 1980s. In its stead, some are discerning a more 'caring' attitude towards people, communities, and the wider environment.

At the same time, lack of job security, and reduced expectations of promotion, seem to be leading some young people towards 'alternative' career paths, and a greater emphasis on self-fulfilment. There is evidence to suggest that today's population is increasingly concerned with personal growth, personal responsibility, and autonomy at work, and less with the material rewards of success.

The rapid growth in self-employment over the last few years can also be seen as a reflection of these changing values, as well as a response to widespread redundancy. And it seems that some self-employed people are now striving to ensure that their enterprises reflect their own changing values, rather than the traditional concerns of big business.

In the second half of the chapter, we turn to an examination of how some innovative organisations are responding to these changing values. We find evidence of a new approach in some new initiatives in training and development, and in increased attention to flexible working
conditions.

Non-profit making organisations, in particular, are reflecting changing attitudes in a more democratic, grass-roots, community-oriented approach to their work. And of course, more than one organisation is finding that there is money to be made from the increasing popular concern about the environment.

We conclude with a cautionary look at some of the wilder out-posts of New Age management thinking.

*Only when the last tree has died and the last river has been poi-
soned and the last fish has been caught will we realise that we
cannot eat money.*
Native American Chief

*I don't think we know what our values are any more. I don't think
anyone has asked us these questions in decades ... What do we
care about? What do we stand for? What are our priorities? We
simply don't know, and we're already paying the price.*
Steve Jobs, Chief Executive Officer, Next Inc.

In this chapter, we take a look at some of the further shores of
innovative management, sometimes collectively described as 'New
Age management'.

This expression is increasingly being used to describe a whole
range of activities, some of which may have more apparent legiti-
macy than others. However, what many so-called New Age management theories seem to have in common is the idea that human
values have changed so much in recent years, and are likely to
change so much more in future, that a wholly new approach to
management is needed.

The development of New Age ideas in management also represents a growing awareness of the importance of these new values to
the world of work. Some would argue that work is now one of the
most influential aspects of our lives. As other forms of community
have withered, work has taken on a corresponding increase in
importance, at least for those who are employed. As an increasingly
influential social institution, it is argued, employers should set standards and reflect the new values of the populace. The biggest organisations influence governments, and directly touch the lives of million of people. Why should they not play a larger, more responsible
role in society?

There are signs that some organisations are beginning to accept
at least some of the thinking behind New Age ideas, and many of
the innovative practices described in other chapters of this book

are a testament to this growing acceptance of their wider role. In this chapter, we take a look at some of the new values at the root of these developments, and examine how they are affecting the way at least some employers run their businesses.

NEW VALUES

In 1979, President Jimmy Carter chastised Americans for their failure to recognise that 'consuming things does not satisfy our longing for meaning'. The world seems to have suffered an excess of individualistic materialism, even in the United States where the consumer used to be king. As the world struggles with slower growth, and a more competitive economy, there is a growing awareness of other values.

Many people believe that, since the 'loving' 1960s, a more self-ish drive has become apparent in world affairs. There are those who believe that some of our current ills, including drug abuse and high crime levels, are related to what George Bush has called a 'moral emptiness'. There are signs that people are getting scared. The worry seems to extend beyond fear of losing a job to fears about what will happen to the world.

The recent trend, recessions notwithstanding, for people to move around frequently in pursuit of a career is seen to have created a more mobile, but correspondingly less stable, society. People are becoming less and less involved in their communities than before. And despite achieving increasingly high standards of living, with both men and women going out to work, almost everybody in the West seems to have stopped saving, and just spent more.

In Britain, increasing materialism was seen by many as a keynote of the Thatcher years. Measures like the right to buy council homes, and the privatisation of public utilities, were trumpeted as offering 'empowerment' of the people. But some commentators have seen these developments as an incentive, not to greater freedom, but simply to greater greed. Consumer debt rose dramatically on the underlying assumption that, somehow, there would always be more money to pay off debts. The advent of the recession, and the scale of the debt now being experienced at all levels of society, has proved a sobering antidote.

Social commentators are claiming to discern a new movement away from the raw values of the market towards a more 'caring' attitude to people, communities, and to the wider environment.

The changing economic climate has also led to a rapid change in people's attitudes to their work. Even those working for previously 'safe' companies are feeling insecure, and this insecurity is taking hold at all levels.

There is evidence that corporate restructuring has discouraged many high-flyers from seeking posts in large corporations. In America, it seems that even graduates are beginning to reduce their expectations, and many are not even considering the business world as an option. Some, with a mixture of idealism and practicality, are taking alternative routes, such as joining the Peace Corps, and accepting the fact that they may be relatively poor for quite some time. Conspicuous consumption is increasingly seen as unacceptable, and self-fulfilment is in.

There is an apparent rejection amongst young people of the idea that success at work, and the conspicuous display of its material rewards, should be the prime focus of their energies. Some would argue that the short-termism that is seen to have done so much damage to the economy is the result of just such a materialistic value system.

Along with the changing personal values that have accompanied the end of the spendthrift 1980s, there is evidence of a deeper, longer-term change in people's values, especially as these relate to work. Much of this evidence has emerged from the studies carried out by organisations like Taylor Nelson[1] and Applied Futures.[2] whose market research is used by governments to identify long-term trends.

From such studies it appears that increasing numbers of people in the working population want work which permits personal

[1] Taylor Nelson Research Limited, 44–6 Upper High St, Epsom Surrey
[2] Applied Futures, 83–9, Kingsway London WC2

growth and offers opportunities for increased personal responsibility and autonomy. Surveys carried out in the UK in 1988 found these values being expressed by a large and growing proportion (38 per cent) of the work population. Just one third of the population was primarily interested in work as a source of high earnings, status, position and power, while a declining number (28 per cent) looked to a job simply for a secure weekly wage.

These studies have also identified a very small new group of people who judge their work experience in terms of the total range of experiences it allows them to enjoy, and of the contribution it enables them to make to their community and to the wider environment. This group has moved a long way from the predominant assumption of a few decades ago that the main function of work was simply to supply a living and to fill the time between leaving school and retirement.

Applied Futures' research suggests that tomorrow's European will increasingly be characterised by:

- Concern for the environment
- Concern for self-development (mental, physical and emotional)
- Acceptance of individual responsibility
- Enjoyment of complexity and ambiguity
- Informality, and rejection of conformity
- Egalitarianism
- Kinship with those of like interest, cross-nationally
- Acceptance of regulations for collective efficiency, rather than order giving.

THE LURE OF SELF-EMPLOYMENT

One of the groups being hardest hit by the redundancies of the 1990s is the middle managers, and jobs like these are unlikely ever to come back. White collar workers are increasingly getting the message that Bruce Springsteen gave to blue-collar workers in the early 1980s:

*They're closing down the textile mill across the railroad
tracks.
The foreman says these jobs are goin' boys,
and they ain't comin' back ...*

Those who are likely to survive in the corporate world are not the
supervisors but the doers, not the 'bosses' but the 'team leaders',
and the team players. Those working for large organisations are
likely to be called on less to take control of others, and more to
take responsibility for their own successes and failures. For those
middle managers who cannot face such a radical move, one of the
few solutions is to take a bigger job in a smaller company. But this
is an option that will be open to few.

One of the results of this trend has been that many more employees, especially former middle managers, are now starting to look
elsewhere for self-fulfilment, either working in the community, or
starting their own businesses.

Particularly if they feel themselves to have been sacrificed on the
altar of big business, many of those setting up in business for themselves decide to run them on the basis of quite different values.
Many have demonstrated, indeed, that social responsibility can be
profitable. In 1992, *Fortune* magazine reported the case of a bakery
in San Francisco that employs 240 people. Last year, the bakery's
employees teamed up with the local prison to turn the waste ground
next to the bakery into an organic kitchen garden. This garden is
now looked after by prisoners on parole, and by homeless people in
the city. The bakery and a local restaurant buy produce from the
garden, and the 80 gardeners share the proceeds. Five of the former
prisoners have now got jobs with the bakery. As a result of this initiative, several other businesses in the area are planning to open
new gardens and sell their produce to supermarkets.

Small businesses may offer one of the solutions to our need to
balance profit-making with a renewed commitment to the community. As one entrepreneur has said, 'If business is to be the domi-
nant social institution of the future, we have to mix social goals
with business goals. The bottom line should include whether you

hired more people and that you improved your products, your workplace and your community – not just your profit.'

Of course, all is not rosy in the world of self-employment, and there are considerable personal risks in taking this route. It is difficult not to be 'on call' 24 hours a day when the business is your own, and many self-employed people find it hard to find the time to relax, enjoy life and recharge their batteries. This is especially the case when self-employed people still hold the values of a large corporation. Without changing their own values, it is unlikely that those who leave corporate life to run their own businesses will get the satisfaction they seek.

Self-employment is certainly not the universal panacea some would have us think it is. And in some of its manifestations, it can present as many problems as working for a big company. One of the fastest-growing sectors of employment for managers is temporary or contract management. Here, the manager works on a short-term contract for a company which can thereby meet its immediate needs without incurring the cost of a permanent employee.

For some, of course, self-employment can open the door into a new world of discovery. For others, though, leaving a big organisation can feel like bereavement. To succeed, a self-employed person needs to be creative, and to adjust fast in order to find something new for themselves.

NEW CORPORATE VALUES

In this chapter so far we have looked at some of the new values emerging in our society, and at some of the new attitudes to work resulting from the current turbulent changes in the business environment. Let us now turn to some of the ways in which organisations are responding to these changing values. One of the major corporate responses to the new values can be seen in a new attitude to training and development. Some firms are now devising programmes in conjunction with educators and parents to offer students job training, or, at least, training for job readiness.

Grand Metropolitan, for instance, has so far committed two million dollars to the launch of an education programme called 'Kapow': kids and the power of work. Volunteers from the company's US operations, including Pillsbury, Burger King and Haagen Dazs, lead one-hour classes once a month at their local primary schools. Pedigree Pet Foods, who employ 1,200 of its 1,500 workforce around Melton Mowbray in Leicestershire, vary their local support from a cheque to a quiet word with suppliers who might be able to help a school or charity with savings on a project. In another example, Salomon Brothers have formed a partnership with a local business and technology school in Brooklyn. More than 70 Salomon Brothers employees act as mentors for students, and the company has also offered student scholarships. McDonald's, on the other hand, pays its young employees to study before or after their shifts.

Other organisations are responding to the changing values of their employees in different ways. For example, in response to its employees' expressed need for greater flexibility in order to meet their other needs, Oxfordshire County Council offers a scheme called 'flexiplace'. This allows employees flexibility to decide where and when they work. Arrangements are tailored to individual needs, and follow one of three models:

- Working at home and in the office, usually with an agreed number of 'core' hours or days when the employee is in the office
- Working at home with only short periods in the office
- Working entirely at home.

The three departments piloting the scheme have provided their staff with fax machines, mobile 'phones, answering machines, pagers, and laptop computers. Of course, home working is not unusual nowadays, and many organisations allow it informally. What is perhaps unusual in this scheme is that this way of working is officially recognised as part of company policy.

The idea that there is more to life than work, and more to work than profit, is an important component of the new value system that organisations are having to accept. Linda Hamilton, an American woman, was standing at the supermarket checkout one day when she had what she later described as a revelation. She suddenly realised that the checkout offered an ideal opportunity to get people to donate money to hunger relief campaigns. By catching them when they were buying food for themselves and their families, such a campaign would be more likely to encourage giving than one which targeted people in their own homes.

Although she recognised that she had a great new idea, Linda Hamilton had no idea how to put it into practice, nor did she have any contacts in the food retailing business. However, she pushed on, and within months had an outline of how the idea could work: hunger relief coupons would be sold to customers at the checkout, with the supermarket forwarding this money to the relief organisations.

A local grocery store agreed to trial the scheme, and with some funds from early supporters, the programme got under way. Within a year, one of the largest supermarket chains in America had signed up. Today, Food for All is a national non-profit making organisation, with thousands of stores participating in the coupon scheme. Only 10 per cent of the funds raised are used for administrative expenses. To achieve this, most of the staff work either voluntarily or for very low salaries. Seventy-five per cent of the remaining funds support projects in the local communities where the money is donated. Emphasis is placed on programmes to empower the poor and hungry to support and feed themselves. The developing world receives the balance of the funds.

The organisational structure of Food for All reflects its values:

- Local committees have complete control over fund distribution.
- All ideas come from the bottom up. Emphasis is on local, grassroots participation. It is recognised that a top-heavy structure would stifle the almost missionary zeal and values of the organisations' workers.
- At the national level, advisory boards work with the directors to establish policy. This enables the programme to access the

expertise of people in the food industry and those in public relations. This use of a wider community of ideas is seen to benefit both individuals and the organisation as a whole.

In some examples closer to home, Traidcraft, the Third World trade and development company, promote trade with the Third World countries, but have a very strong objective to prove that it is not only a 'good' thing to do, but it is also commercially feasible. It is based on an industrial estate in Gateshead, supporting 115 jobs as part of its commitment to the North East. Its trading policies reflect its impact on overseas suppliers, its workforce, supporters, shareholders and commercial neighbours. The Cooperative bank in May 1992 extended its ethical policy by refusing to speculate against the pound during the international monetary crisis. It also refuses to be involved with factory farming, the animal fur trade, blood sports, tobacco manufacturers, arms delivery to oppressive regimes or 'any regime or organisation which oppresses the human spirit.'

THE ENVIRONMENT

We have saved perhaps the most radical change in popular values to nearly the end of the chapter. After decades of devastation brought on by a culture that worships at the altar of economic advancement at any cost, it seems that business is finally waking up to the dangers of destroying its own habitat. Although there is evidence that many organisations see the environment as just one more convenient bandwagon, there is a genuine awareness amongst some of the more forward-thinking companies that preservation of resources can be excellent long-term business sense.

'Our products create pollution, noise and waste.' This statement on the cover of a Volvo brochure acknowledges the company's responsibility for the 'adverse environmental effects' of its products and activities. The brochure also carries a policy statement that commits the organisation to act in environmentally responsible ways in developing products and processes and in conducting environmental research. Volvo is one of an increasing number of organisations making such commitments.

One of the clearest examples of the money to be made from increasing environmental awareness is, of course, the Body Shop. Anita Roddick has made her environmental beliefs the bedrock of her business. The company sells only biodegradeable products from natural sources, recycling waste, providing refillable containers, and immersing the company, and its customers, in environmental causes such as the preservation of the rain forest and endangered animal species.

The Body Shop's environmentalism is not limited to its external campaigns. The company has an entire department devoted to environmental projects, which monitors the firm's compliance with its own environmental principles. This department carries out a six-monthly audit of all the company's activities, from production to human resources.

The auditors meet regularly with environmental groups, to hear their suggestions for improvements. The results of this work have been reflected in the Body Shop's recycling programmes, its reduction of paper waste, and the minimisation of its water use. The company has recently replaced some of the directors' company cars with smaller, more fuel-efficient models. It also subsidises the purchase of a bicycle for any employee who wants to ride one to work. More than 500 bicycles have been bought under this scheme, and the company has built a shed to house them. The Body Shop recently collaborated with Volvo to create aerodynamically-sound delivery lorries that cut energy use by half. The company's employees are educated about environmental issues through seminars and dissemination of literature.

The Body Shop's well-publicised environmental stance has probably been responsible, at least in part, for its huge growth. Despite some of the hype that inevitably goes with such an organisation, it still stands as a commanding example of a company that has merged good business practice with emerging popular values, and as a result has been extraordinarily successful.

Other organisations, too, are taking the increasing importance of environmental values to heart. Esprit Corporation, a clothing retail operation, offers its employees the chance of a paid holiday during which they can work on community projects. Employees can have up to 10 months to work on the public interest projects of their choice so long as they contribute an equal amount of their personal time as well. Esprit has set up a grant fund to support these projects.

NEW AGE OR JUST PLAIN CRANKY?

In this chapter, we have been looking at some of the ways in which new popular values are affecting the way organisations do business. But we cannot end without casting a glance at some of the more off-beat manifestations of the so-called 'New Age' movement in management.

The ease with which some of the more esoteric products of New Age thinking have been able to make their way into executive boardrooms should, perhaps, be seen as a cause for alarm. The merchant banker who refuses to make a move without 'consulting his crystal' is not alone in his adherence to the more cranky aspects of popular culture.

Some of the further shores of New Age thinking have offered a surprisingly congenial home to some successful City types who had the stuffing knocked out of them in the recent rounds of redundancies. Some dropped out of business life altogether, and became interested in alternative confidence boosters. Others have seen the possibility of a fast buck in putting on huge 'personal development' events: seminars which cram hundreds of people into a conference room for a day or a weekend, and give them a 'moving' experience. This is usually achieved by encouraging people to break down into tears in public, and then telling them that they are now free to be anything they want to be. There are strong grounds for the view that this kind of event does not manifest a 'new value', just an updated version of a very old one...

Some business leaders are showing enthusiasm for 'shaman' workshops, which examine the mystical side of leadership. In America Robert Bly's well-publicised 'wild man' theories have led to the current huge popularity of male encounter groups. In a world which is rapidly changing, the need to belong to a well-defined group is clearly becoming increasingly strong.

Although it is easy to mock some of the crankier ideas emerging from New Age theories, this should not cause us to ignore the undoubtedly accelerating pace of the changes taking place in popular values. It is perhaps indicative that the new leader of the free world is a young man, brought up in the 1960s, with, apparently, a very different value system from that of the last US President. It is inevitable that the policies adopted in the US over the next few years will have a strong knock-on effect in this country. While it remains to be seen whether Bill Clinton's tenure will bring about genuinely new ways of doing things, what seems certain is that the current pace of rapid change in our values is set to increase even further into the next century.

APPENDIX
Further Reading

Agor, W., *Intuition in Organisations* (Sage Publications, 1989).

Block, P., *The Empowered Manager: Positive Political Skills at Work* (Jossey Bass, 1986).

Bransford, J.D., and Stein, B.S., *The IDEAL Problem Solver* (W.H. Freeman and Co., 1984).

Bridges, W., *Transitions: Making Sense out of Life's Changes* (Addison Wesley, 1980).

Eden C., Jones S., Sims D., *Messing about in Problems* (Pergamon Press, 1983).

Goldberg, P., *The Intuitive Edge* (Jeremy P. Tarcher, Inc., 1983).

Lindaman, E., *Thinking in the Future Tense* (Broadman Press, 1978).

Majaro, S., *The Creative Gap* (Longman, 1988).

McGee-Cooper, A., *You Don't Have To Go Home From Work Exhausted!* (Bowen and Rogers, 1990).

Miller, W., *The Creative Edge* (Addison Wesley, 1987).

Pfeffer, J., *Managing with Power* (Harvard Business School Press, 1992).

Phillips, N., and Sidney, E., *One to One Management* (Pitman Publishing, 1991).

Rowan, R., *The Intuitive Manager* (Gower, 1986).

Storr, A., *The Dynamics of Creation* (Penguin, 1972).

Vaill, P., *Managing as a Performing Art* (Jossey Bass, 1989).

Weisbord, M., *Discovering Common Ground* (Berrett-Koehler, 1992).

Weisbord, M., *Productive Workplaces* (Jossey Bass, 1987).

INDEX

Magnetic Healing

Advanced Techniques for the
Application of Magnetic Forces

By Buryl Payne, Ph.D.

LOTUS

Library of Congress Cataloging-in-Publication Data
Payne, Buryl
Magnetic Healing
ISBN 0-914955-42-X
1. Subject   I. Title
Library of Congress Catalog Card No. 98-67862

Published By:
Lotus Press
P.O. Box 325
Twin Lakes, Wisconsin 53181

Dedication

To Richard and Mary Broeringmeyer,
pioneers in the magnetic diagnostic technique
for glands, organs, and injuries. Their work has
helped to transform magnetic therapy
from an arcane art into a science.

Table of Contents

TABLE OF CONTENTS

Magnets are probably the least expensive, most effective
alternative medical device that a person can use.

Preface

Magnetic therapy is both one of the oldest forms of medical treatment, and one of the newest. We are only just beginning to explore this remarkable healing modality, but the results are already impressive.

Although it seems incredible that something as simple as a magnet could alleviate in minutes or hours a headache, sore tooth, or other pain, it is nevertheless often the case. Whatever the ailment or condition, someone probably has tried to help it with magnetic treatments. Perhaps as many as four out of five ordinary aches, pains, and common ailments are helped by proper use of magnetic therapy. Few methods of conventional Western medicine work that well!

Magnetic therapy can help the body heal stiff necks, some headaches, premenstrual cramps, back pains, and about thirty other common and serious ailments. To do the therapy yourself you have to know some basic principles, and for serious conditions you may need to know how to do a full magnetic diagnosis and treatment of all glands and organs. (See chapter 4.)

Although magnetic treatments do seem to work wonders at times, they are no cure-all, no magic panacea. They operate more like a jump start for a car. If there is gas (proper nutrition) and a good charging system (proper exercise), the car will start and keep on running.

One of the ways that magnetic forces interact with the body is by altering the spin orientation of some protons, the tiny particles that make up the nuclei of atoms. Perhaps this is the reason why they help a wider variety of ailments than many chemicals or drugs that operate only on the more gross molecular level to alter or attack specific bacteria or viruses, or to change a particular chemical imbalance.

Magnetic forces help the body to heal itself by stimulating the biochemistry of the body so natural healing can take place.

After years of being considered a folk remedy, magnetic healing is finally becoming an accepted medical treatment. In Europe, an estimated 5 million people have been treated with pulsed-magnetic-field therapy instruments. In Japan and Asia, over 10 million magnetic necklaces have been sold. The Japanese equivalent of the FDA has approved magnetic therapy devices and it is estimated that 10 percent of the people use them in one form or another.

Many solid research studies that clearly support the therapeutic value of magnetism have been published in major medical journals. There are now trade journals, newsletters, and yearly international conferences dealing with research on the biological effects of magnetic forces. These include: *Newsletter of the BioElectro-Magnetics Institute; The International Society for the Study of Subtle Energies and Energy Medicine; Bioenergy Newsletter; The Journal of Psychoenergetics;* and *Bioelectromagnetics.* An international conference on magnetic healing was held in Madras, India, in 1992, sponsored by the Institute of Magnetobiology and *The Journal of Electromagnetic Therapy.* The Bioelectromagnetic Society holds annual meetings at which papers on magnetic therapy and other related topics are presented. Although none of these journals and newsletters are entirely devoted to magnetic healing, they have a preponderance of articles on the subject. In January of 1998 the third conference of magnetic therapists was held in Los Angeles. A professional journal is planned, as well as yearly meetings.

Research programs on magnetic healing are under way at private clinics and universities around the globe. The largest company in the business of manufacturing pulsed magnetic force instruments does over $50 million in gross revenues each year. Popular magazines such as *East West Journal* carry occasional articles on magnetism and healing, and magnetic healing devices are shown on infomercials on a regular basis. Magnetic necklaces and backpads are popular items.. Public awareness is constantly on the increase.

We stand today at the threshold of a new yet ancient science that will probably transform our health-care practices in a few decades.

But researchers in laboratories cannot do everything. You, the reader, can play a major part in finding what works for you and your friends. The purpose of this book is to help you do that as efficiently and economically as possible. Magnetic therapy is an ever-expanding field. Who knows what you will discover?

Buryl Payne, Ph.D.
Santa Cruz, California
September 1996

Acknowledgements

This work, like most scientific work, does not stand alone. Magnetic therapy rests solidly upon the research of scientists who have dedicated their lives to the study of Earth's magnetic field; the research of physicians, chiropractors, and other healers who have often carried on their work in spite of the negative opinions of others; the work of electrical engineers, physicists, and technicians who have developed the techniques for making powerful magnets and electromagnets; and those few of the millions of people who have benefited from magnetic therapy who have been willing to speak or write about it.

Disclaimer

The procedures described in this book are not intended to replace traditional medical advice or treatment. Magnetic forces are thought by many, including this author, to help the body to heal itself; they do not cure diseases.

Do not stop taking any medications, and do make your physician or practitioner aware of your use of magnetic forces and any changes in your condition.

Magnetic treatments may be compatible with other forms of conventional or alternative treatment if used correctly. Serious, life-threatening diseases should be monitored by a physician only.

Chapter I
Introduction

Personal History

In the late 1970s, I had the good fortune to attend a lecture on magnetic therapy by Dr. Ralph Sierra, a Puerto Rican chiropractor and electrical engineer. At that time I directed a holistic health center in the Boston area, and was always open to new treatment methods. Dr. Sierra found my work in biofeedback, bioenergetics, hypnosis, and several other therapies interesting, so he invited me to visit his laboratory in Puerto Rico and study with him. I did this once a year for several years until Dr. Sierra passed away with some of his secrets still unknown.

I continued the study of magnetism and healing. I spent several years evolving the design of a simple and inexpensive portable pulsing magnetic force instrument. By 1982 I had made several, but wasn't too excited about them because I tried them on myself a few times and didn't notice any effects. Then one weekend I went skiing and dug a ski into a snow bank. Although my knee got a good twist, I ignored it, kept skiing, and then drove four hours home. The next morning that knee hurt! I'd intended to go for a short walk, but when I got to the front porch, I just lay down in agony. I thought of trying my magnetic instrument. After about thirty minutes of treatment, the pain in the knee was about ninety percent gone! I was skeptical, since as a professional hypnotist I know how powerful the mind can be in facilitating healing. I figured that I'd just psyched myself out of the pain. Nevertheless, I was glad to be largely free of pain and passed a quiet day. The next morning the pain returned, though not as intense as before.

1

After another thirty-minute treatment, the remaining pain left. It did not return, and I went skiing the next weekend.

Before the skiing accident, I'd had only the experience of others to go by and while that was positive, I'm the kind of person who likes to test things for myself. After the experience with my knee, I was ready to continue developing my magnetic instrument.

I improved the design, constructed several more prototypes, and began doing library research. I soon found out that I had reinvented the wheel; magnetic instruments had been in use in Europe for about fifteen years before I made my first one. But my work hadn't been for nothing—my instruments were easier to use in the home, and were much cheaper. (Today a refined version of my device, named the Pulsar after stars that pulse with giant magnetic fields, sells for one-tenth the cost of the European instruments.)

A few weeks after I'd done my library work, a local physician friend of mine came by for a visit. I mentioned my instrument, and he said he'd like to try it on his sore shoulder. After twenty minutes, the pain went away, so he bought one for use in his walk-in clinics. He later told me that it was helpful for about eighty percent of the people who came in with aches and pains, and that it usually began to help them within about seven minutes of treatment.

Some time later he invited me to work in his office and formally treat some patients who were suitable for this kind of treatment.

Early Case Studies

One patient was a young woman who had, six years earlier, broken bones in both ankles and feet in an automobile

2

accident. She had been on anti-inflammatory medication and narcotic pain killers ever since. The ankles were arthritic, but had no particular swelling or erythema (redness). There was chronic pain in both feet and in her back. Following are notes about the treatment of one patient I kept for myself and the supervising physician:

Session 1

Treated with two pulsed magnetic force applicators, one on each ankle. She reported feeling a little tingling and warmth in her ankles.

Session 2

Put two applicators on her ankles and one on her hip.

Session 3

She had been used to feeling pain on rainy, foggy days, but on the day of her third treatment, which was rainy and foggy, she said she had been almost skipping around. She had taken only five Motrins® (pain killers) in the two weeks, compared with the four per day prior to treatments. She was able to lie flat on her stomach at night, which she had not been able to do before, and had noticed big improvements in general. Treated her on both ankles and hip again.

Session 4

Several days had passed; as she came in she said, "I have come a long ways. The knee is good. The other leg is fine. The right foot is better. I used to feel like I was walking on marbles, and now I don't feel that. I completely stopped the Motrin®." She said on the previous night she had sat cross-legged on the floor, something she had not been able to do since the accident.

Session 5

Reported that she no longer had foot cramps at night. Treated her right leg, which was tender above the ankle.

At the end of this session she said to the physician: "I'm so tickled with this!" She purchased a small pulsing magnetic force instrument for her own use and was never heard from again.

Another of the doctor's patients had injured her back when she slipped on a freshly mopped floor in the local supermarket. She had been in pain for several months and nothing had helped. Applying the magnetic instrument to the lower spine did not help either, but one day it occurred to me to treat the top of her head. After only one treatment she said she felt better and when she returned the next week, she reported that she could sit on the floor without pain. Two more treatments and she completely recovered.

Several of the physician's patients experienced dramatic improvement in those early years of my experience, stimulating me to continue my work.

Several years later I was in Washington, D.C., presenting a workshop on magnetic therapy. I was a house guest of one of the participants. His wife had painful arthritis in both feet. She was highly skeptical that my tiny little instrument would be helpful, but reluctantly consented to try it on the more painful foot. She received a twenty-minute treatment and thought that there was some slight improvement. She was advised to treat that foot again for fifteen minutes before bed.

The next morning she reported with great delight that the treated foot did not hurt when she first woke up—normally the period of greatest pain. She let go of all skepticism and began treating the other foot as well as other arthritic areas of her body.

In 1986, I met Drs. Mary and Richard Broeringmeyer, chiropractors who had worked with magnetic therapy for many years. They taught me the method of magnetic diagnosis they had developed with Walter Rawls, another magnetic therapy pioneer.

Allthough the Broeringmeyers worked primarily with permanent magnets, their techniques work as well or better with pulsed magnetic fields. Their work has transformed magnetic therapy from guesswork into specific procedures which can be taught and replicated by anyone. Much of that process is described in this book, for I want you to have access to the techniques regardless of where you live or what your financial situation is.

Magnetic therapy is simple to apply, effective, and inexpensive. If magnetic therapy works as well for you as it has for me, you will be very pleased indeed.

Chapter II
A Brief History of Magnetic Healing

The use of magnets in healing extends back in time at least as far as there are written records. Egyptian nobility were reported to wear magnetic jewelry to preserve youth and beauty, a property of magnetic treatments just being rediscovered. Many thousands of years earlier, one African tribe apparently used magnetic ores in food preparation; it has recently been rediscovered that magnetic fields can alter the flavor of some foods.

Magnetic therapy (therapy using magnets) has been used in China for more than two thousand years, according to Minda Hsu and Chikuo Fong, two modern researchers of biomagnetism. The oldest known medical book, the *Chinese Yellow Emperor's Book of Internal Medicine*, is thought to have been written around 2,000 b.c., and mentions the practice of placing natural magnets on acupuncture points. Hsu and Fong describe a report of patients eating magnetic ore for paraplegia, rheumatism, and arthritic swellings of the limbs. Magnetic therapy has been used in the Orient in many forms right up to the present. Today, the practice has evolved to the use of very tiny magnetic beads applied to acupuncture points.

In the West, Aristotle wrote in 300 b.c. about the use of magnets for healing purposes. In a.d. 100, Pliny the Younger, a Greek physician, wrote about the use of magnets for healing eye diseases. Galen, a third-century Roman physician, observed that magnets can help constipation—a finding I have often verified when friends who had this complaint tried placing a magnet on the abdomen over the colon for a few minutes.

In a.d. 400, a French physician (name unknown) wrote of using a magnetic necklace. Recently, a reference dating from a.d. 750 was found that described the work of a Chinese physician who treated wounds with magnetic powder to stop pain and accelerate healing.

The use of magnets continued for centuries. Writing in 1530, the physician Paracelsus seems to have been the first to mention using the different poles of a magnet for different purposes. This important observation appears to have been lost until this century.

In 1600, William Gilbert, English scientist and physician to Queen Elizabeth, wrote a comprehensive book in Latin called De Magnete that created widespread interest in magnetism, especially for healing.

In 1777, the Directors of the French Royal Society of Medicine appointed two experts to verify the value of magnets in the treatment of disease. After a careful study, the experts supported the value of magnetic therapy. A few years later, succeeding directors of the Royal Society condemned the notions of the famous Austrian physician and hypnotist Mesmer, whose early experiments involved using magnets as an aid to hypnotizing people. With his very valuable work discredited, Mesmer left Paris. Six years later, other directors of the Royal Society again approved the use of magnets in the treatment of disease.

In the early 1800s, Baron Von Reichenbach was condemned and disbarred from practicing as a physician, apparently because of his use of magnets. Like Mesmer, he was one of the first people to state that some of his patients could see colored sparks or rays at the end poles of a magnet, and that when they became well, this perception faded away.

It should be noted that these centuries marked the beginning of rational thought and the scientific method.

The Dark Ages were over. Only things that could be observed, measured, and put into the framework of mathematics were acceptable; all else was considered superstition, or, at least, not within the realm of science. "If you can't see it and measure it, then it doesn't exist," was the motto of the age. Since no one could explain how magnetism could possibly work to help the body heal, it had to be rejected as a medical treatment. Besides, it was too simple!

In spite of attempts to suppress or ridicule the use of magnets to help the healing process, their use has persisted to this day—because they work. People keep rediscovering the value of magnets over and over again. Now that powerful permanent magnets are commonly available, more and more people are discovering this simple and natural healing method.

In the 1880s, Dr. C. J. Thacher of Chicago sold a full line of therapeutic garments with hundreds of magnets sewn into them. Collier's magazine called Dr. Thacher the "king of the magnetic quacks." Thacher sold caps, coats, insoles, vests, and back braces. No doubt they worked, but because no one knew how, they were not fully accepted. Around the same time, a physician's wife made and sold a magnetic liniment for the treatment of rheumatism.

Magnetic Healing in the Twentieth Century

In 1936, Albert Davis rediscovered that the two poles of a magnet have biological effects. Davis carried out repeated experiments on the effects of different magnetic poles on rats, mice, and other animals, as well as seeds and plants. His research, reported in several books, has been repeatedly verified by others working in the field of biomagnetism. Davis' basic finding was that one pole stimulated living organisms, and the other pole calmed them.

Around this time, it was observed that people who had arthritis and had been staying at the South Pole for several months experienced an improvement in their arthritic conditions. At first it was assumed that the extreme cold of Antarctica was the factor, and a number of unfortunate arthritis sufferers endured much trauma and misery by having their hands and feet partially frozen at regular intervals. Eventually, magnetism, not cold, was recognized as the healing factor. It was also found that besides reducing arthritis, magnetic treatments helped heal sprains and broken bones. As wounds healed, the treatments also reduced scar tissue formation and sped the healing process.

In 1948, physicians in the Soviet Union reported that magnetic treatments would reduce pain after amputation of limbs. In the 1960s, the Canadian Ministry of Agriculture was reported to be researching improvement of germination achieved by exposing grain to magnetic forces.

Japanese research on magnetic effects has been extensive. Many experiments have been done in the past fifteen years, and several companies now market magnetic devices, including necklaces, bracelets, and beds. It is estimated that ten percent of the Japanese population use magnetic beds or other magnetic devices. The Japanese Health Ministry has fully approved magnetic healing, which is now the twentieth largest industry in Japan.

Magnetic treatments are now widely used all over the world. In Europe, electrically generated pulsed magnetic forces have been used by some health spas since the 1970s with great success. There are newsletters, organizations, and frequent workshops and seminars.

The United States lags behind other countries in this area of medicine, but interest and use are beginning to increase.

In 1993, the National Institutes of Health set up an organization to accept grant proposals for alternative therapies, including magnetism. Today, mainstream medical doctors are routinely using pulsed magnetic force instruments to help heal fractures. Magnetic coils are sometimes embedded inside a cast so that continuous treatment is easily possible.

Careful research carried out in the past twenty years with the aid of powerful microscopes and other sophisticated equipment and techniques has solidly supported the value of magnetic forces in the healing process. There are no doubts as to its efficacy, and rarely are adverse effects reported.

Swiss physician Marcus Weber (1992) describes a study of the results of pulsed magnetic fields on 1,712 patients with inflammations, joint and organ disorders, fractures and acute injuries, and circulatory disorders. Over 60 percent of the physicians evaluated the results as either very good or good; no side effects were observed.

Although mainstream medicine is rapidly incorporating the use of pulsed magnetic forces in bone healing, the use of permanent magnets has been largely bypassed, perhaps because pulsed magnetic instruments are more expensive and thus are more worthwhile for companies to manufacture and sell to physicians. Permanent magnets have their uses, too. Although they may not work as rapidly or effectively as pulsed magnetic forces, they are less expensive and readily available to the average person.

Most of the techniques and applications in this book can be made with either permanent magnets or pulsed magnetic forces. The next two chapters will describe the different types of magnets and how to apply them to the body.

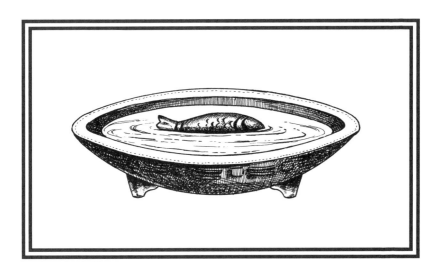

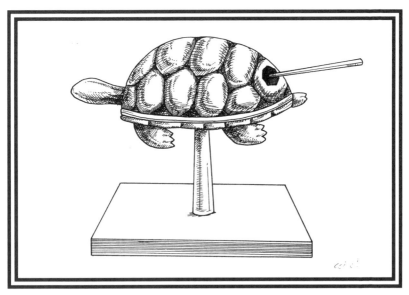

Figure 1: Early Chinese compasses

CHAPTER III

What are Magnets?

Pieces of iron that twist, attract, or repel other pieces of iron are called magnets. An older English name for natural magnets was lodestones, meaning leading stones because they led or pointed to the north if they were suspended by a string. The observation that lodestones attract or repel each other has mystified people for centuries, and today the basic nature of magnetism is still a mystery to most people.

The name magnet was introduced into Western culture about 2,000 years ago when lodestones were rediscovered in the mountainous Magnesia region of Greece. Other cultures had different names long before that. Magnetism is just a word used to describe a phenomenon that is no more or less unusual than many other forces and events that occur all around us every day. Magnets seem more mysterious, probably because we can directly experience the physical attracting and repelling force as we hold them in our hands. The invisible force we feel between two magnets eternally fascinates people and has stimulated much research and speculation.

Figure 2: Magnets are Puzzles

13

TYPES OF MAGNETS

Natural Magnets

Natural magnets, or lodestones, are formed when molten lava containing iron or iron oxides cools and is magnetized by the great magnetic force of Earth. When the lava is molten, it does not exhibit magnetic properties, but as it cools, the tiny molten particles of iron twist around to align with Earth's magnetic poles, and are trapped in this position when the iron solidifies. Since different mountains have erupted at different times in history, it is possible to determine changes in the direction of magnetic north by examining lava from different places and eras. The orientation of these lava magnets indicates that Earth's magnetic poles have altered their positions by hundreds of miles, and even completely reversed every few hundred thousand years or longer.

How did Earth itself become a magnet? No one knows for sure, but it is now believed that Earth's magnetic force is mostly generated by spinning molten iron within the interior of the spinning planet. Spinning appears to be a necessary condition for any planet to have a magnetic field. But how did the Earth start spinning in the first place? This may be a misleading question because spin appears to be a fundamental force in the universe, along with gravity and electricity. (See chapter 10.)

Electromagnets

For thousands of years, the only magnets available were natural magnets or lodestones, which were primarily used

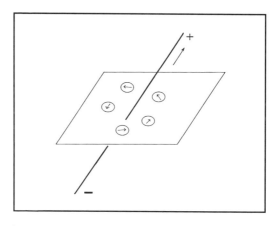

Figure 3: Five compasses around a wire showing circular force

as compasses. They were only occasionally used for healing. Magnets remained one of nature's mysteries.

Major advances in understanding came in the 19th century with the development of batteries. On March 20, 1800, Alessandro Volta discovered how to make a continuous-current battery using copper and zinc discs separated by moist cloth in a weak acid solution. This enabled

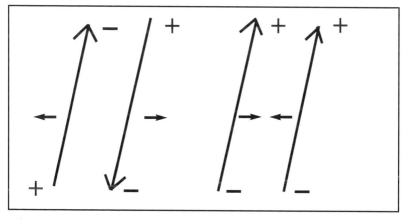

Figure 4: Magnetic repulsion and attraction between two wires

research on electricity to progress rapidly, and in 1819 a Danish scientist, Hans Oersted, discovered a connection between electric current flow and magnetism. He found that when a compass was placed under a current-carrying wire, it would turn at right angles to the wire. When it was placed on top of the wire, it would turn at right angles in the opposite direction. This fundamental discovery rapidly led to many others.

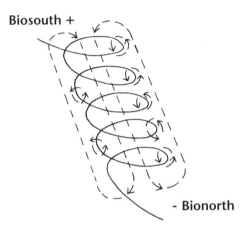

Figure 5: Counterclockwise coil as seen from the top

Oersted soon discovered that two wires conducting current and placed side by side will attract each other if the current is in the same direction, or repel if the currents are in the opposite direction.

Soon other researchers found that by shaping wire into a coil, the magnetic force around each wire segment would add up to produce a concentrated magnetic force in the center. These coils were called *electromagnets*. Discovered only 180 years ago, the electromagnetic coil led to the invention of electric motors and generators—machines that make possible today's world of refrigerators, washing machines, and thousands of other devices, including electric automobiles and pulsed magnetic healing instruments.

Once electromagnetic coils were known, other discoveries followed in rapid succession. Some unknown genius discovered that the magnetic force in the center of a coil could be increased even more by placing a piece of iron inside the coil. Once placed inside a coil, a piece of iron would still hold its magnetic force for a while after the current in the coil was turned off. This finding quickly evolved into a means to artificially make magnets, which freed people from the necessity of finding natural magnets in lava fields.

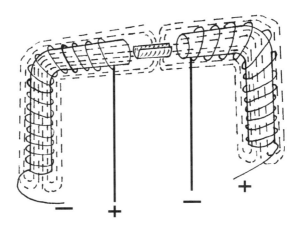

Figure 6: Iron alloy being magnetized

Permanent Magnets—Made by Electromagnets

Magnets are alloys made by adding different metals to finely ground iron, heating the mixture to the melting point, and pouring it into molds of different shapes. Magnets are given an initial magnetization while still in the molten form, but after they have cooled and hardened, they are demagnetized, shipped to distribution points, and then strongly remagnetized at room temperature prior to their sale.

Manufactured magnets are fifteen to thirty times stronger than lodestones. Artificial magnets can now be made that are more powerful than electromagnets of about the same weight, even those using large currents.

Today, all artificial magnets use iron as the primary ingredient. Iron, with twenty-six electrons, is by far the most magnetic element. Iron is unique: it commands a central place in the periodic table, forms the basis of our current metals technology, and holds a central position of power in our organisms. Iron is the key element in hemoglobin, which carries oxygen from our lungs to every cell in the body. Iron is also the heaviest atom manufactured in our sun. Within the iron atom are a few electrons that are free to change their spin orientation. When external magnetic forces are applied, these few electrons in each atom will align with the applied magnetic force. The aligned magnetic spin fields of adjacent atoms reinforce each other. When enough electrons in enough atoms are organized in this manner, the iron or iron alloy manifests the property we call magnetism.

Even research physicists specializing in magnetism still don't know exactly what goes on in iron to give it its unique magnetic properties. Those readers interested in some of the details can refer to chapter 10, in which I describe magnetism and its relationship to spin.

Magnetic Polarity

One of the most intriguing things about magnets is how they attract and repel one another. If you've played with magnets, you know that one end of a bar-shaped magnet will be repelled by one end of a similar magnet,and attracted to that magnet's opposite end.

> Please keep in mind that, polarity in this book refers to the direction of magnetic force, not some special kind of "energy" or mysterious field.

In the past, people have believed that there were two aspects of magnetism known as polarity. A magnet was said to have a north and a south pole. Because these words are nouns, a common misconception occurred: that magnetic poles were separate objects or attributes of a magnetized thing. This semantic error has led to some false ideas about magnetism, including the notion that there could be a magnetic monopole. Magnetic polarity refers only to the direction of magnetic force. There is no intrinsic difference between one pole and another because there aren't such things as poles; there are only directions of a magnetic force, as shown in Figure 7. If this description seems strange to you, keep reading. More details are given in chapter 10.

Pole Terminology

Several systems for naming magnetic poles are in use. The two most common systems use the terms *north* and *south* for opposite poles.

Another system calls the poles positive and negative; this is confusing, since these terms have long been used for electricity. Moreover, it gives the false impression that magnetism is like electricity and that magnetic currents flow between poles like electrons between electrodes. Furthermore, the terms positive and negative have connotations of good and bad. For these reasons, I recommend that these terms be dropped from general use (the term *magnetic pole* should probably also be dropped, but it is already too entrenched in the language).

The terms we use for magnetic poles are arbitrary. We could just as well call them yin and yang, black and white, or sweet and sour. The latter would even be useful, for one pole will sweeten fruit and the other will make it sour.

North and South Poles

Albert Davis, the researcher mentioned in chapter 2 who discovered that the poles (force directions) of a magnet have different biological effects, called the pole (or force direction) which stimulated plant growth, the healing of wounds, and the fermentation of fruits the *south* pole. His *north* pole decreased inflammation and slowed down biological activity. However, in marking his magnets north and south, Davis used the opposite definition of that which is used in industry and science. This mistake has created much confusion. The National Bureau of Standards has defined the *north* pole of a magnet to be that end which seeks the North Pole of Earth (a bar magnet suspended by a string will swing to line up with Earth's field).

> The end of a compass needle that usually points to the North Pole of Earth will point to the bionorth pole of a magnet.

Unfortunately, it seems too late to change now. The biological terminology is becoming more well known than the traditional physics definitions. Therefore, the terms used in this book are **bionorth** and **biosouth,** short for biological north and south as used by Davis.

This definition is easy to use in practice. Simply place a compass near a magnet face or end of unknown polarity. The side or pole of the magnet that attracts the North-Pole-seeking end of the compass needle is defined as: **the bionorth pole of the magnet**. In other words, the magnet acts like a little Earth, where the north pole is called *bionorth*.

Color-Coding Magnets

Following the practice of others, I color-code all the magnets I use for healing, and recommend that you do also, regardless of the terminology you use for magnet poles. Keep the color-coding standard to save time. When I pick up a magnet in my lab or office, I don't have to stop and think about bionorth or biosouth; I just glance at the color and use the magnet accordingly.

Color-coding systems are fairly standard. The stimulating biosouth pole is usually color-coded red, the soothing bionorth end color-coded blue, white, or green.

If you plan to work with ordinary household magnets, you may mark the biosouth end with red nail polish. The other end can be marked with white paint or white typewriter correction fluid. If you prefer a nicer and softer feeling marking system, you can buy colored plastic tool dip material; larger hardware stores usually stock it. Magnets coated with this material are easy to use, won't chip when they knock against each other, and are softer against the skin.

21

Common Confusions with Magnet Terminology

Some people have written that one pole of a magnet has a clockwise spin around it, and the other pole a counterclockwise spin. This is incorrect. If you consider how magnets are made, you will see that the force around a magnet is either in toward the center of the magnet, or out away from the magnet.

The direction of force around a bar magnet is not clockwise or counterclockwise, it is either into the end of the bar or it is out of the end of the bar and changes continuously in between.

Not This   **This**

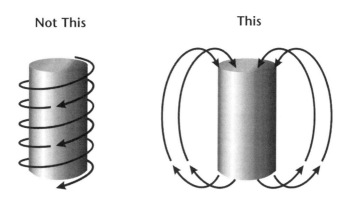

Figure 7: Magnetic force direction changes

A number of terms have been used in popular accounts of magnetism. These terms are often used inappropriately and can be confusing. For instance, the writer of an article on magnetism used the terms: *magnetic force, magnetic energy, magnetic waves, magnetism as polar, magnetic current, magnetic circuit,* and *magnetic field* all in just four pages! After reading that article, anyone would be confused, as most probably was the writer himself. I recommend using only the term *magnetic force.*

Magnetism is not energy and magnetic currents do not flow, nor do they make waves between the north and south poles of permanent magnets.

The term *magnetic field* is usually applied to the region around a permanent magnet or around a current-carrying wire. However, this term is an abstraction and I generally prefer to use the term *magnetic force* when a direction is implied, and *magnetic strength* when the magnitude of the force is of interest. The glossary at the end of this book may help clarify the terms.

The underlying physics that suggests magnetic forces may be a special type of spin force, or torque, is explained in chapter 10.

Magnet Strength

For healing work, magnet strength is less important than choosing the correct polarity, but sometimes strength is important. We might need a strong magnet to get through a thick cast, a large low-intensity magnet to treat a sore muscle, or a small high-intensity magnet to cure a toothache. How do we measure and compare the strengths of magnets?

A magnet exerts a twisting and pulling force on some of the electrons in iron atoms. Since the electrons are bound in atoms, they aren't free to jump out, so the entire piece of iron moves toward the magnet. The force of attraction is called a *gauss*, after the German mathematician Karl Fredrick Gauss. When we speak of a magnet's *gauss strength*, we usually mean the pulling force measured at the surface of the magnet. However, magnetic forces operate on other atoms besides iron in the body. (See chapter 11.)

Limitations of the Term "Gauss"

As one moves away from a magnet, the magnetic force diminishes according to the inverse square law. This law states that intensity varies according to the formula $F = 1/r^2$, where F is the force intensity and r is the the distance from the source. The practical effect is that if the intensity at a certain distance from the source is 1, the intensity twice as far from the source is only $1/4$. (See the glossary at the end of the book for more on the inverse square law.)

Measured gauss strength will be much less a short distance away from the surface of the magnet. Even a coat of thick plastic or a layer of cloth will make a difference. Therefore, the term *gauss* may only correctly be used if one also states the distance from the surface under discussion.

A second problem with using gauss strength to compare magnets relates to their physical size. One can have a magnet the size of a pea with a gauss strength of 1,000 at the surface, and another magnet about the size of a domino with a gauss strength of 300 at the surface. If we just look at gauss strength, the larger magnet seems only one-third the strength of the smaller one. But if we make a measurement a couple of inches away from the small magnet, its gauss strength may reduce to 100; six inches away, its gauss strength may be only 50, while the larger magnet still gives a gauss reading of 100.

A good way to visualize this is to imagine two light bulbs, one tiny and brilliant, and the other large and dim. Close to the bulb, the tiny light illuminates your hand more brightly. If you are illuminating a room, the larger bulb will do a better job. (Light intensity also follows the inverse square law.)

In order to compare two magnets, it might be better to refer to their magnetic strength multiplied by the weight in ounces (g x w). This would produce a number we might call the gauss-weight, or gw number. For example, the common domino-sized ceramic magnet mentioned above has a weight of 1.8 ounces and a gauss strength at the surface of 1,000. Its gw number, therefore, is 1,800 gOz (1,000 x 1.8). A 1″ diameter, $1/4$ -inch thick super-strong magnet weighs exactly one ounce. Its gauss strength when measured near the surface is over 2,000. Its gauss-weight number would be 2,000 gOz (2,000 x 1), so the smaller super-strong magnet has about 10 percent more magnetic force.

Determining Gauss Strength

A gauss meter costs several hundred dollars. Fortunately, it is possible to gauge a magnet's approximate strength by using a comparison magnet.

To do this, set a compass in the middle of a ruler laid on an east-west axis so the compass needle will be perpendicular to the scale. Set the magnet of known gauss on one side of the compass so that it just pulls the needle, and then place the unknown magnet on the other side, with opposite polarity so the forces balance out. The ratio of the square of the distances will give you a comparison of the forces of the two magnets.

Types of Permanent Magnets

The three main types of artificially made, iron-based permanent magnets are **alnico, ferrites,** and **rare earth**.

These names come from the elements added to the iron to increase its magnetic permanence, which include nickel, barium, boron, cobalt, samarium, strontium, and neodymium. For example, alnico contains iron, nickel, aluminum, and trace amounts of cobalt, copper, or titanium. Although magnetically stronger than pure iron, alnico magnets need to be attached to an iron shield known as a **keeper** when not used in a motor or other application, or they will slowly lose their magnetism.

Ferrites—The Best Buy

Barium and strontium ferrite magnetic materials are lumped together and called *ferrites* or *ceramic* magnets, because they are made by pressing a powder into a die under many tons of pressure and at a high temperature. They can be pressed into a die of practically any shape and size. After they are pressed, they are fired at a high temperature to form a ceramic.

Ferrites have slightly different strengths and are divided into grades from 1 to 8. Grades 5 through 8 are stronger. They are made stronger by first applying a strong magnetic field to the pressed mixture before firing. This causes the tiny particles to flip around and orient to the external magnetic field. Then, when the pressed materials are fired, a stronger magnetic material is formed.

Barium is no longer used because in some forms it is toxic (not those used by magnetic manufacturers). While strontium is slightly more expensive, it is still cheaper than cobalt. Strontium ferrites are the most common magnets

Figure 8: Some typical magnets

available. They are the most value for the money, and are especially useful for biological applications, since they are readily available in many different forms. These magnets can be made powerful by making them quite large. Ceramic magnets are brittle, like ceramic pots, and will break if dropped.

Strontium ferrite magnetic materials are also combined with a vinyl compound to form the commonly available magnetic materials used to close refrigerator doors tightly, and to hold papers and signs on metal surfaces; they are used in many toys. This material is not brittle, but it is magnetically weak.

Rare Earth Magnets—The Most Powerful

Samarium or cobalt magnets have been used for biological applications in the past. These magnets are mixtures of elements, not a chemical compound. The magnets are almost as strong as the neodymium ones described below, and as expensive. They retain their magnetic properties at high temperatures.

Neodymium magnets are today's delight. They are super-strong! Like ceramic magnets, neodymium magnets don't need a keeper. Neos, as they are called, degrade at temperatures over 140 degrees. They are expensive at this time (1996).

Unlike barium ferrite magnets, neos and samarium-cobalt magnets cannot be made stronger by making them larger. For maximum strength, the maximum thickness that rare earth magnets can be is about $^3/_8$ to $^1/_2$ inch. They often come in rod or disc shapes between $^1/_4$ and $^3/_4$ of an inch in diameter. Neodymium magnets come in grades numbered 27 to 60, with the higher numbers being stronger.

All magnets rust since they are mostly iron; however, neos can be purchased with color-coded red (biosouth) and blue (bionorth) plastic cases from suppliers which makes them much easier to handle.

Most of the techniques and applications in this book can be made with either permanent magnets or pulsed magnetic forces. The next two chapters will describe the different types of magnets and how to apply them to the body.

Some of the permanent magnets commonly used today are described in the table that follows

Types of Artificial Magnets

Iron	Soft Iron	The first type of permanent magnet made; much stronger than natural lodestone. But pure iron won't stay magnetized very long. Heating or dropping a magnetized iron bar will demagnetize it.
	Alnico	The first type of alloyed magnetic material. Alnico is made by mixing nickel and aluminum with iron. Alnico needs a "keeper" across the poles to retain its magnetism.
Ferrites (Ceramic)	Barium Ferrite	Barium combines with iron atoms to form barium ferrite, a stronger magnetic compound than alnico. It doesn't need a keeper, and can be powdered, melted, and cast into any desired shape or size, then magnetized. Barium ferrite magnets have been manufactured in the United States since 1954.
	Rubber Magnets	A flexible plastic material is mixed with powdered barium ferrite to produce a material that is fairly strong magnetically and won't break. It's usually magnetized in strips of alternating polarity.
	Strontium Ferrite	Strontium also combines chemically with iron to form a magnetic compound. Like barium, it can be powdered and cast into different shapes.
Rare Earth	Samarium-Cobalt	Samarium and cobalt can be mixed with pure iron to produce a very strong magnetic material. It, too, can be cast, but produced only in small sizes. It is expensive.
	Neodymium	The most recently discovered and most powerful type of magnet material is made by combining the rare earth element neodymium with iron and a little boron, a common element. Basic crystals in neodymium magnets are made out of 56 iron atoms, 8 neodymium atoms, and 4 boron atoms. This material can be cast and shaped in small sizes only. It is expensive.

Comparison of Magnetic Field Intensities

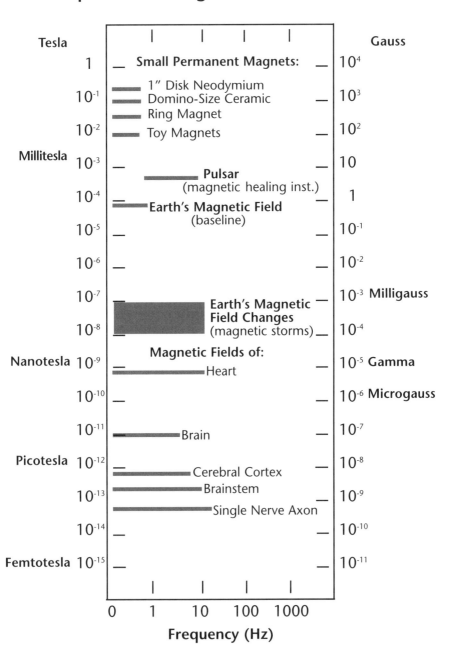

Chapter IV
General Principles of
Magnetic Diagnosis & Treatment

The application of magnets to the body to stimulate healing is very simple. By following the procedures described in this chapter, you can quickly and easily help your body heal itself.

Some Basic Advice

Basic Facts

- The biosouth pole (red) stimulates and promotes healing, growth, and activity.

- The bionorth pole (white, blue, or green) calms, sedates, reduces inflammation, and also promotes healing.

These are observations based on experiments by many people over many years. They are not absolute; research continues.

The Basic Rule

- If it feels better, keep doing it! If it doesn't help, or makes the condition worse, wait a short time and then apply the other polarity.

You are the ultimate judge of whether something is working. Applying magnets to your body and paying close attention to what happens will help sharpen your inner senses.

Five Don'ts

- **Don't treat tumors, cancers or infections with the *biosouth* (red) pole at the site of the problem.**

Since the biosouth force stimulates growth, it could stimulate the growth of bacteria, viruses, or cancer cells. It is OK to stimulate the blood supply and the thymus gland, which is working to destroy the invaders. At the same time, you can sedate the inflammation or infection with the bionorth polarity.

- **Don't treat pregnant women around the uterus area.**

Growing tissues are more susceptible to magnetic fields, although most likely there would be no adverse effects.

- **Don't treat people who have pacemakers with magnets around the chest area.**

Although it's unlikely that a magnetic force would disrupt the pacemaker, there is no need to take chances.

- **Don't treat a condition with magnetism if it worsens when either polarity is applied.**

- **Don't use strong magnets around the head, neck, glands, or organs for long periods of time every day.**

Most likely you would not do harm, but moderation is the wisest course. Although probably nothing much would happen, you could overstimulate something and throw the entire endocrine system out of balance. Fortunately, the body is so well balanced that in most cases overstimulation by a magnet will not be harmful. Once the endocrine system is in balance, it will tend to stay that way.

Which Magnetic Pole To Use

There is often some uncertainty about whether to use north or south polarity. In part, this confusion arises from an incomplete understanding of magnetism. A common misconception is that north and south poles are intrinsically different, when in fact they are simply terms describing the direction of magnetic force. To think of north and south as separate is to take a simplistic black-and-white view of what is a circular force, with as many directions as there are points on a compass. These different directions affect the biochemistry differently. The direction known as biosouth increases plant growth, enhances the flavor of water, sweetens fruit, and stimulates healing for many ailments. The directly opposite magnetic force does not necessarily produce opposite effects. For example, bionorth magnetic forces also help many ailments heal and increase plant growth. Although the reader can go by the general principles described in the table below, it should be kept in mind that this is a simplistic, two-valued approach. It is best (as of 1996) to use muscle testing procedures (described later in this chapter) to determine which direction of magnetic force should be applied to a person. Most permanent magnets accentuate only the north or south magnetic force directions, as does a flat coil from a pulsed magnetic generator. While usually either north or south, and sometimes both, work, there may be an optimum magnetic force direction. Moreover, the direction required by the body may change from time to time.

Some magnets come already color-coded. Red is usually used for the stimulating biosouth pole, while white, blue, and green are all used for the bionorth pole. Test each new magnet to be sure of the polarity before using it on the body. Color-coding makes it easy to remember which pole you should use for what purpose.

BIOLOGICAL PROPERTIES OF POLARITIES	
Biosouth	**Bionorth**
Tonifies Stimulates Increases circulation Expands	Sedates, Inhibits Slows, Soothes Reduces inflammation Shrinks tumors Acute conditions
Alternating North/South	
General use for chronic conditions	

Magnets come in many different shapes, types, and strengths; some are more useful for treating the body than others. For instance, horseshoe magnets don't produce uniform forces and are not ideal for healing purposes.

You can obtain magnets at hobby stores or magnetic supply houses. Permanent magnets vary in cost from less than a few dollars up to $70 for a large block magnet. You can prepare your home medicine kit with a good supply of magnets for less than $100.

Before you begin using magnets, be sure to mark all of them in some clear way. You can use a test magnet or compass to determine their polarity.

Some magnets are formed with north and south poles on the same surface. These multipole magnets may not work quite as well for helping all injuries heal, but they do seem to

> *The side or end of a magnet which attracts the north-pointing end of a compass needle should be color-coded blue or green. This is called the bionorth pole.*

work in many cases, and have the advantage that you don't need to determine which polarity to apply to the body.

Do not apply multipole magnets to tumors.

What To Treat

You can treat any condition with magnets; it will either respond or it won't. There are rarely any harmful side effects, except on tumors, cancers, or infections. In these cases, the biosouth (red) pole may stimulate the growth of abnormal cells or the invading organism. Treat these conditions with the bionorth (blue) pole only. Once an infection has passed the inflammatory stage and is healing, it may benefit from red pole treatments; use magnetic diagnosis to find out. (See the Magnetic Diagnosis Section of this chapter for directions.)

Magnetic therapy doesn't seem to help bacterial infections once they have made a strong inroad in the body. Other treatment procedures are recommended.

Magnetic therapy works for about 80 percent of common ailments. Healing takes time, no matter what the treatment. I recommend multi-level approaches that include nutritional supplements, massage, and manipulation, and some form of psychotherapy where appropriate.

Where To Treat

The first place to treat is obviously the site of the injury, or where there is pain, tightness, or a feeling of constriction. If the condition is general, such as depression, weakness, or anxiety, treat the chest area or up and down the spine. Since magnetic fields penetrate most materials, you can place magnets of high to moderate strength over clothing.

Secondary treatment sites are glands that might be related to an injury or illness, or organs that could be associated with the problem. Chinese physicians have found connections between many ailments and the major organs.

Acupuncture points along relevant meridians or reflex points in the feet may be treated. In fact, any sore point on the feet or anywhere else on the body is a candidate for treatment. Acupuncturists Hannamann, Prince, and Sierra have written about the use of magnetic stimulation of acupuncture points. Apparently, these men did not use the muscle-testing technique of magnetic diagnosis to determine the appropriate magnetic polarity for each acupuncture point, gland, organ, or injury site. When their work is combined with this technique, it will probably be even more effective.

How To Treat

Treating most conditions with magnets is simple and straightforward. In most cases, you will want to do a magnetic diagnosis, covered later in this chapter, to determine which polarity to use, where to treat, or how long to continue treatment.

Headaches, colds, sore throats, tightness in the chest, stiff necks, sore muscles, stomach cramps, premenstrual symptoms, and a host of other minor and suddenly appearing aches and pains usually respond to soothing bionorth (white) pole treatments during the initial, inflammatory part of the ailment. The red pole is likely to help the body in the healing phase. Treatment is more likely to help if applied at the very first awareness of an imbalance.

Chronic muscular or joint conditions usually respond well to biosouth (red) pole forces which stimulate healing. If there is pain and inflammation, treat with the bionorth (white) side until the pain goes away, then with the red side for long-term healing effects. Chronic soreness around glands or organs may need either bionorth or biosouth polarity, depending on whether the organ or gland is under- or overactive. If you already know that a particular gland or organ is underactive, treat with the red pole. Otherwise, use magnetic diagnosis to determine the correct polarity.

If specific areas of the body are injured, stiff, or sore, treat directly over the area with a bionorth pole or pulsed magnetic force applicator. If it's a chronic injury, or one in which the pain and inflammation have subsided and it's in the healing phase, treat with a red pole. Use magnetic diagnosis for confirmation of the proper polarity.

If someone is tired, depressed, or weak, apply the biosouth (red) pole to the chest area, throat, or around the eyes and forehead. Don't overstimulate!

> *Don't apply high-gauss red-pole (biosouth) magnetic forces to the head area for more than 15 minutes at a time—this can cause mild headaches.*

Sometimes, the area of the body that hurts is not the place where the trouble is. For instance, some headaches may be connected with liver problems. If a headache does not go away in a few minutes, check the liver for a magnetic reaction. If a shoulder hurts, check the spine at the back of the neck.

You might also try treating a headache by applying a magnet to the inner side of both wrists about two inches up from the joint, which is a significant acupuncture point.

Multiple ailments can be treated simultaneously with magnets. For example, one can treat the pancreas, the liver, the throat, and a sore wrist or neck all at once. Adverse side effects are rare.

If the problem is a generalized one, such as hypertension, widespread arthritis, or general fatigue, then a magnetic bed, magnetic jewelry items, or magnetic shoe inserts may be helpful.

When a person is ill, the chances are high that the endocrine system is out of balance. If they become so ill and weakened that the body is unable to bring the endocrine system back into balance, the condition can last much longer. Magnetic diagnosis and correction is simple, safe, and very effective. I have seen weak and ill people achieve normal energy levels within hours from a short-term sudden-onset illness, or within days for a major illness such as chronic fatigue syndrome (with daily treatments).

If the Pain Increases, Reverse the Polarity

In general, if any minor condition worsens within five to fifteen minutes of treatment, reverse the polarity. If a condition worsens when either polarity is applied, do not treat that condition with magnetism. This is unlikely to occur. Because magnetic forces affect the overall biochemistry, they are usually beneficial.

A slight increase in pain, stiffness or discomfort can sometimes mean the magnet is too strong. Large, strong magnets are not necessarily better. Moreover, large, heavy, powerful magnets are difficult to hold in place on the body. Lightweight electromagnetic coils can be used in place of permanent magnets in many applications.

Ultimately, you or whoever is being treated must decide whether or not a treatment or polarity is helping. Always respect the persons being treated by allowing them to tune into the wisdom of their own bodies and choose what is right for them. (A hypnosis tape is available to help people do that. (See resources.)

How Long to Treat

Sheet magnetic material or pea-size magnets used on acupuncture points may be taped on and left on for a day or two if desired, as may magnetic strips or permanent magnets up to an inch or so in diameter. Large plate magnets may be placed in contact with the body for an hour or more. Magnets larger than two inches in diameter may be uncomfortable or awkward to tape or hold on the body.

It is not advisable to place powerful neodymium magnets on the body for more than a day or two at a time. Neo magnets are strong enough to overstimulate an area.

> It is important to treat any kind of chronic condition for a few days after the pain is gone, so complete healing and even strengthening will occur. If this is done, a relapse is less likely.

Treatments of fifteen to thirty minutes twice a day are sufficient for most conditions if pulsed magnetic forces are used; half an hour to several days if permanent magnets are used; or up to 30 or more days if magnetic flex pads or magnetic foils are used. Larger magnetic strength or longer treatment times are not necessarily better, although they won't be harmful. Since the required treatment time will vary from individual to individual, use muscle testing to help determine how long to administer the treatment. When a person tests equally strong with either polarity, the body is in balance and will no longer appreciably benefit from magnetic treatment. However, it may be desirable to treat with biosouth for a few more days in order to strengthen that body part and possibly prevent a recurrence. People often have a clear sense of when they have had enough treatment—body wisdom that should be respected. The part of the body being treated may feel irritated when the treatment is continued past the optimum time.

What to Expect

For acute conditions (recent painful injuries or the sudden onset of an illness), improvement may be observed in anywhere from a few minutes (a simple headache) to after five or six treatments. If any improvement at all occurs, more may be expected with continued treatment. If no improvement is observed after five or six days, then continued magnetic treatments probably won't help that condition.

In the case of chronic or long-term ailments, it naturally will take longer for effects to be observed. It depends on the condition, the general health of the person, whether or not the whole body is involved, and other individual factors. Sometimes improvement will be noticed after a few treatments, but it may take a month or more of daily treatments.

It is often said that a condition has to get worse before it gets better. The patient is supposed to experience a healing crisis—a worsening of the symptoms or an outpouring of the condition. While this may happen with other forms of treatment, it is not my experience with magnetic therapy. **If magnetic treatments are going to help at all, only improvement takes place, not a worsening of the condition.**

While magnets can temporarily rebalance the body, the individual must then maintain this healthy state with a positive mental attitude, the proper diet, and sufficient exercise to clear out toxins. Remember: **Magnets don't heal; they help the body to heal itself.**

Are Magnetic Treatments Safe?

In the published literature there are few reports of adverse reactions to magnetic treatments.

Magnetic Resonance Imaging (MRI) applies 650 gauss to 15,000 gauss forces to the whole body. The FDA has approved MRI instruments, implying approval of weaker magnetic forces. Some people occasionally have unpleasant reactions to MRI, however.

In 1994, four physicians published an article in the Journal of Rheumatology on the value of pulsed magnetic fields for treating arthritis. They stated that over 200,000 patients (most in Europe) have been safely treated with pulsed magnetic forces with no toxic side effects.

Two Chinese physicians and acupuncturists, Hsu and Fong, reported in a 1978 *American Journal of Acupuncture* article that:

41

"From an experience of several tens of thousands of cases, observed clinically in departments of internal medicine, surgery, pediatrics, traumatology, neurology, dermatology, etc., covering nearly one hundred types of complaints, no contra-indications have been found. Of all said patients, no complications have ever been recorded. A few patients felt light-headed, tired, or sleepy after treatment, but this went away and did not affect the ailment, which usually improved. A few patients did not benefit from the treatments and occasionally felt worse. In such cases, magnetic treatment was discontinued, and all reactions promptly disappeared, leaving no after-effects."

Long-term monitoring of blood cells of people who received magnetic treatments did not show any adverse changes, according to Hsu and Fong.

On the other hand, several people have reported to me that magnetic beds were irritating or too stimulating for them. One woman reported that her face broke out when she simultaneously applied a permanent magnet and a pulsing magnetic field applicator to her sinus area.

A friend strained his thumb hammering nails all day. He applied a magnet to it and after a few minutes exclaimed, "This hurts worse!" He was advised to reverse the polarity, and in a few minutes the thumb was pain-free.

Improper use of magnets can interfere with the body chemistry. Nausea, headache, or irritability can be temporarily produced by using the wrong polarity or too strong a magnet. Be careful, prudent, and use common sense. If a symptom or condition worsens when a magnet is applied, the chances are that the wrong polarity has beem applied. Wait a few minutes and then apply the other polarity, perhaps with a magnet of lesser strength. Pay close attention to how the patient feels. Trust your intuition, or support the patient in trusting his or hers.

Magnetic Diagnosis

Proper balance of the endocrine system is fundamental to good health, and hormones interact in complex ways. While treating one particular gland or organ may help, you may need to know the full pattern to provide effective therapy. This can easily be determined by following a systematic testing procedure using any of the diagnostic methods described in this section. Magnetic diagnosis will indicate which polarity to use for treatment. The basic idea is simple.

Muscle Testing

If the correct magnetic polarity to heal a particular condition is applied, the body will strengthen. If the wrong polarity is applied, it will weaken.

By going over the entire body with a test magnet or the magnetic applicator from a Pulsed Magnetic Generator, one can map the energy balance of the entire glandular and organ systems, as well as major joints and muscles.

A magnetic diagnosis may be made using a stack of magnets about three inches high so that there will be some pole separation between the ends of the stack. Six disc magnets about $1^{1/2}$ inches in diameter will work well for this practice.

When it was commonly believed that there were magnetic poles and each pole had a characteristic "energy," it was mistakenly assumed that one pole did one thing and the other pole another. Therefore, it was believed that it was necessary to shield one pole from possibly affecting the body in this testing in order to obtain a pure polar effect. But since there are no magnetic poles, just magnetic directions, it is only necessary to reverse the magnetic direction to do a muscle test. Separation of the poles by a few inches is sufficient.

Muscle testing for magnetic diagnosis was developed by Drs. Mary and Richard Broeringmeyer, chiropractors who based their work on the observations of magnetic therapy pioneers Albert Davis and Walter Rawls. The Broeringmeyers found that when a magnetic force of the wrong direction is applied to a gland, organ, or site of an injury, every muscle in the body will weaken.

Muscle Testing Basics

Any place on the body can be used as a test point for magnetic treatment; the principle is the same. Simply place the test magnet or magnetic applicator on that point and test muscle strength. If one polarity increases strength, then treat with that polarity. If you know acupuncture, check points along the entire meridian. If you know polarity therapy, use the polarity points. If you know reflexology, you can test the tender foot points. If you don't know, experiment.

If there is an illness or imbalance on one side of the body, that side will usually be weak and will not give reliable test results. Use a muscle from the other side, or a site more removed from the location of the injury.

Muscle testing is not 100 percent accurate. Occasionally, the person may be too ill or too weak to be tested. If an imbalance is marginal, the test will be inconclusive.

For example, the Broeringmeyers have been diagnosing and treating stomach ailments with magnets for several years. By holding the magnet over the stomach and testing muscle strength, one can determine whether the stomach is underactive or overactive. An underactive stomach has become more alkaline than normal in its response to the body's demand on it. There is less acidity and digestion is slowed down. The hydrogen ion concentration has apparently been decreased. When the blue (bionorth) pole of a diagnostic magnet is placed on the stomach, the body is weakened because the problem is made worse.

> When a gland or organ is overactive, any muscle will become weaker when the red (biosouth) pole of a magnet is placed at that point. If a muscle is weaker when the blue pole is placed over the test point, the organ is underactive.

When the stomach is too acidic, it will be overactive. The hydrogen ion level is higher than it needs to be. When the biosouth (red) pole of a diagnostic magnetic is placed on the stomach, the condition is made worse and the body's muscles are weakened. When the stomach is too acidic, ulcers are more likely.

Clients sometimes know which gland or organ is out of balance because they have had medical tests or have sensations or pains in those areas. When knowledge such as this has been available, it always has concurred with the muscle testing procedure in my experience.

Details on the significance of, and symptomology associated with, hyperactive and hypoactive glands and organs are described in the Broeringmeyers' book *Energy Therapy*.

Further information on muscle testing is given in my previous book, *The Body Magnetic*.

Arm and Leg Strength as Indicators

Ask the person you are testing to lie down on their backs and raise one arm straight up. Have them gently close the hand into a fist. Explain that you are going to move their arm down towards their hip and they are to resist as hard as they can. Before you apply any force, say in a clear, loud tone, "Lock...and resist." Speak slowly so that they can have time to

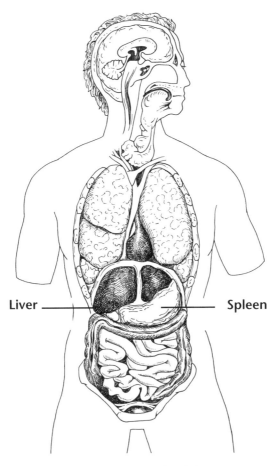

Liver ——————   —————— Spleen

Figure 9: View of the body's organs

inhale and hold their breath, or exhale and hold, whichever is their preference. People are sometimes stronger in one phase of the breath cycle. Simply allow plenty of time to "get set" before you push on their arms; most people will automatically hold their breath at the point that is right for them.

You should wait a second or two, then push or pull the arm down a few inches towards the hip. Carefully make a mental note of how strongly they can resist, whether you feel the arm lock solidly in place as you make initial contact with it, and whether the arm feels strong as you apply firm pressure. There are two aspects to the test—the initial locking of the muscles and the strength to resist firm pressure. Both will show a reaction to magnetic forces if there is an imbalance in the body.

After you have made a control test, apply the diagnostic magnet or pulsed magnetic applicator to each gland or organ in turn, using first one side or polarity, and then the other. Muscle test each magnetic polarity to determine the strengthening or weakening effect. Make a note of each

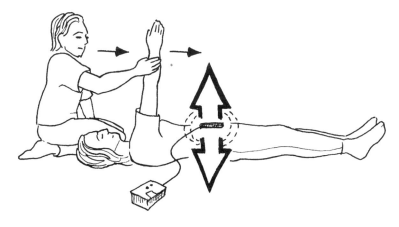

Figure 10: Muscle testing procedure: front

place of weakness for later treatment. Magnets or magnetic applicators can be applied over the clothing for diagnosis or treatment.

If a site is weak with one polarity, treat it with the opposite polarity. A site that tests strong for both polarities generally does not need treatment. A site that tests weak with either polarity may be treated with both polarities.

A muscle test in which the person does not experience a clear difference is not one that can be relied upon. For best results, the person being tested should clearly know by their awareness, not yours, that they are weaker or stronger. If there is not a clear difference to them, the test may not be accurate, and/or a magnetic force treatment may not be appropriate for that ailment or condition.

Treat with the polarity that makes the person stronger.

Sometimes a person does not properly muscle test. In that case, Dr. Mary Broeringmeyer suggests slowly moving a tape demagnetizer over the body, then muscle testing again.

Notes on Locating Specific Points on the Front

The pituitary is in the middle of the forehead. People sometimes refer to this test point as the "third eye."

The thyroid consists of two lobes, located on each side of the neck. Sometimes these lobes show different reactivities to magnetic testing.

The thymus, governor of the immune system, is located just below the collarbone. It apparently moves downward with age, so adjust your test position accordingly.

There are four test points to use in testing the heart. Usually, one general area test will be adequate, but if a

Testing Tips for Consistent and Accurate Results

- Apply pressure at the same place on a person's arm, usually at the wrist.
- Always place yourself in the same body position and use, for example, only two or three fingers to push or pull.
- Be loud and clear in your statement to "Lock... and...resist," and always test at the same time after you give the command. Speak slowly.
- Pause for a few seconds after the word "lock" so the person can have time to breathe the same way each time and to prepare the muscle to resist.
- Ask the person being tested not to look at you; it is all right to close the eyes.
- Allow the person to rest the arm after a few tests. You can also switch arms.
- Watch the person's face when you muscle test. The body is so wonderfully designed that, when a person's muscle does go weak, other muscles will automatically take over its task. The person may make a grimace as other muscles compensate, so you will know that a weakening of the primary muscle has occurred.
- Always ask the person which polarity feels stronger, especially if there is no obvious difference. People usually know when they are stronger or weaker, and it is good to encourage their awareness and participation in the procedure.

Test Points

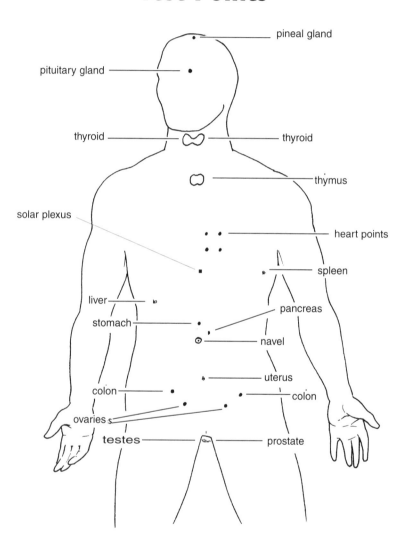

Figure 13: Test points—front view

weakness is present, test more specifically at four points in the region of the heart.

The solar plexus point is located where the ribs come together. The pancreas test point is one inch up from the navel and one inch to the left side of the body (as seen from within). The stomach is a large organ, so you may need to test several points in the region. The uterus is about halfway between the navel point and the top of the pubic bone. The ovaries may be tested by locating the top of the pubic bone in the middle and moving an inch or two to either side to test each one. On men, both testicles should be checked. The prostate is tested by placing the test magnet between the anus and the genitals (I generally ask the clients to place and turn over the test magnet themselves in the genital regions).

After you have completed the tests on the front of the body, ask the person to turn over and test the adrenals and kidneys.

Notes on Locating Specific Points on the Back

The adrenal test points are located just below the shoulder blades, although the adrenal glands are actually located near the kidneys. If the test points below the shoulder blades are sensitive to a firm pressure, then you know immediately that there is an imbalance in those glands. The kidneys may be located by first locating the top of the hip

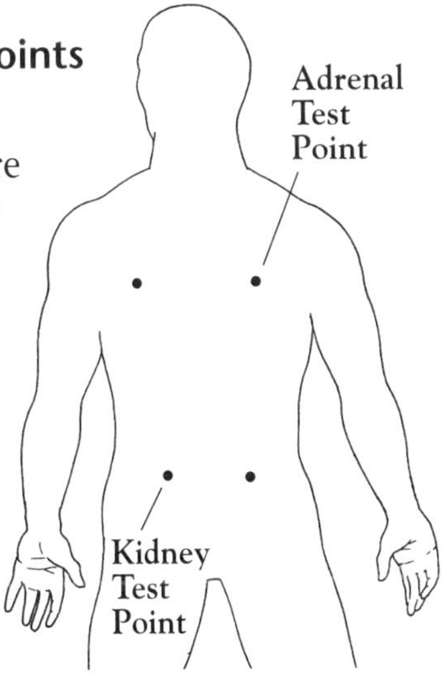

Adrenal Test Point

Kidney Test Point

Figure 11: Test points: back view

bones, then moving to the spine at that level, then moving up two vertebrae and out two inches on either side. For test points on the back, use the leg, lifted and bent at the knee (see illustration on the next page). Push the foot back towards the floor and ask the person to resist as before.

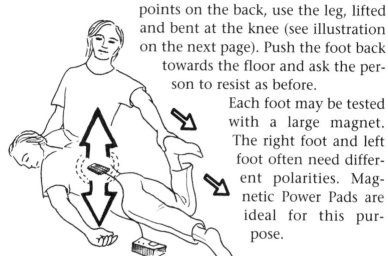

Each foot may be tested with a large magnet. The right foot and left foot often need different polarities. Magnetic Power Pads are ideal for this purpose.

Figure 12: Muscle testing procedure: back view

Finger Strength as an Indicator

A simple yet remarkably accurate muscle test uses just one finger and thumb. Have the client push his or her thumb and forefinger, or thumb and middle finger, together as tightly as possible while leaving the other fingers extended. Then give a verbal signal such as, "Lock... and resist," and attempt to pull them apart.

Note the strength of resistance when each magnetic pole is applied to the test point. Treat with the side that makes the person strong. Because the finger strength test uses only a couple of muscles rather than several, as in the arm test, it is often a more accurate indicator of the appropriate magnetic polarity needed by the body. I often use the finger test as a check on the arm test.

Figure 14: The finger strength tester

The Electronic Muscle Tester as an Indicator

This device makes muscle testing more objective. It consists of a small transducer that is squeezed between a finger (any finger) and thumb. A meter needle indicates the strength reading. In use, a person squeezes at about two-thirds maximum pressure and attempts to hold a reading steady for about one second, then relaxes. First, one magnetic polarity is applied and while in place, a strength test is made. Then, the person relaxes a few seconds, the other magnetic polarity is applied, and the process is repeated. If there is a difference in strength when the red (biosouth) pole is applied versus the blue pole, then one knows that the magnetic polarity that makes the body stronger is the proper one to apply in treatment. If the body doesn't need a specific magnetic polarity, the person's strength clearly remains the same. It's difficult to fool the instrument.

One of the greatest values of the Electronic Muscle Tester is that you can easily use it on yourself. It can also be used to test the efficacy of vitamins, herbs, and homeopathic remedies, or to indicate if there is any weakening effect on the body from nearby power lines, computer terminals, microwave ovens, or fluorescent lights.

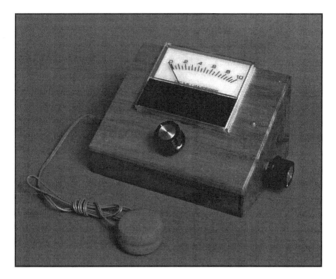

Figure 15: The Electronic Muscle Tester

The **Electronic Muscle Tester** is available from PsychoPhysics Labs.

Leg Length as an Indicator

You may also use leg length as an objective test. This has the advantage of taking the client's psychological state out of the testing procedure. No resisting effort is required. Simply lift both legs (the client lies on his/her back) and check to see if one leg contracts due to the presence of the test magnet's force. The contraction may be as much as 1/4" and is easily perceived. The client may be barefoot or shod, but it is usually easier to perceive changes if shoes are worn which have clearly defined soles. If there is a contraction, treatment with the opposite polarity is indicated. It may be helpful before beginning this procedure to lift both legs and give them a gentle tug and a shake. Lower them and check the lengths with no test magnet applied. Then begin the testing procedure. The disadvantage of this method is that it is a bit more awkward and takes a little more time. It can be useful to confirm the arm muscle test.

Vascular Autonomic Syndrome as an Indicator

Another objective diagnostic test makes use of something called the Vascular Autonomic Syndrome, a slight change in pulse amplitude when the body is presented with a stimulus. This test is described in Dr. Laurence Badgley's excellent book, *Energy Medicine.*

Chapter V
Picking the Right Magnet for the Job

A wide range of magnetic materials, strengths, and shapes is available today, compared with what the magnetic therapists had to work with 100 years ago. There are tiny BB-size magnets used by acupuncturists, oval shaped button-size magnets, dime-size neodymium magnets, domino-size ceramic magnets, cookie-size disc magnets, rectangular block magnets from 2" x 4" to 4" x 6" bar magnets up to 3/4" thick, and flexible magnets of any size and shape desired. Magnets may have one pole on each end or face, or the poles may alternate across a face. Since ceramic magnets can be made in any shape, hundreds of variations are available.

When magnetic powder is embedded in plastic, it can be made into even more diverse shapes. All these shapes, sizes, and kinds can be mounted on or in various bandages, tapes, vests, and shoe inserts, or they can be strung on a necklace, made into a bracelet, or used to cover a whole mattress.

As discussed in chapter 3, there are several kinds of permanent magnets. Alnico was the first type of magnetic alloy manufactured. Today, ferrite or ceramic magnets are most common; they are generally the best buy among permanent magnets. Ferrites can be powdered and cast into nearly any shape, or mixed with flexible plastic to produce magnetic strips or sheets. Rare-earth magnets are most powerful, but they're expensive and come in limited sizes and shapes.

Magnets are available at the larger hardware stores and at some hobby stores. Some fabricators of magnetic devices also sell magnets, but most don't want to deal with individual buyers. Magnets from all three sources are unlikely to be marked with their strength and polarity, so bring a compass or test magnet when shopping. Mail order companies sell a large selection of magnets and magnetic devices. (See resources.)

It's difficult to sort out the statements made by manufacturers of magnetic devices. In part, this is because practically everything works, at least on a few people. (As previously mentioned, there is also a placebo effect of about 13 percent.) In part, this is also because magnetic companies are not allowed by law to make healing claims; hence, it is necessary to make your own evaluations and inferences about what works best for you.

Some companies have designed their own magnet shapes, pole configurations, garments, beds, or other devices, and make claims for uniqueness, perhaps so they can develop a special advertising program. Shop around before buying.

Permanent Magnets For Healing

Only some of the magnets commonly available in hobby supply and hardware stores are suitable for healing, and are unlikely to be labeled with strength and polarity. If you can't find what you want locally, mail order sources provide an excellent selection of permanent magnets, as well as magnetic instruments and devices.

The most generally useful common magnets have only one direction of magnetic force on one end. Multipole magnets, manufactured with bands or strips of alternating polarity on the same face, are useful for treating certain kinds of aches, pains, and irritation, but cannot be used when one force direction only is needed. The pole strips should be at least 1/4" wide to work effectively. When in doubt about a magnet you are purchasing, use a compass to check the polarity.

Ceramic ring magnets with holes in the center are used exclusively by Richard Hopkins, a San Diego magnetic therapist. Because there iis a polarity change in the center, they act like thin, flexible multipolar magnets, but they are much stronger.

For most uses, you will want magnets with the poles on the large faces, not the ends, because you will want to lay the face with the correct polarity against the body of the person being treated. Two such magnets, one inside and one outside the clothes, will hold each other in place. Discs up to several inches in diameter, without holes, are ideal, as are domino-shaped magnets.

The most inexpensive way to do home treatment is usually with permanent magnets. If you have a large area to treat, pulsed magnetic healing devices may be cheaper and more quickly effective. Use the following sections to familiarize yourself with what's available.

You can probably stock your home medicine kit with a good supply of magnets for under $100. It's good to have a variety of shapes and sizes and strengths for different applications. For example, for treating a sore tooth a small, strong magnet (a neo) would be good. For helping a broken leg heal, a large, strong magnet would be best to penetrate through the cast.

The type and size of magnet to use depends on the condition you wish to treat.

If you are treating acupuncture points, tiny disc magnets can be taped on the points and left for several days. A fractured leg or arm may be treated by the largest block magnets available (4"x6"x1") or 6" diameter magnetic pads. Minor aches and pains, sprains, and sore muscles may be best helped by a large-area, medium-strength ceramic magnet, or by placing a low-strength flexible multipole magnetic strip over them. A more serious ailment may call for a high-strength neodymium magnet for a short time. A toothache will often benefit from a neo magnet, bionorth (blue) pole on the cheek, for ten to fifteen minutes.

There are a bewildering array of magnet shapes and stengths available now. For magnetic therapy, it seems that almost everything works to some extent, and it's not just a placebo effect. As long as you don't use strong biosouth poles on tumors, and apply magnets in moderation, you will have no difficulty. Of course, anyone using magnets should not keep a magnet on their body if it makes any symptom or condition worse.

Beads

Acupuncturists commonly tape tiny magnets over acupuncture points. They come in convenient packages with sticky tape included, and are available mail order. Check the polarity of the beads—do not trust the manufacturer's markings. Gauss strengths vary, but this is probably not as important as selecting the proper polarity.

Beds

Magnetic beds come in several varieties. Basically, they consist of magnets embedded in pads that one sleeps on. Different manufacturers use magnets of different sizes and shapes, each claiming that theirs is the best, cheapest, or most unique. Exercise caution when considering a purchase. Is your body generally in balance? Is the bed's polarity right for you? Magnetic beds are best used for tonifying by people whose bodies are already in balance.

Most magnetic beds have only the bionorth pole towards the body, although some can be turned over to provide biosouth polarity. Muscle testing may show which polarity the body predominantly wants, but parts of the body needing different polarities may be made worse by using a bed pad. If a person has an illness, the thymus may need stimulating, the adrenals sedating or calming, the liver stimulating, and so forth. Using a magnetic bed with only the sedating polarity might even make the condition worse. People with whole-body arthritis could be made worse by using a magnetic bed pad with the bionorth polarity facing the body, whereas people with leukemia would be made worse with biosouth.

Several types of magnetic bed pads are now being made in the United States and Canada. In an effort to produce uniqueness for the marketplace, designers have added crystals, copper wire designs, mineral mixtures supposed to be helpful, and various other materials and devices. I cannot say whether or not these variations are just for show or actually produce positive results. Of course, individuals are different; some people are extremely sensitive to subtle energies that others completely ignore.

It's possible to make your own bed. You could use a cotton futon, rather than a plastic foam pad which may not be good for the body. Magnetic sleeping systems are also available from many biomagnetic supply companies.

Bargain Basement Magnets

Sometimes surplus electronics catalogs, people at flea markets, used electronic parts stores, etc. will have assorted magnets salvaged from tape recorders, computer disc drives, and other instruments. These magnets may often be neos, available at bargain prices. They will be fine for body treatments. Just be sure to have one standard test magnet color coded so you can mark the polarity of every magnet you pick up.

Magnets with more than one pole on one face may not be quite as useful for biological applications, but you can experiment and form your own conclusions.

Block Magnets

The largest commonly available magnet is about 6" x 4" x 3/4". With a gauss strength of one thousand, these ferrite (ceramic) magnets are useful for big jobs. Placing them under feet (muscle test for correct polarity!) for short periods of time can be helpful.

Bracelets

In Europe and Asia, magnetic bracelets have been found to relieve stress and ailments such as minor arthritis pain, nervous disorders, and insomnia as well as improving circulation and the health of the muscular system in general.

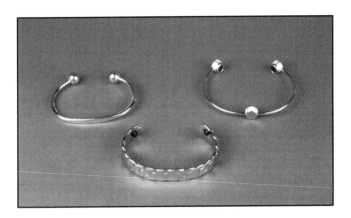

Figure 17: Magnetic bracelets

My favorite magnetic bracelet is called the Stress Bracelet. Although it holds only three or four small magnets, I have been amazed at how much it strengthens my body when I'm feeling low. (Whenever I feel a sniffle coming on, half an hour or so wearing the Stress Bracelet usually cures me.) Made of copper, zinc, and a combination of other alloys, and finished in 24-carat gold, it comes with a lifetime guarantee. The magnetic elements of the Stress Bracelet must be in close proximity to the body, although it is not necessary for the magnets to touch the skin. The bracelet can be worn loosely on the wrist.

Disc Magnets

Disc magnets without holes in the center are available in diameters from 1/3 inch to over 2 inches.

Flat discs about $1\frac{1}{2}$" in diameter and $\frac{3}{16}$" thick (called cookie magnets) are handy for treating minor aches and pains. They cover a wider area than a domino-shaped magnet (1.8 sq. in. versus 1.3 sq. in.) with just over half the gauss strength (650 G versus 1000 G). Cookie magnets are easy to apply in pairs to the body. One can be placed inside a garment and one outside, so they hold each other in place. They are thin, lightweight, and unobtrusive.

Domino Magnets

About the size of dominos, domino magnets are also called "Briggs and Stratton" magnets because they have been used by the millions in small gasoline motors of that name. With a gauss strength of 800 to 1,000, they have many applications. They are the best buy for the money because they are so widely used.

Latch Magnets

Latch magnets have been used by the millions to close cupboard doors. They are flat rectangles about 1" long by 3/4" wide, with a 1/8" hole in the center. Gauss strength may vary from 400 to 800.

Magnetic Foils

Magnetic foils with alternating magnetic polarities are inexpensive and easy to apply to the body. Do not be taken in by advertising which claims special designs are better than others. The least expensive product will be fine.

Magnetic foils are often effective in relieving pain, and have been found to increase body temperature. Peter Kokoschinegg (*Magnets In Your Future*, April 1991), who thoroughly studied their effects, writes of positive effects occurring after several months of continuous treatment (a few weeks or less of intermittent treatment with pulsed magnetic fields would probably produce similar results).

Magnetic Garments

Magnets have been added to practically every garment imaginable. You can buy magnetic garments or make your own. Be aware of polarity and weight. Some garments are made with all bionorth side toward the body, some with biosouth pole, and some with a mix. For some applications you will want to get a garment where the polarity can be reversed. For others you don't—bras should always have bionorth pole toward the body so as to discourage the growth of tumors.

Magnets are heavy. Tiny neodymium magnets can provide gauss strengths equal to much bigger ferrite magnets, but they are expensive. If you need to treat a big

Figure 18: Magnetic insoles

area, permanent magnets may not be practical. Electromagnets are generally lighter and have stronger biological effects. If you are making your own magnetic clothing, be sure to mark the magnets with their polarities before you begin. Make sure your magnets can't flip once the garment is assembled, or that you can get at them if they do. One advantage of using latch magnets is that you can use the tiny hole in the center to stitch them down.

Magnetic Power Pads

Six-inch diameter color-coded blue and red pads are user friendly for treating water, sweetening fruit, placing under the feet, on the back, chest, or stomach while lying down. Their gauss strength is over 1,000 over a large area, so they are quite powerful.

Applying magnets to the body takes some ingenuity. Taping them on becomes awkward with magnets larger than domino size, and removing tape from hairy legs or chests is not much fun. Elastic sweat bands can be used for applying magnets to heads, arms, or legs. Magnets can be slipped inside socks or pockets, or placed on the floor of your car as foot rests.

Necklaces

Magnetic necklaces were first reported to have been used by a French physician in a.d. 400. They could only have been made out of lodestones, so they must have been very heavy! In modern times, several companies in Asia have made lightweight high-gauss necklaces from samarium-cobalt-iron alloys. They are gold-plated and look elegant. My personal favorite is called the Longevity Necklace, which I wear for days at a time because it keeps my neck loose and spending hours at a computer is not good for the neck. Another attractive type is made from hematite, a shiny gray-black iron ore. Cut like crystals, these strongly magnetized necklaces look beautiful and work amazingly well.

A hematite or samarium-cobalt-iron magnetic necklace has many uses. It can be wrapped around the head when one feels a headache coming on; it can be wrapped around a wrist, elbow, knee, foot, or hand; or it can be formed into two small coils and placed over the eyes to give them a soothing magnetic rejuvenation.

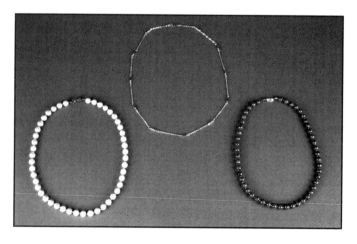

Figure 19: Magnetic necklaces

Besides helping stiff necks, magnetic necklaces are also effective for sore shoulders. In some cases they help improve the condition of the whole body. They do not seem to help major ailments. One researcher stated that the necklaces were more effective for healthy individuals in their everyday lives than for persons with serious illness.

Neodymium Magnets

Neodymium magnets do not come in large sizes. A common useful neo for magnetic therapy is 1" in diameter covered with a red and blue plastic case. Other sizes and shapes are available.

Plastic Magnets

The magnetic strip keeping your fridge closed and the flexible magnet sticking notes to the door are both plastic magnets. This type of magnet is manufactured with strips of alternating polarity, but the pole strips are too close together to be effective for healing. Magnetic foils with at least 1/4" wide strips are better.

Ring Magnets

Ring magnets seem to work for healing even though the hole in the center makes the magnetic force non-uniform. The most common ones are about 1" in diameter and 1/4" thick, with a gauss strength around 300. Ring magnets up to 3" or 4" outer diameter are also available.

Electromagnetic Instruments

Just as we are no longer dependent on scouring old lava fields for magnets, and can now make them to suit our needs, we are likewise no longer dependent on fixed-force (permanent) magnets. Electronic circuits are available at reasonable cost which produce magnetic forces of varying strengths and waveforms. Battery-powered pulsed magnetic force instruments can be small, lightweight, and easily applied to any part of the body. Pulsed magnetic forces of a few gauss are biologically equivalent—in terms of therapeutic value—to permanent magnets of several thousand gauss.

There are thousands of different frequencies and patterns to choose from. The possibilities are as endless as musical compositions. It may be that the complex molecular and atomic structures within the body respond differentially to different magnetic wave-forms. This is now being investigated in many laboratories, but it will be years before people know what works best.

Pulsing magnetic forces seem to be more biologically active than forces put out by a stationary permanent magnet. Much lower gauss strengths can be used for the same effect, and healing often takes place much more quickly.

I do not recommend coils or instruments that run from the 110-volt wall socket. Even if the 60-cycle current is rectified to transform it into direct current, there is still some 60-cycle wave pattern that leaks through. This frequency is not optimum for the body. Also, there is a small but real possibility of electric shock hazard any time you plug into the 110-volt system and have wires going near the body.

The Pulsar

The *Pulsar* has a small disc-shaped applicator that can be placed in a pocket, held in place by elastic bandages, tape, or sweat bands, or tucked in between articles of clothing. A thin wire several feet long connects the applicator to the rechargeable batteries and pulse generating circuit, both of which are contained in a box about the size of a Walkman®.

I often treat my chest by dropping the applicator down my shirt front and clipping the wire to the neck of my shirt with a large paper clip.

Figure 20: The *Pocket Pulsar*

The *Pulsar* is easy to use while you work or drive. This pocket-size magnetic force instrument generates pulses about 16 times per second. A thin 3" diameter applicator produces biosouth pole forces on one face, bionorth pole on the other. Rechargeable batteries are built into the unit, and a recharger provided.

The Power Pulsar

Much stronger than the *Pulsar*, the *Power Pulsar* has a 9" diameter coil applicator that's flexible and comfortable to use. It gets slightly warm in use. The magnetic force will penetrate completely through the body. The rechargeable power supply and electronics are housed in a box about the size of a laptop computer.

Larger electromagnetic coils are available, some large enough to encircle a double bed. Coils can be sewn into cloth garments of all sizes. Bear in mind that you may end up carrying a ten-pound battery along to power the coil, as well as some electronic circuitry.

The *Power Pulsar* is the most powerful instrument available in the United States. The coil carries the maximum amount of current possible; to carry more would result in overheating. The 6" diameter flexible coil can be bent around shoulders, elbows, or legs, placed behind the back, sat upon, or positioned around the head. A 12-volt, 7-amp-hour rechargeable battery powers the unit. The *Power Pulsar* is about one-fifth the cost of similar units made in Europe or South America.

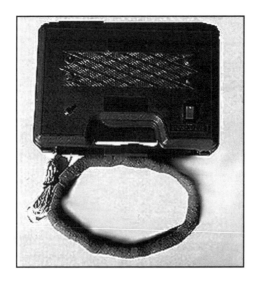

Figure 21: The *Power Pulsar*

Stocking Your Home Magnetic Therapy Kit

If you have a specific ailment you need to treat, tailor your magnet purchase to the job. If you want to stock a general-purpose medicine kit, use the recommendations below to help you choose your purchases.

Home Healing Kit for $100 or Less

- 4x6 Magnetic Foils
- 8 Cookie Magnets
- Magnetic Necklace
- 8 Domino Magnets

The $200 Magnetic Medicine Chest

- Add two 6" diameter Magnetic Blocks or Power Pads™
- 10 Gold-plated Neo Discs (3/8")
  (for acupuncture point treatment)
- Back Belt

Chapter VI
Treatments for Specific Ailments

Because a treatment benefits one person's ailment does not mean that everyone with the same condition will benefit from identical treatment. Most diseases and ailments, and many injuries, have different causes in different individuals, and may even have multiple causes in one individual. Nutritionists maintain that food allergies or improper diet can bring about countless symptoms. The cures range from fasting to eating only grapes for seven days, from eating raw foods to cooking food over gas flames for hours, and so forth. Homeopathic remedies and herbal preparations help thousands. Innumerable case studies support every conceivable treatment. And with every treatment there is a placebo effect for about 17 percent of the people, according to one FDA study.

As a psychotherapist and hypnotherapist, I have seen a number of symptoms clear up when psychodynamic factors are brought to light and released, or when the patient has learned and applied self-hypnosis. Great is the power of the mind!

Nevertheless, after years of experience and association with many different kinds of health practitioners, it is clear to me that magnetic treatments help more ailments more quickly than any other treatment procedure. And they usually stay helped. That is, the pain or condition does not return, at least not for a long time.

Magnetic treatment is only one of many possible modalities for helping the body heal, but because it is simple, relatively inexpensive, and almost entirely free of adverse side effects, it ought to be tried as soon as initial first aid or medical treatments have taken care of threats to survival. Chapter 8 describes other alternative means for helping the body heal; in any ailment, a multi-level approach is obviously worthwhile. After all, we are very complex beings—much more than mere machines!

Any ailment, condition, or part of the body may be treated with magnets. Use the magnetic diagnosis techniques described in chapter 4. Sometimes the condition may be treated directly over the problem area, or one may test relevant glands or organs and treat them as well.

In the following sections, I describe treatment procedures for many conditions and give a summary of research findings and reports by others as well as my own experiences.

Bear in mind that while a treatment may have helped thousands of others, whether or not it will help you with your particular condition cannot be determined in advance.

Ultimately, you must make your own tests and evaluations on your unique body.

I would like to caution those of you taking prescription medicines not to discontinue them without consulting your doctor, even if you get immediate relief. Make your doctor aware of your improvement.

Magnetic Therapy for Specific Conditions

Acute Injuries

Aches, pains, strains, bruises, and bone breaks are known to respond quickly to the application of magnets. Black and blue marks will often go away within hours or not even occur if the site of the injury is treated with the bionorth pole as soon as possible after the injury.

In general, it is desirable to treat an acute injury with the bionorth pole until the pain and inflammation is gone, then treat with the stimulating biosouth polarity to increase blood circulation, tissue oxygen saturation level, and cell division rate.

Some books on magnetic healing state that only bionorth polarity should be used when treating injuries, but this is incorrect. Both muscle testing and the general principles of how magnets heal indicate that the biosouth pole is needed for many conditions. My experience completely supports this notion, as does that of Dr. Mary Broeringmeyer, who has many years of experience.

If someone has a major wound or injury, it is advisable to wait until bleeding has stopped, then apply the red pole to the chest area to increase tissue oxygen levels and blood circulation.

Any injury may also be helped by psychological or hypnotic re-enactment of the injury. (See resources.)

Adrenal Insufficiency

The adrenal glands can be stimulated or sedated by treatment with magnets. They are located a few inches above the waistline on the back, just above the kidneys. According to Dr. Mary Broeringmeyer, one can also stimulate them by placing magnets on the adrenal test points just below the shoulder blades.

Magnetic stimulation or sedation of the adrenal glands may only be a temporary or partial aid. **Continual stimulation of any gland or body part can eventually become ineffective when the body learns to compensate for it.**

The endocrine system works as a whole; therefore, check all the glands as described in chapter 4. If adrenal secretions are increased too much, they could decrease the activity of the pancreas (see Diabetes Section, p. 92). Keep testing the adrenals and other glands to make sure you don't overtreat.

Do not use large or strong neo magnets every day on any glands or organs. While they would probably do little harm, it is possible they could overstimulate something and throw the entire endocrine system out of balance. Fortunately, the body is so well balanced that in most cases overstimulation by a magnet will not be harmful—it just won't work.

People often believe or have been told that their adrenals are low. The adrenal glands are complex and secrete 22 or more different hormones which fall into two classes. In normal functioning, there is a balance between the two classes of hormones, called gluco-corticosteroids and mineral corticosteroids. If the adrenal gland is not working properly, there may be too low an amount of one class or the other. Such deficiencies may be associated with some general health problems. The table below gives some guidelines, although exceptions occur. The body is a complex, interacting system.

Low Gluco-corticosteroids	Mineral Corticosteroids
Asthma	High Blood Pressure
Eczema	Gout
Allergies	Arthritis
	Ulcers

If your problems are clearly in one side of the table, appropriate psychological techniques may be helpful. For example, if you characteristically hold in the expression of anger, allergies may be present, indicating low gluco-corticosteroids. Expressive therapies such as bioenergetics, psychomotor, primal scream, movement therapy, and vigorous exercise may be helpful. If you characteristically lose your temper easily, high blood pressure may be more common as well as the other symptoms on that side of the table. Stress reduction techniques such as self-hypnosis, meditation, and relaxation training will be helpful for you. (See chapter 8).

Alcoholism

Magnetically test the energy balance of the liver, kidneys, spleen, adrenals, and pituitary—the glands and organs most often affected in excess alcohol consumption. Treat as indicated. Also use multivitamin therapy, exercise, and hypnosis to help the body rebalance. (See chapter 8.)

Allergies

Some allergies are related to adrenal imbalance. As mentioned above, the adrenal glands produce two classes of hormones, called gluco-corticosteroids and mineral corticoids. If the gluco-corticoids are insufficient, allergies are more likely to occur; if mineral corticoids are insufficient, ulcers and hypertension are more likely. At this time, I do not know how to use magnetic treatments to alter the balance of gluco-corticoids and mineral corticoids, but a magnetic diagnosis may indicate whether or not the entire endocrine system is out of balance, and rebalancing can occur with appropriate magnetic treatment.

There are psychological and physical exercise techniques that can also be helpful. (See chapter 8.)

Allergies may also be related to a hyperactive thymus gland. If the thymus gland reacts to a relatively innocuous substance as if it were a threat to the body, it will increase inflammation to attempt to rid the body of that substance.

Treating the thymus with a magnet may reduce those annoying allergy symptoms of runny nose, red eyes, and wheezing.

Anxiety

Leanne Roffey, a physical therapist in Houston, Texas, recommends treatment with the biosouth pole along the spine for some psychological conditions such as anxiety, paranoia, and manic depression.

I have found that an anxious person will often calm down and sometimes become drowsy if I place the bionorth pole of a magnet on his or her chest, but I have seen very few cases. You will have to experiment for yourself.

Appetite Control

Magnetic earrings worn on the acupuncture points can be moderately helpful. Another acupuncture point is located just two finger widths below the kneecap. A small magnet, biosouth towards the body, could be taped there for a few days.

Hypnosis can be helpful for weight control. (See Weight Control Section, chapter 8.)

Arthritis

This scourge of humans can often be helped by magnetic treatments. If the condition is painful and inflamed, treat with the calming blue polarity, then after the pain is gone, treat with the biosouth or red pole to stimulate healing.

Arthritis is not a specific disease; the word means joint inflammation, and there are over 100 different types. Gout and rheumatism were names commonly given to this condition in the past. Now rheumatoid and osteoarthritis are commonly used terms. Ankylosing spondylitis is a term used for inflammation of the spine; gout refers to inflammation of the big toe.

Magnets have been known to help stiffness in joints for centuries, but natural magnets were not that common. Now that strong artificial magnets and electromagnets are readily available, everyone has access to a simple and effective remedy.

Furthermore, much more is now known about how magnets heal, so their use is becoming more widely accepted in the traditional medical profession. Magnetic treatment is no longer an *experimental* therapy for arthritis.

Blood Flow and Absorbed Oxygen

Dr. Ulrich Warnke in Germany and Dr. Benjamin Lau of Loma Linda University in California both did careful studies showing that the blood flow and blood oxygen content dramatically increased upon treatment by pulsed magnetic forces. They found an increase of up to a factor of 4 for blood flow. Their research is discussed in detail in chapter 9. Increased blood flow is a general mechanism which helps every disease improve, including arthritis.

Calcium Deposits

Magnets have been used for many years to prevent calcium in water from depositing in pipes and boilers of heating plants. Although the exact mechanism by which this works is still unclear, it is definitely the case that it works. Many research papeers have been published. Several companies sell magnet devices to attach to home water systems as well as industrial ones for these purposes. One of the largest companies in the United States has found that the biosouth polarity works best for this application.

Could it be that the application of biosouth to people with arthritis will help keep the calcium in circulation?

Calcium Migration in Nerve Cells

Dr. Ross Adey of Loma Linda University, San Diego, found that a specific frequency of pulsed magnetic force would increase the migration of calcium ions in nerve cells. The frequency he found, 16 Hz, is also about the same optimum frequency that Dr. Lau found for increasing blood oxygen and Dr. Warnke found for increasing blood flow (15 Hz). It's possible that calcium ions migrate in the body fluids as well as the nerve cells.

Application of pulsed magnetic forces can help broken bones mend by stimulating the addition of calcium ions, help reduce bone spurs by stimulating the removal of calcium, and help arthritis by redistribution of calcium. Dr. Adey's finding that there is an exact resonance with the calcium ion of 16 Hz may prove to be more than a coincidence.

Case Studies—Arthritis

To round out the theoretical notions and formal research on arthritis, I've included a few case studies from my own experience while working with others. Magnetic therapy works particularly well on arthritis.

♦ Arlene S. had painful arthritis in both feet. She was highly skeptical that a magnetic treatment would be helpful, but reluctantly consented to try it on the more painful foot. She received a twenty-minute treatment and thought that there was some slight improvement. She was advised to treat it again fifteen minutes before retiring. The next morning she delightedly reported that the treated foot did-n't hurt when she first woke up—normally the period of greatest pain. Letting go of her skepticism, she has continued treating other arthritic sites on her body.

♦ A fifty-eight-year-old woman who was in constant pain with arthritis so severe she had to walk with a cane came into the medical clinic where I was using magnetic force treatments on a physician's difficult cases. After seven hours of treatment, distributed over several weeks, she was pain-free and no longer needed the cane.

♦ A visitor happened to mention that she had some arthritis in one finger. Her husband purchased a pulsing magnetic force instrument, and on the long drive home she treated the finger. The pain and stiffness went away. One year later it had not returned.

♦ Another visitor complained of severe arthritis, mostly in one finger. Her finger was noticeably swollen and inflamed. An acupuncture treatment had helped to some degree, but only temporarily. After about twenty-five minutes of treatment with a red pole magnet, the finger had visibly reduced in size.

More individual case studies could be cited; the results are pretty much the same—a person has arthritis and treatment with magnets dramatically helps. However, it should be noted that not all cases of arthritis are helped by magnetic therapy. Some more formal research studies are briefly described below; more details are given in chapter 9.

Formal Studies—Arthritis

One of the most recent formal studies was done on osteoarthritis by Connecticut physicians David Trock, Richard Markoll, and others. They observed an improvement of about 50 percent in arthritis patients using pulse magnetic therapy.

Sarada Subrahmanyam, M.D., and Sanker Narayan, Ph.D., at the Madras Institute of Magnetobiology in India, treated 1,000 people with arthritis. About seventy-five to eighty percent of the patients with rheumatoid arthritis and osteoarthritis recovered most of their lost movement and became pain free, and with only two exceptions, no recurrence was noted after two years. More details are given in chapter 9.

Another highly positive study on arthritis was carried out by Dr. Benjamin Lau, a physician at Loma Linda University. He treated nineteen patients with severe to moderate stiffness of joints. After about three weeks of daily treatment (time, pulse rate, and polarity not specified), sixteen of the nineteen reported no more stiffness and very little or no pain.

In yet another research study done at the Sniadecki Hospital in Wloszczowa, Poland, about two hundred people with rheumatoid arthritis were treated with pulsed magnetic forces for twenty to twenty-five minutes per day. Pain generally decreased after five or six treatments although the treatment time continued for ten to fifteen sessions. It was judged to be 73 percent effective, compared with 45 percent effectiveness for short-wave diathermy treatments carried out on a control group. The good results lasted for several months.

None of the foregoing studies mentioned polarity. Both polarity and pulse repetition rate are important variables.

Future studies on arthritis might take this into account following the principles described in this book, thereby obtaining even better results with arthritis. Each person may need his or her own particular magnetic frequency and treatment time at which there should be a change from the inflammatory reducing bionorth to the stimulation of healing with biosouth polarity. These parameters can be determined with the Electronic Muscle Tester or by applied kinesiology.

Nutritional Approaches for Arthritis

Cod-Liver Oil

A physician in Vermont reported that cod-liver oil was helpful for arthritis. A second physician was skeptical, but did his own study which confirmed the results of the first physician. Cod-liver oil contains large amounts of vitamins A and D. I've been taking it for years; I found it greatly reduces colds and sore throats and keeps my skin smooth and healthy.

Aspirin

Aspirin has been used for the treatment of arthritis for many years. However, if as many as eighteen to twenty tablets per day are required, then unpleasant side effects may be present. There are at least eleven other drugs used for relief of arthritis, none of which are curative. Glucosamine sulfate has been found to relieve pain and inflammation of osteoarthritis, according to Michael Murray, M.D., writing in the January 1994 issue of *Health World*. Cortisone is sometimes given for arthritis sufferers since it is a strong anti-inflammatory hormone. Usually it is a last resort because of side effects.

Asthma

Sometimes, placing a bionorth pole on the chest area will ease an asthmatic condition within minutes. Dr. Broeringmeyer recommends a red pole on the back at the same time. It's best to treat asthma as early as possible, and will be helpful to treat the chest routinely when the individual is not having an attack.

The adrenal gland should also be tested by applying either a red or blue pole and muscle-testing to determine if magnetic stimulation is needed (see the section on Adrenal Insufficiency). The adrenals produce cortisone which decreases inflammation. Taking cold showers or swimming in cold water will also stimulate the adrenal glands.

At the psychological level, inhibition of anger can result in adrenal suppression (see Hans Selye's The Stress of Life) and reduced production of cortisone, thereby contributing to asthma. Asthmatics may benefit from expressive therapy.

For bronchial asthma, acupuncturists tape small magnets on the points CV-22, CV-17, CV-14 and so forth, following the established principles of acupuncture.

Denise Perron, a chiropractor in Montreal, uses magnetic therapy in her work with asthmatic children. She told me that she achieved good results by treating the feet with pulsed magnetic fields.

Back Injuries and Chronic Back Pain

Back pains can arise from several different causes. The hips or pelvis may be out of alignment, especially if pain is felt in the lower part of the back and to one side. Muscles may have been stretched, throwing the delicate back vertebrae out of alignment. Consulting a chiropractor is advisable.

Another common cause of back pain is obesity. The back is not designed to support a large stomach; the angle of support is wrong. There are no bones below the stomach to hold it up.

Lack of muscle tone is an indirect cause of back pain. Moderate exercise and special movements can help restore back muscles and relieve back pain. I've written a booklet, *"Ways to Relieve Stiff Necks and Stiff Backs,"* detailing movements for the back.

Magnetic forces will not realign hips or backbones, or build strong muscles; they can be helpful if back pains are a result of injuries, even ancient ones. (See chapter 9 for studies and case histories.)

To treat back injuries, place magnets up and down the spine and even at the top of the head. Muscle testing will tell which polarity to use. Several different magnetic garments may be used. One of the most common ones is the use of belts which contain small disc magnets. These magnets are usually oriented either all bionorth towards the body, or alternating north and south. However, muscle testing has indicated to me that biosouth is often needed, especially for old injuries or chronic back pains. It's possible to reverse the magnetic belts.

Many people have reported good results in getting rid of back pains by sleeping on a magnetic bed. I have no doubt that this works, since I often sleep on one myself. From experience with muscle testing, I would expect that only some types of back pains would be relieved.

Two formal studies on magnetic treatment of back pain have been done by Japanese researchers Dr. T. Okinio, who used a plaster magnet, and Dr. Y. Ooi, who used magnetic belts. Both procedures were successful, but magnetic belts are easier to use.

Bladder Weakness

Walter Rawls, one of the early magnetic therapy pioneers in this country, claims that a weak bladder can be strengthened by application of a biosouth or red pole magnet on a daily basis. Since this is not an acute or chronic injury, the usual technique of muscle testing may not give you clear results. You will have to experiment for yourself.

Biosouth treatment of the bladder area could overstimulate the production of sex hormones. There is also the danger of aggravating prostate problems, including cancer or precancerous conditions. For this reason, older men should have a prostate test before using biosouth magnetic fields around that area of the body.

Brain Injuries (See Head Injuries, p.94.)

Cancer

There are many positive reports on cancer and magnet therapy. (See chapter 9.) **Every magnetic therapist agrees that only the bionorth pole should be applied at the site of cancer, since biosouth forces could stimulate the cancer cells to increase.**

Stimulating the thymus, which regulates the immune system, with the biosouth polarity could help the body destroy the cancer cells. Stimulating the liver may help that organ get rid of toxins. It is all right to treat glands and organs with biosouth forces unless there are tumors nearby or the cancer has begun to spread throughout the body. Use magnetic diagnosis to determine which organs and glands to treat with what polarity.

Unless the cancer is in the chest area, it is a good idea to treat around the heart with biosouth in order to increase blood flow and blood oxygen throughout the body. More oxygen can help the cells do their work.

> If you have cancer, early treatment is essential. Don't waste time reading reports, all of which have found positive results. The principles are well enough established so that with caution and common sense, magnetic therapy can be a useful adjunctive therapy with any established medical treatment.

Naturally, life-threatening diseases should not be treated in a casual or experimental manner. Unfortunately, there are not many magnetic therapy practitioners in the United States who are also medical doctors. Magnetic treatment is not yet approved by the FDA except for healing of fractures. An individual with cancer may have to go to Mexico to receive magnetic therapy, where it is routinely used in some clinics. A list of magnetic therapists is available from Bio-Electro-Magnetics Institute. (See resources.)

Swedish scientist Goesta Wollin described remarkable success with cancer treatment using high-strength neo magnets directly over tumors (bionorth polarity). His work was the subject of a major article in the April 1988 issue of *Magnets in Your Future*.

In Germany, treatment of human patients has been carried on for many years, according to a report in my possession. The (unidentified) writer states that, starting in 1963, Swedish engineer Ivan Troenig worked with magnetic therapy for twenty years and obtained fair results in the treatment of cancer. In 1983, he began using stronger equipment of his own design and obtained much better results.

Eighty percent of clients using his equipment at home recovered. Home treatment is superior because it can be done several hours per day at the convenience of the client, who can usually do sedentary work like writing or phoning while the treatment is taking place. The report claims that the greater the strength of the magnetic force, the greater the therapeutic effect. According to Troenig, whole-body treatment was found appropriate even for cancers located in only one part of the body. A magnetic strength of 200 to 300 gauss over the entire body was used. Troenig also developed an instrument called a cancer-cannon, which produced a strong, narrow magnetic force of around 1,000 gauss at the surface of the pole.

An herb tea called Essiac appears to have remarkable healing effects on cancer (ask for it at any health food store).

Cancer Prevention

One of the most striking experimental studies involved the irradiation of mice with a combination of pulsed 1200-gauss magnetic forces and electromagnetic waves of 17 megahertz and 9 gigahertz. Mice treated with this combination could not be given cancer by inoculation with cancer cells. The same treatment worked with rabbits.

In order to prevent breast cancer, a magnetic bra has been developed in China. These bras have small pockets containing magnets. In a newspaper article dated July 17, 1990, Dr. Bruno Grosse quoted Dr. Hu Chow, one of the Chinese physicians who tested the bras at a clinic in Beijing, as saying, "So far there has not been one woman who hasn't experienced positive benefits from wearing this brassiere. And we've tested hundreds. Further testing reveals that the magnetic bra is just as effective in shrinking breast lumps. Prevention is the best medicine when dealing with cancer." The bionorth pole would be indicated, since women often have small benign lumps in their breasts that could develop into cancer if stimulated by biosouth polarity.*

An excellent discussion of general health, aging, and cancer prevention was written by Richard Broeringmeyer, D.C., in the December, 1985, issue of his *Bioenergy Health Newsletter*.

*Special soft, flexible magnetic bra inserts are now available from PsychoPhysics Labs.

Carpal Tunnel Syndrome

This condition can be helped by wearing wrist bands or wraps containing small magnets. There are several types with three different magnetic configurations—bionorth towards the body, biosouth towards the body, or alternating. What the individual needs depends on the state of the wrist. If prevention is desired, biosouth might be the one to use. If only mild symptoms are present, alternating magnetic forces may be just fine, and if the condition is advanced, with inflammation and pain, bionorth polarity may be called for. Use magnetic diagnosis if you are in doubt. Stronger, pulsed magnetic instruments could help a severe case, bringing increased blood flow to the wrist area.

Rena Davis, an iridologist in Oregon, has found that the small multipole disc magnets (those with alternating poles on the same side of the magnet) work well for this condition. Wrist wraps are also commonly available. Changes in the type of work the patient is doing may be necessary, at least until healing is complete.

Another treatment now being used for carpal tunnel syndrome is low-level laser therapy. Tracy Standridge, a chiropractor, wrote that the light of cold light lasers can penetrate the skin up to three inches, promoting increased blood flow, thereby helping stimulate healing.

Cataracts (See Eye Problems, p. 93.)

Cholesterol, High

Research is currently being conducted to measure the effectiveness of using magnets. Bionorth pole treatments have been helpful according to Dr. Philpott's *Biomagnetic Therapy Handbook*, but he did not specify where the magnets were placed. Presumably, one would treat the entire blood supply, which could be done by treating the region near the heart. The application of large, high-gauss bionorth pole magnets to the heart area can make the patient drowsy.

Chronic Fatigue Syndrome

Magnetic diagnosis usually reveals that nearly every gland and organ of people with this debilitating ailment is either hyperactive or hypoactive. This extreme condition seems to be a characteristic of CFS, with the result that the person "wears out" or quickly fatigues.

Apparently, when one gland or organ becomes overactive or underactive, another one will attempt to compensate by going the other way. This may be a natural mechanism for self-regulation, but in CFS the mechanism appears to be out of control, or the body is too weak to restore balance. When the pattern of overactivity and underactivity has been determined by magnetic diagnosis, each gland and organ can then be treated with magnets of the appropriate polarity. Treatment times of fifteen to thirty minutes for each gland or organ are recommended if pulsed magnetic forces are used; treat an hour or more if using permanent magnets.

Every day or two, the magnetic diagnosis should be repeated and treatment altered accordingly. With each diagnosis, the tester will probably find fewer glands or organs that need rebalancing, until the body is completely back in balance. This could happen within a week to ten days, and if the individual is normally healthy and vital, he or she will be able to maintain balance indefinitely.

Margie, a client I diagnosed and treated, recovered completely within a week. One year later I called her to see how she was doing. She never experienced a relapse of any kind.

Other professionals using magnetic treatments have also reported success with chronic fatigue syndrome. According to Washnis and Hricak (1994), magnetic therapy has been used extensively in Japan and a few other countries. They say that people with CFS who have made regular use of magnetic beds report improvements. Dr. Philpott reported success treating only the pineal gland with the bionorth pole. Since this is a master gland, a change in its activity will affect the other glands. Dr. Bonlie said that he treated seven cases of CFS successfully, using a magnetic bed plus a magnetic bracelet or necklace.

While these general treatments apparently work, the more precise treatment based on magnetic diagnosis of the whole endocrine system seems more likely to be useful.

Constipation

If temporary, this is one of the easier ailments to treat. Simply place a magnet of about 1,000 gauss over the colon with the red stimulating polarity facing the body (muscle test to verify that red is needed). A fifteen-minute application is usually sufficient. Sometimes results are experienced within a few minutes, so it is not advisable to wander too far from a convenient bathroom. Note that there are two parts of the colon that may be involved: the ascending, on the right, and the descending, on the left.

The Japanese use a magnetic belt for constipation, either biosouth polarity or alternating.

Diabetes

Diabetes in some people may be helped by placing a red pole magnet over the pancreas for thirty minutes twice a day. This can stimulate the pancreas to produce more insulin, thereby reducing the need for externally supplied insulin.

Also check the adrenal glands. There is a connection between the pancreas and the adrenals such that if the adrenals are overactive, the pancreas shuts down. This leads to low blood sugar levels, and the person may be incorrectly diagnosed as diabetic. If the adrenals are overactive, application of the bionorth pole will bring their activity back to normal.

If a person is anxious or stressed, learning self-hypnosis can be helpful. The aim, of course, is to reduce the amount of insulin the person is required to take, for too much insulin produces undesirable side effects.

Any self-administered treatment for diabetes should be monitored by a physician, and blood sugar levels should be checked as needed. Magnetic treatment is probably more useful for those people who have been diagnosed as pre-diabetic, and are not required to take insulin.

Eye Problems

Some people have reported that magnetic treatments reduce cataracts. I have not seen any formal studies, but anecdotal reports are common. Davis and Rawls reported that 60 percent of the cases they treated (bionorth towards the eyes) showed improvement, and 20 percent experienced total recovery.

About ten years ago I began to see spots before my eyes. It was also getting difficult to focus clearly on the tiny electronic circuit board components I was putting together for research instruments. After a few treatments with the bionorth magnetic pole, the spots disappeared and focusing became easier.

Magnetic eyeglasses (they have tiny magnets glued around the rim) are available. The manufacturers claim they are restful, and they probably are. Magnetic treatments do not seem to improve nearsightedness.

Headaches

Most, but not all, headaches will be helped by the use of magnetic fields, usually within a few minutes. The bionorth polarity is generally recommended. Treatment at the very first sign of tension or pain works much better than if you wait until you've got a full-blown headache.

Stress headaches and headaches from eyestrain are usually quickly relieved by north pole treatment on the forehead.

Migraine headaches may require treatment around the entire head area. Sometimes the pain will shift from place to place rather than go away. Regular treatments, especially when there is no pain, are important.

Magnetic headbands are commercially available, but you can make your own by obtaining small magnets and gluing them onto the outside of a cap, bionorth pole facing towards the head. Color-code them before you start, then check and double-check the polarity as you work. When you turn your back on a magnetic device under construction, gremlins can appear and flip your magnets over before the glue dries!

If a headache doesn't respond immediately to magnetic field treatment, look elsewhere in the body for a possible cause or alternative treatment site. Some respond to magnets placed on acupuncture points on the inner side of each wrist about two inches up from the joint.

Some headaches may be connected with liver or bowel problems. Test the liver and colon for overactivity and underactivity as described in chapter 4. Treat with disc magnets, one inside and one outside the patient's clothing so they hold each other in place. They are inconspicuous and will stay in place while the person sits or walks.

Head Injuries

Since magnetic forces bring more blood to the area treated, help the tissues absorb more oxygen, and increase cell division rate, enzyme activity, and other biochemical processes, it seems reasonable that they would help head injuries. Magnetic therapy pioneer Walter Rawls claimed that head injuries could be helped. There is at least one paper on nerve regeneration in rats treated with magnets (Ito, 1983); it is likely that nerve regeneration happens in humans as well.

One study was done in India by M. Sambasivan (1988). He studied rats, and then humans. One hundred people were divided into two groups; one group received treatment, one did not. The treated cases showed improvement.

I have only an abstract in my possession, so I don't know what intensities and frequencies were used.

Be cautious in your treatment. **Applying large-area magnets of over 1,000 gauss to the head for more than ten or fifteen minutes at a time could produce headaches or throw the endocrine system out of balance.** I would suggest use of a Pulsar, which only generates three gauss. It might be appropriate to apply a pulsed magnetic field at a frequency of about 10 Hz, that of the alpha brain wave rhythm produced during meditation and dream sleep.

Treatment of the chest area of a head-injured person with the red pole will increase oxygen saturation of all the blood, and thereby indirectly help healing throughout the body. Psychological or hypnotic re-enactment of the injury may also help. (See chapter 8.)

Hemorrhoids

Inflammations should be treated with bionorth polarity. It's easy to sit on a small magnet, such as a 650 to 1,000 gauss disc. Naturally, each case is different, so time of treatment will vary.

Hypertension

Overactive adrenals can contribute to high blood pressure. A simple magnetic test will determine this, but the adrenal gland alone is not necessarily the cause. Psychological factors are often present; biofeedback training which teaches a person to relax at will often makes a big difference. A biofeedback-hypnosis training kit is available at very low cost. (See resources.)

Another place to treat high blood pressure is the acupuncture point LI-11, located on the outside of each elbow. Tape small magnets on them, bionorth pole toward the body, and leave them on for a day or two at a time.

Insomnia

Sometimes use of bionorth will help insomnia. This is one of the best uses for a full-body magnetic pad or bed with the bionorth side towards the body. However, if a person has any specific place on the body which requires biosouth for healing (such as arthritis), a bionorth pole bed will irritate it. I had a cold one season and used my pulsed magnetic bed to help me sleep. It worked very well, but after three nights on the magnetic bed, one of my knee joints began to hurt. I had to stop using the magnetic bed for a few days while I treated the knee with biosouth forces.

An alternative method is to treat the chest area with bionorth polarity for fifteen minutes before retiring. This has a calming effect on the emotions.

Some people have placed large, strong bionorth magnets around the head to help induce sleep. While this might work, it could throw the endocrine system out of balance if used on a continual basis.

Jet Lag

Bead-size magnets used by acupuncturists may be taped on certain acupressure points to help reduce jet lag. The points are Liver 3 (Lv 3), found between the big toe and the second toe, halfway up the web towards the ankle; and Large Intestine 4 (Co 4), located in the middle of the webbed area between the thumb and the first finger. Don't leave the magnets on during sleep periods, as they may keep you awake. They come in convenient packages with sticky tape included. Gauss strength is not critical, but higher strength may be more effective.

I applied a bionorth pole magnet to my chest at the beginning of a cross-country daytime flight. The magnet made me drowsy. I slept for hours and awoke at the end of my flight refreshed and ready for action. You may wish to experiment for yourself.

Kidney Problems

Diagnose as described in chapter 4 and treat accordingly. Infections will probably be helped by bionorth poles and sluggish action by biosouth. Disc magnets may be worn for hours at a time, or treat with larger magnets for fifteen to thirty minutes once or twice a day.

Knee Problems

Knees are tricky. There are many kinds of problems, several of which can be present at the same time. Sometimes magnetic treatments help, and sometimes electric currents are helpful.

One common magnetic device consists of a nylon wrap which contains many small magnets. These are available in three types—with the magnets oriented bionorth towards the body, biosouth towards the body or alternating north and south. It may be necessary to have one of each type to test which works for you. I have used these with moderate success; they do feel comfortable and are good to wear when your knee hurts and you have to do a lot of walking.

I strained my knee swimming in heavy surf in March of 1994. It was painful, and I could not walk very well. The application of a small though powerful neodymium magnet did not help, nor did the low-gauss pulsed fields put out by the *Pulsar.* The knee was still hurting a bit a month later. At that time, I applied the *Power Pulsar* which produces a much larger force over a greater area. As an experiment, I first applied the bionorth pole for thirty minutes or more per day for seven days. There was no improvement; in fact, the knee became slightly more painful. Then I applied the biosouth polarity and the knee pain cleared up after only two treatments. I was able to resume jogging and swimming and have not experienced any knee pain. This knee had been marginally painful for several years.

Muscle testing indicated that the biosouth polarity was strengthening, but since one or two magnetic therapists have claimed that only bionorth should be used on the body, I wanted to make my own test. The results confirmed again what I have often observed: many ailments, especially chronic ones, respond well to biosouth polarity, not bionorth.

Sometimes, knee problems can be helped by pulsed direct current, rather than magnetic forces. The mechanism of healing is different. Anyone who has a knee problem might like to try both magnetic and electric treatments. The negative electric polarity is usually applied to the site of the pain or injury. (Pulsed magnetic instruments can also provide pulsed electric currents with suitable electrodes.)

A chiropractic adjustment can also be helpful, not only to the knee itself, but also to the back. Sometimes foot, ankle, back, or pelvis misalignments can throw a leg off kilter, resulting in knee pain. As in almost all ailments, the body works as a whole. Treating just one symptom may be insufficient. So, if you treated a knee with a magnet and the pain went away, but returned a few days later, have a chiropractor check out the entire leg from the toes to your lower back. Perhaps you need corrective shoe inserts or a more comfortable chair.

An acupuncturist told me that if the kidney is out of balance, the knee may hurt, so the kidneys should be checked as well.

Liver Disease

Stimulate a clogged liver with red polarity. Help an infected liver with the white or bionorth polarity. The liver is a large organ, so small magnets probably won't affect the whole organ. It would be better to treat with a large area magnet for up to an hour once or twice a day. Muscle test to determine which polarity is needed.

Avoid eating sugar at night, because the liver has to store unused sugar, and one may awaken with dark circles under the eyes since the liver is connected to the eyes.

Menstrual Cramps

Cramps are usually alleviated within a few minutes by the application of bionorth polarity. Emotional upsets may require a more thorough magnetic diagnosis of the endocrine system and treatment of each gland as indicated.

Migraines (See Headaches, p. 93.)

Multiple Sclerosis

Good results have been obtained by application of the stimulating biosouth polarity to the entire spine and the base of the head. Pulsed forces have a more powerful effect than permanent magnets, but either can be used.

One of the most careful studies of magnetic therapy ever made was done on multiple sclerosis patients by researchers in Czechoslovakia. Positive results were obtained on the majority of 124 patients in a careful, double-blind study. The patients were hospitalized, which indicates that their illness was well advanced.

Patients received treatment on their upper backs, lower backs, and legs once a day for fifteen days. (I have found that magnetic diagnosis can also reveal a need for treatment at the very top of the spine or base of the head.) A 300 Hz sine wave was applied to the coil in bursts of six milliseconds. The burst frequency was between 2 and 50 pulses per second. This produced a field of 60 gauss, which is large for a pulsing field instrument. Overall, 80 percent of the 124 patients showed some improvement, which decreased slowly after four to twelve weeks but could be readily re-established with additional treatments.

While the study showed good results, perhaps even better results could have been obtained with instruments now available. According to the literature and my own experience, a 300 Hz sine wave, presumably producing alternating magnetic polarity, is probably not as effective as a 16 Hz square wave producing only one polarity. For less severe cases, permanent magnets of the proper polarity could probably be worn many hours a day with beneficial results, although weight could be a problem since the whole spine must be treated.

A magnetic rod or bed could be useful if the proper polarity were used. Some magnetic beds can be turned either way.

Neck Pain

Neck and shoulder pains will likely be helped by wearing a magnetic necklace. Magnetic necklaces have a 1,600-year history, and studies show that their effectiveness rate is high. Since so many people get stiff necks from driving, sitting at desks all day, typing, and watching computer terminals or television screens, it seems most people would benefit from wearing one.

Although I didn't have a stiff neck, I wore a magnetic necklace as an experiment for several days. By the fourth day, I noticed that it was easy to turn my head enough to look out the back window of my station wagon. It definitely increased my neck flexibility. For research data on necklaces, see chapter 9.

Operations

Sometimes surgery is the only recourse. If this is the case, the use of magnetic fields afterwards can help speed the healing process and reduce scar tissue. Usually the body will respond well to bionorth in the beginning when there is pain and inflammation, and then to biosouth as healing begins, but it depends on where and for what the surgery was done. It would not be wise to treat a cancer operation with a biosouth. The same technique works on minor wounds and cuts.

Overweight

Some acupuncturists found that the appetite could be suppressed by stimulation of relevant points in the ear. Since most people don't care to walk around with needles in their ears, magnetic earrings were developed to provide the necessary stimulation. These earrings combine magnetic force and pressure on acupuncture points to suppress hunger. The few people I know who used the magnetic earrings reported that their appetites were slightly reduced.

Dr. William Philpott stated that weight reduction could be helped by placing bionorth pole magnets over fatty areas, using stronger magnets for larger fat deposits. The weight loss occurs slowly, according to him.

In many cases, hypnosis also works for weight reduction. I have prepared four hypnosis programs for helping people tune into the wisdom of their bodies, and consequently eat more sensibly. Two of these tapes are described in the resources.

Pancreas Insufficiency

The pancreas may be stimulated with biosouth polarity. This gland is located one inch up from the navel and one inch over to the left. A couple of $1\frac{1}{4}$" diameter disc magnets can be placed inside and outside clothing to hold each other, and worn comfortably for several hours. The adrenal glands may be involved as well, since there is a link between the two. (See Adrenal Insufficiency, p. 75, and Diabetes, p. 92.)

Premenstrual Syndrome (See Menstrual Cramps, p. 99).

Prostate Enlargement

Tumors in this gland are fairly common in older men and can often be treated by the daily application for an hour or two of bionorth polarity. Sitting on a magnet such as the Magnetic Power Pad is a reasonably comfortable method of treatment. A towel or light cushion can be placed over the magnet to make it comfortable. Do not treat tumors with biosouth polarity!

Shoulder Stiffness and Pain

If a shoulder hurts, check the top of the spinal cord, because what is called "referred pain" is sometimes present. The pain is felt in the shoulder, but is caused by a misalignment of the neck vertebrae that can interfere with nerve impulses, giving a false signal to the brain. Magnetic treatments may or may not be helpful, but a chiropractic adjustment will probably help.

Magnetic necklaces are often highly effective for shoulder pain. (See Neck Pain, p. 100.)

Sinus

Magnetic foils (resources) or other small magnets can be applied directly over the sinuses. These may be taped on. Perform magnetic diagnosis for proper polarity, although bionorth will probably be indicated for reducing inflammation. I have found that while direct application of magnets to the sinus area works, the effects are often only temporary. A more careful analysis of the entire endocrine system may be helpful. Dr. Broeringmeyer reported that magnetic treatment of the kidneys was beneficial for some sinus problems.

Stomach Upsets

Temporary stomachaches may come from an imbalance of the acid-base balance, or sluggish digestion chemistry. Often the application of a large-area, moderate-strength magnet will provide relief within a few minutes. Muscle test to determine which polarity is indicated.

Stress

Stress is a general condition of excessive wear and tear, whether psychological or physical. Magnetic treatments are easily applied to back, knees, chest, eyes, teeth, neck, etc., in order to help the body relax. The bionorth pole will reduce specific aches and pains resulting from overuse, and the biosouth will help to strengthen the body to counteract the effects of stress.

I advise against using magnetic fields every day to treat stress symptoms. Use common sense and moderation. A change in life style may be needed to address the root causes of the stress. Learning self-hypnosis could be valuable in order to change psychological habit patterns. (See chapter 8.)

Toothaches and Tooth Problems

If there is inflammation, infection, and soreness, try the bionorth pole. Be sure to muscle test, though. I have found biosouth often more strengthening than bionorth. Toothaches respond quickly to magnetic treatments. Magnets won't fill cavities—see a dentist.

In an English study, half of the patients studied received an hour's magnetic treatment after a tooth was pulled, and half did not. Both swelling and pain were rapidly reduced by the magnetic treatment (Washnis 1993, p. 140). I always treat my teeth after a visit to the dentist.

A water pick that magnetically treats the water is now available. The inventor claims good results, of course. I just acquired one, but it's too early for me to tell whether or not it works, and that might be difficult to carefully research in any case. Still, every little bit helps, and the unit is well designed and not expensive. It has two small permanent magnets between which the water flows. This is claimed to produce a slight but significant change in the electrical properties of the water molecule, which in turn is supposed to inhibit bacteria and foreign molecules from clumping together. Supposedly, plaque can't form as easily on the teeth, and bacteria can't grow in large colonies. Therefore, both are swept away more readily by the natural circulation of the mouth. Similar magnetic treatments have been effectively used to prevent scale formation in boilers for years (Nord, 1992). To possibly improve the operation of my waterpick, I glued three domino-sized magnets on the outside of the water holder with the north side towards the water.

A magnetic toothbrush is also available. There are two small magnets in the head of the brush, north pole towards the bristles. The inventor reports on a Chinese study of 120 patients with various gum problems. Patients had gingivitis, swollen gums, tooth decay, tartar, tooth abscesses, and plaque build-up. Within two months, eighty percent of the patients significantly improved. I own one of these brushes. It's a good quality toothbrush, although it's impossible for me to test its effectiveness.

Ulcers

When the adrenals produce an excess of gluco-corticosteroid hormones, the natural inflammation of the stomach is reduced. This natural inflammation serves to protect the stomach lining from digestive acids. Therefore, overactive adrenals could result in some types of ulcers. Check the adrenal test points as indicated in chapter 4 and treat accordingly. Also, applying the blue or bionorth force directly over the ulcer area will be helpful. Albert Davis and Walter Rawls reported that drinking magnetically treated water (bionorth) was helpful for people with ulcers.

At the psychological level, people with ulcers may be hyperactive or temperamental. Stress reduction techniques such as relaxation training, meditation, or self-hypnosis will probably be more effective than dietary changes or medications. A powerful and effective autosuggestion is simply: "Take time to let the body rebalance itself." Taken from the Edgar Cayce readings, this suggestion is incorporated into the basic hypnosis training tape which accompanies the Hypnosis Training System. (See resources.)

Whiplash

Cervical adjustments by a chiropractor can be helpful. However, if there is pain and inflammation, adjustments might not be possible right away. Application of the bionorth pole may help reduce inflammation and pain. After the initial pain has subsided, and x-rays and spinal adjustments have been made, application of the biosouth polarity may be useful (if called for). It's important to muscle test to determine what polarity strengthens the body.

Application of a pulsed magnetic force to the neck area helped one woman in only two sessions. She had suffered from whiplash for a month, and had tried many other remedies to no avail. After major recovery has taken place, wearing a magnetic necklace would probably be helpful.

This list of injuries, ailments, and disease could be almost indefinitely extended, but ultimately the individual must be willing to try magnetic therapy for his or her own condition. If the individual is also receiving medical help or taking herbs, medicine, homeopathic remedies, or other treatments, it may not be possible to know which treatment was most effective in promoting healing. Most of us are more interested in getting well than in doing health research, so a multi-pronged approach makes the most sense.

Chapter VII
Preventive Care Strategies

Stress, aging, and constitutionally weak bodies call for prevention techniques. Magnetic force treatments are ideal for this, since they are easy to apply, have virtually no side effects, are inexpensive, and can be used in the home, office, or car without interfering with quiet work or recreational activities. Sleeping in a magnetic bed, for instance, requires virtually no attention. Such whole-body treatment is desirable every week or so, except for people who have particular spots or areas of imbalance that may need treatment with magnetic polarity opposite to that provided by a magnetic bed.

At least two parts of the body can be treated in a preventative fashion: the heart area and the thymus gland.

The Heart Area

The amount of oxygen in the blood and tissues is a significant factor in general health and energy. Tissue oxygen is definitely increased by the application of pulsed magnetic forces. (See chapter 9.) According to a Dutch publication, the ability of the white blood cells to divide can be restored by exposure to a weak electromagnetic force. Blood oxygen increases are believed to be responsible for this.

Treatment with a moderate-strength permanent magnet around the heart area will probably increase tissue oxygen saturation. I say "probably" because the studies were all done with pulsed magnetic fields; in general, permanent magnets seem to have similar effects to pulsed magnetic fields, only not as strong. A permanent magnet of 100 to 1,000 gauss in any convenient size may be used. A 2,000 neo may be too strong. If a pulsed field is used, the optimum frequency is about sixteen hertz, the optimum strength under 5 gauss. This treatment will be generally helpful for the entire body, although no obvious effects will be felt unless a person is vigorously exercising and perhaps pushing his or her limits at times. Activities such as marathon running, high-altitude skiing, mountain climbing, surfing, basketball, and soccer can be made easier by the routine application of magnetic forces.

Permanent magnets of a few hundred gauss placed over the heart area to treat the entire blood supply for a few hours or an entire day will not be a health risk. The biosouth pole is recommended for stimulation. Application of bionorth to the heart area will be calming and may cause drowsiness. This effect may be helpful for people who have trouble sleeping; it probably won't decrease oxygen, although I do not know of any studies which show this.

The effect may diminish with time as the body adjusts to it; you will have to experiment and find out what works for you. Please remember that a stronger magnetic force is not necessarily better. Naturally, it is unwise to place magnets over the heart of a person with a pacemaker or known heart problem.

The Thymus Gland

Many people have weakened immune systems due to stressors, eating habits, age, or other factors. The thymus gland is a primary factor in the immune system. Located just below the collar bone, it may be stimulated by applying a low gauss biosouth pole. Fifteen minutes a day should be adequate. Overstimulation could produce allergy-like symptoms.

If the thymus gland overreacts to relatively innocuous substances, such as roses and ragweed, thereby producing allergy symptoms, application of the white or bionorth pole to the thymus gland may calm it down. Each person is different—experiment!

Drinking Magnetic Water

Magnetically treated water increases plant growth. Dr. Peter Kokoschinegg, a researcher at the Institute for Biophysics and Ray Research, of IBS-Bericht, Germany, found that plants watered only with magnetically treated biosouth pole water increased their growth compared with control plants watered with tap water. Plants watered with bionorth pole treated water grew less than the controls.

Dr. Mary Broeringmeyer reported to me personally that plants watered with biosouth treated water grew faster. She also said that she places freshly cut roses on bionorth magnets to make them last longer, whereas the biosouth pole made them open more quickly and lose their petals.

Davis and Rawls, early pioneers in magnetic therapy, also reported that plants watered with biosouth treated water grew faster. I started two trays of wheat sprouts, watering one with bionorth treated water and the other with biosouth. The tray sprayed with south pole water grew more abundantly, but the sprouts didn't grow appreciably higher. The taste also seemed slightly better.

Water is not a simple substance; it can form nine different three-dimensional structures. Magnetic forces apparently can influence what kind of structures are formed. The effects last until the water is boiled according to Dr. Kokoschinegg, who took Kirlian photographs of magnetically treated water, showing it was apparently more organized by the applications of magnetic forces.

Dr. Glen Rein, a biochemist in Boulder Creek, California, measured the ultraviolet transmission of water treated overnight with a south pole magnetic pad and a north pole magnetic pad. The control, or untreated water, showed an absorption of 1.01 (relative units), the north pole showed an absorption of -1.32, and the south pole showed an absorption of -2.59. In other words, both north and south directions of the magnet force decrease the amount of dissolved oxygen, for it is the dissolved oxygen that alters the ultraviolet absorption. Dr. Rein also said that he heard a French scientist report on experiments treating water with magnetic fields and making measurements with Ramon spectroscopy which could indicate something about the structure of the water molecules. The French scientist inferred from his observations that permanent magnets promoted the production of more free water molecules and alternating magnetic fields produced more structured water. Obviously, the significant parameters are not yet clear, but it is clear that the two different directions of magnetic force produce measurably different effects.

Drinking magnetically treated water is recommended by Dr. Bansal of the Indian Institute of Magnetic Therapy and Dr. William Philpott. Dr. Bansal recommends washing the eyes and skin with it. Dr. Broeringmeyer reported it helped bed sores. Dr. Yoshitaka Ohno did an exciting study on giving magnetized water to people with Alzheimer's disease. The successful pilot study was followed by one with 75 people.

Many magnetic therapists maintain that water should only be treated with the north pole, but I repeatedly find that the south pole treated water tastes better. Since the south polarity also sweetens fruit and increases plant growth, it seemslikely that it might help people too. I drink it every day. However, if one had an ulcer or acid stomach, the north pole might be better to use. You are invited to do your own experiments. Besides water, you might try treating juices, wine, beer, milk, soda pop, or vegetable juices.

Old Injuries and Genetically Weak Body Parts

As bodies age, weak areas tend to show up. For one person, it may be knees; for another, eyes, or some other organ or gland. I recommend routine treatment of areas, glands, or body parts which have exhibited weakness in the past or which have been injured, even if there presently is no problem.

When a person has an injury or severe illness, the body may end up with a weakened condition. For example, a broken shoulder may be indefinitely weakened and can impair lung capacity or even colon activity, since the acupuncture meridian for the colon passes over the shoulder. Hepatitis may leave one with a chronically weak liver. Bronchitis can lead to diminished lung capacity. These areas can be routinely treated with magnets, although results may be only marginally evident unless one is stressing the body to the limit as in marathon running or strenuous mountain climbing. Routine treatment with magnetic forces is recommended for prevention of cancer and other degenerative diseases. If one is in good health, use of a whole body magnetic bed system is recommended. If not, it may be necessaary to first treat specific glands, organs, or parts oof the body with the appropriate polarity until the condition is alleviated, and then to treat the whole body.

Magnetism and Youthing
Reversing the Aging Process

For thousands of years, magnets have been used for healing. Although being healthier obviously helps prolong life, it's now known that the proper use of magnets can directly prolong some life forms. Until recently, magnetic effects upon biochemistry and cell metabolism were not understood; this has slowed acceptance of magnetic treatments for aging, and research has lagged. Although major long-term tests have yet to be done on human rejuvenation, positive results have definitely been found in animal studies.

Animal Studies and Aging

Dr. Hajime Okae of Tokyo's Kyorin University kept mice in a magnetic force of 4,200 gauss for fifty-nine days. After they were removed from the magnetic field, the average life span of their red blood cells in a culture increased from 70–100 days to 120 days. Dr. Okae also reported that when subjected to the 4,200-gauss force, mice lived 400 days, or almost 1/3 longer than the average mouse life span of around 308 days (polarity not stated).

Presumably these were Japanese mice, because in India another researcher stated that a mouse grows old in about 400 days, then the aging process sets in, and it dies a few months later. If, at the time of the appearance of aging symptoms, it is treated twice daily for one hour with a magnet of 3,000 to 4,200 gauss, and these treatments continue for three or four months, the mouse looks younger, becomes as active as before, gains weight, and sheds all of its aging symptoms. It behaves like a six- to eight-month-old mouse. A 250-day-old mouse lived 615 days in good health after treatment (polarity not stated).

112

Davis and Rawls reported that mice and rats lived longer if exposed to the stimulating biosouth magnetic pole—if they weren't allowed to copulate. If they were exposed to the calming bionorth magnetic pole, they also showed an increased life span, apparently because the growth process was slowed down. In mature rodents, exposure of the testicles to the biosouth pole resulted in more sperm production, more sexual activity, and a shorter life span. For some humans, a difficult choice may be required!

Experiments were done by Davis and Rawls on chickens, worms, and other animals. Similar experiments have been done on plants with positive results on seed yield, vitality, and growth. Biological activity is clearly enhanced by magnets of the proper polarity. General principles and findings have emerged and been replicated by other researchers.

When the external magnetic force is reduced below the prevailing level of Earth's one gauss, living organisms often suffer. In tests of reduced magnetism, mollusks, protozoa, and flatworms were observed to become less active. Birds became disoriented, and their egg-laying capacity drastically lessened. Among mice and rats, a decreased magnetic force adversely alters enzyme activity. The longer an organism is deprived of magnetism, the less fertile it becomes, the more shriveled its tissues and organs, and the shorter its lifespan.

Colonies of bacteria kept in a magnetically shielded environment below Earth normal for 72 hours showed a reduced reproduction capacity by a factor of 15 according to Dr. Broeringmeyer (*BioEnergy Health Newsletter*, May, 1990).

Chinese acupuncturists Minda Hsu and Chikuo Fong reported an experiment on extending the life of tadpoles. Five each were placed in glass beakers filled with water. One beaker was treated with a magnetic field of 800 gauss (polarity not specified), the other left alone. No food was given to the tadpoles. The ones in the magnetically treated beaker lived an average of twenty-seven days, versus twenty-one days for the non-treated tadpoles.

Plants and other small organisms grew faster and bigger when magnetically treated according to the same authors. Mice placed in a cage and shielded from all natural Earth magnetism died sooner than a control group.

Youthing and Humans

Wrinkles have been observed to diminish when magnetic treatments have been combined with application of a cream. In Holland, a company markets a magnetic massager and skin cream. They claim that treatment for two to five minutes several times a day for two weeks is sufficient to produce a large reduction in deep wrinkles, and that after the initial two weeks, treatments may be quickly reduced to once a month.

Dr. Kenneth MacLean, founder of the Institute of Biomagnetics in New York, experimented on himself for many years. He was observed to look much younger than his chronological age and retained his youthful hair color well into his sixties.

Dr. MacLean also noted that elderly people treated with his strong electromagnets showed a darkening of their white hair and became more energetic. According to him, after ten half-hour sessions under his "electro-magnetic activator," some of his patients' white hair definitely darkened. A small percentage of patients with cancer also showed remission.

I recently spoke with a physical therapist in New York who knew Dr. Maclean and had a treatment from him. The apparatus used consisted of two large permanent magnets which were physically moved by a motor both to and fro and in and out to produce a pulsing pattern.

> In general, wherever there is a weak or injured gland or organ, treat it! Keep treating it, even when it feels fine. This will strengthen it, and may keep it from being injured again.

My acquaintance reported that he was so charged after the treatment on his pituitary area, he worked in his garden all day and stayed up writing until 2 A.M.. He verified that Dr. MacLean had brown hair and acted and looked much younger than his stated age.

Mechanisms of Youthing

It is known that pituitary and thymus gland extracts, when given to older people, will rejuvenate aging bodies. In one study, done at the Veterans Affairs Medical Center in North Chicago, twenty-one healthy men ranging in age from sixty-one to eighty-one years were given a pituitary growth hormone. They gained almost 9 percent in lean body mass, dropped nearly 15 percent in body fat, and regained a youthful appearance to their skin. In many respects, the treatment was observed to cut almost twenty years from their bodies. The researchers reported that not everyone benefited from the hormones.

In another study, 450-day-old aging mice were treated with thymus gland extracts taken from young, healthy calf thymuses. They showed a definite age reversal. In humans, thymus extracts have been helpful in treating certain types of diseases, including AIDS.

The pineal gland also decreases its secretions of the hormone melatonin with aging. It has been found to be sensitive to the daily cyclic pattern in Earth's magnetic field. Melatonin secretion may be changed by application of permanent magnetic force of about the same value as Earth's force of one gauss.

Apparently, the pineal produces a growth hormone shortly after one goes to sleep. In older people, this hormone production is decreased, but it may be increased again with the proper application of magnets at the proper time. If so, this could possibly be a better way to slow the aging process than the injection of hormones, since side effects are unlikely. Stimulation of the pituitary tends to produce an increase in sexual drive. Although it is possible that artificial stimulation of the pineal or pituitary by very strong large magnets (over 2,000 gauss), for several hours every night could produce an imbalance in the rest of the endocrine system, **low-gauss short-term exposure seems perfectly safe.** I am constantly experimenting on myself and have noticed only positive effects, such as increased energy and the need for less sleep, or no effects at all. It is my hypothesis that if a person's endocrine system is in balance, it will not be easily pushed out of balance by magnets of moderate strength even if they are wrongly applied.

Other glands can also be stimulated with pulsed magnetic forces by putting the applicators on the surface of the body directly over the glands. Remember that pulsed magnetic forces are more biologically active than those put out by permanent magnets, and don't overstimulate.

Cell Division Rate

Several writers have mentioned that cell division rates increase under the influence of pulsed magnetic fields.

Although the study in my files was done upon cells in a laboratory dish, it seems relevant to what could happen in the body. It is known that magnetic fields speed wound healing and reduce the formation of scar tissues; perhaps increased cell division is one of the mechanisms. There is a difference between cells dividing out of control, such as in a cancer, and cells that divide vigorously in a healthy manner.

Earth's constantly changing magnetic field can play a part in cell division rate as well. There has been some speculation that power line frequencies possibly interact with Earth's field to produce increased cell division that can lead to cancer.

Youthing Treatments

A pulsing magnetic bed that generates a large magnetic force is available to qualified professionals. The polarity can be reversed and the frequency can be set between about 1 and 16 Hz. So far, users have noticed greater physical flexibility and increased energy. As mentioned previously, magnetic beds are best used if the rest of the body is in balance. This device is for experimental use only! (It is available from Psycho Physics Labs.) People who wish to experiment on themselves are invited to join the Magnetism and Youthing Project (see Organizations section at end of book).

> Pulsed magnetic forces of high strength and large size permanent magnets, probably should not be applied to the body for long periods. BIGGER IS NOT NECESSARILY BETTER. I would not advise sleeping in the vicinity of large permanent magnets.

117

It's easy to attach a couple of cookie magnets to the chest area, sandwiching them between clothes, or drop them in a shirt pocket. With a sweatband they can be placed on the head at the pituitary point just above the eyes, or on top of the head at the pineal point. The back of the head also seems to be a place where muscle testing shows a strengthening effect of magnets.

Pulsed magnetic fields of the proper strength and frequency may be found to affect each major atomic element in the body. As biophysicists discover the molecules involved in aging, magnetic treatments might be used to restart, stimulate, or unlock the aging keys. (See chapter 12 for more details.)

While some people may think magnetism is an elixir of life, it is not a panacea for every ailment, nor will it necessarily prolong everyone's life span.

References on youthing are in a separate section in the Reference Section.

Chapter VIII
Adjunctive Therapies

Healing modalities that work well with magnetic therapy include vitamins, minerals, herbs, homeopathic remedies, massage, exercise, (including yoga and dance), acupuncture and hypnosis.

Vitamins, Minerals, Herbs, and Homeopathic Remedies

They help. The questions are: Which ones? How much? For how long?

Drs. Mary and Richard Broeringmeyer, who expanded the use of muscle testing to determine which magnetic force direction to use for treatment, also used muscle testing to ascertain which homeopathic remedy to use for a particular disease or injury. Many other health professionals routinely use muscle testing to determine which herb, vitamin, etc., strengthens the patient. It is assumed that whatever strenghens a person may be taken with long term benefit.

Initially skeptical of the muscle testing procedure, I eventually found it useful and accurate for most people.

To further improve the accuracy and especially the objectivity of muscle testing, an electronic device was designed called the **Electronic Muscle Tester**. Somewhat similar instruments have been made in Europe. One well-known type is based on acupuncture meridians and uses a probe placed on some of the points. A meter reading indicates the value of a particular remedy which is also placed in the circuit. Another type, developed in the United States, takes electrical readings from the fingers which are processed by an elaborate computer program to derive recommendations for herbs, vitamins, and other remedies. These devices seem to work, but are fairly expensive (up to $25,000).

The **Electronic Muscle Tester** (available from PsychoPhysics Labs; see resources), consists of a pressure transducer that varies in electrical resistance as it is squeezed between a finger and thumb, showing variations on a meter after suitable amplification by an electronic circuit. To use it for testing vitamins, medicines, and so on, simply squeeze the transducer, note the meter reading, then relax the pressure for a few seconds. Now hold the substance being tested to the chest, or take a tiny taste if appropriate, and squeeze again, comparing the second reading with the first one. If the second reading is higher, the substance is good for you; if lower, or the same, you don't need that particular substance. Try another one. Self-testing this way can be done very quickly, once you get familiar with the EMT.*

With the help of the **Electronic Muscle Tester**, I found I didn't have to take every vitamin and herb the books and all my well-meaning friends recommended for my various real, imaginary, and potential health problems. No more guzzling twenty-seven varieties of colored capsules and liquids for breakfast! I simply sort through my friends' home pharmacies and herbal closets and with the **Electronic Muscle Tester** determine what my body needs at a given time. It does vary from week to week, but some items are

---

*Dr. Sanford Frumker, a long-time practitioner in the science of magnetic therapy and former coworker of the Broeringmeyers, has developed an excellent means for testing the efficacy of remedies, vitamins, herbs, etc. He first finds an organ that shows a weakness when a magnet is applied to it. Then, while the magnet is in place (with the weakening polarity towards the body), he tests different remedies, until one is found that again strengthens the body.

consistently strengthening for me. Everyone will have a different pattern.

If you have an interest in herbs, try Bach flower remedies, or homeopathic remedies. You can first read about what your body might need, then test samples of those items to select which ones, if any, are strengthening for you. You don't always have to take the herb or remedy; you can hold it to your chest or throat, although tasting it will give clearer indications.

Why or how muscle testing works is still a mystery. Nevertheless, I would say it is about 90 percent accurate.

Different colors, crystals, minerals, sound frequencies, and minute electrical signals are also used in helping the body heal. These, too, can be sorted out as to their strengthening or weakening effects by muscle testing. At one show I attended, a visionary artist had a number of "healing mandalas" which he claimed had powerful effects on the body. **The Electronic Muscle Tester** showed that, indeed, his beautiful drawings had strengthening effects for some people.

I have noticed that after using the instrument for a while, my inner sense of what will test strong or weak for me has increased. I don't need to rely on the instrument as much—I intuitively know. Nevertheless, I find that it's good to check on my intuition, because wishful thinking or prejudice can get in the way of accurate intuition.

Therapeutic Massage

There are different kinds of massage, ranging from intense, powerful muscular realignment to acupressure massage, polarity rebalancing, chiropractic adjustments of the bones, and aura massage, wherein the massager moves his or her hands over the body without touching it. All of these have their value.

The **Electronic Muscle Tester** can indicate which person's touch is most strengthening for another. I have found that the touch of another often produces greater meter readings on the **Electronic Muscle Tester** than any vitamin, food, or other remedy—if that person is strengthening for the person being tested. There are large individual differences. Even if you don't have an **Electronic Muscle Tester**, or don't care to use it, just knowing about the personal factor is enough to make you aware and selective when you inquire about receiving a treatment from someone else. Be selective. Your body knows what it needs and from whom it might be best received.

Exercise and Yoga

There are two categories of exercise: exercise that is mind-controlled, and exercise that is allowed to arise from the needs of the body. Mind-controlled exercises consist of two types: those that induce deep breathing, such as running, aerobics, or fast-moving games, and those that are only physical, such as yoga stretching or lifting weights.

Mind-controlled exercises that demand deep breathing and increase circulation and oxygen intake are usually beneficial for the body and help a person feel good, but one needs to be healthy enough to do them in the first place. It sometimes takes a bit of discipline to get the body actively moving. Group games and activities can provide this, so if you feel it's too hard to exercise on your own, join a group, club, or team where motivation will be externally provided.

It's beneficial to exercise hard enough to sweat. Sweating helps eliminate toxins through the skin.

Kundalini Yoga, Hatha Yoga, aerobics, and dance are wonderful exercises. Over the years I have collected 50 of my favorite exercises and had pictures printed on 4 x 6 cards. To make exercise more interesting, I shuffle the cards and pick three or four each morning for my daily routine. There are over 100,000 possible permutations taken four at a time (available from PsychoPhysics Labs).

Although non-mind-controlled movement is not as well known in our speedy society, it can be more helpful in the healing process. This is movement that is allowed to happen by intuition, letting the "mind of the body" or the "moving center" direct the movements. It takes some practice more like Zen or non-mindful action. When this is done, the body will move the way it "wants to" or needs to, and aches, pains, or tensions will be released. Little children move this way, but adults normally are trained to initiate and control all movements from the mind. Mind-controlled movements can lead to repetition of the same patterns, eventually overdeveloping some muscles while leaving others weak.

Most dancing is mind-controlled. Recreational dancers usually move in the same patterns over and over, and while a person may have her own unique style, it often doesn't vary much. Many professional dancers follow carefully rehearsed and preplanned movements. The mind rigidly controls the body. Repetitive movements often leave one feeling tired, but spontaneous movements release tension, leaving one with more available energy.

It doesn't take much teaching, just allowing, and yet it's hard for people over the age of seven to do at first. The mind always wants to take control. If you wish to begin, put on some quiet music, lie on the floor, and relax. Concentrate on the music to help empty your mind, then tune into your body and ask it how it wants to move. Follow your inner guidance. Pause now and then to quiet down, listen to the music, and ask the body how it wants to move. Keep following inner guidance, no matter how strange or bizarre the movement patterns seem to be. The body may want to do some unusual corrective movements to counter the forced patterns you've probably been doing for decades, so if it wants to do something you think is silly, let it.

> When people allow spontaneous, free movement for years, I have found they often find it to be more healing and productive of joy than practically any other activity.

If your exercise regimen is suffering because you are stiff, and you do not have any particular ailment, consider sleeping on a magnetic bed. Using a magnetic bed definitely increased my flexibility, and it worked for my friends, too. Only occasional use is necessary to produce an effect.

A Los Angeles weight trainer uses magnets to improve muscle gain. The magnets are applied directly to the muscle being worked. Known as Captain G, he is very knowledgeable in magnetic therapy of all types.

Acupuncture

Of all the healing modalities, acupuncture is probably the one most closely connected with magnetic healing. The meridian system that acupuncturists use in their work often seems to be activated by magnetic stimulation of acupuncture points, and by magnets applied to the body at the site of injuries. People experiencing magnetic therapy frequently report that they feel a tingling up and down the body, along what appears to be an acupuncture meridian.

Acupuncturists write about "sedating" and "tonifying" a gland or organ. This corresponds to stimulating with the biosouth polarity of a magnet or calming with the bionorth polarity. Many acupuncturists use magnets in their practice. *Magnet Therapy* by Holger Hanneman is one of the most useful books on this technique.

Magnetic treatments are harmonious with acupuncture, so one can needle or magnetically stimulate any meridian point and simultaneously treat the corresponding organ or gland with a magnet.

Biofeedback and Hypnosis

No matter what the problem, it is useful to enlist the power of the mind in the healing process. Most remedies have a placebo effect anyway, and with a bit of mental training one can use this to increase a treatment's effectiveness by perhaps 50 percent or more.

Hypnosis, especially self-hypnosis, is very easy to learn. Training courses costing hundreds of dollars are designed to turn out professionals. You can learn similar techniques in a few hours with a kit that contains a complete workbook on hypnosis, a biofeedback instrument, and a training tape. (See resources.)

The first step in learning hypnosis is to train the nervous system to quiet down so that healing visualizations and affirmations will have greater power. This can be done with the aid of a type of biofeedback called GSR, or Galvanic Skin Resistance. This instrument uses two sensors that are placed on any two fingers to measure the skin resistance. Variations in skin resistance indicate changes in

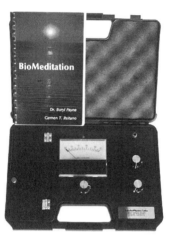

Figure 21: Hypnosis training system

sympathetic nervous system activity, which, in turn, indicate varying levels of emotional tension. The biofeedback instrument transforms the electrical signal from the fingers into a tone of varying pitch. The higher the tone, the more the activity in the nervous system; therefore, one strives to lower one's activity level, which lowers the pitch. This feedback system promotes rapid learning of deep relaxation.

The basic elements of hypnosis are:
1. Deep relaxation (learned very easily by practice with the neurosensor or biosensor)
2. Stating a pre-planned affirmation and visualization with clarity and conciseness
3. Returning to normal alertness
4. Repeating the process once a day for three to ten days

If you have a serious ailment, a few sessions of hypnosis can be an excellent investment, and are good accompaniment for any other treatment modality.

126

Chapter IX
Research and Case Studies

R esearch on the biological effects of magnets would fill several books. As in any field of research, some studies are very thorough with control groups and statistical evaluation, along with personal reports and follow-up. Others are less carefully done, since it is expensive and difficult to do comprehensive studies on human health. Humans are complex, and no single remedy or treatment will help everyone. Some people have good psychological reasons for their illness and may not be ready to change, no matter how effective the remedy.

Aside from the formal studies, there are hundreds of personal reports that have been published. Given that one manufacturer has sold three million magnetic necklaces (in Asia), the number of unpublished experiences must be tremendous.

Sweetening Fruit: Research on Polarity

If you wish to validate for yourself the different effects of bionorth and biosouth polarities, you might try something like the following experiment. I took a bunch of grapes from the same stalk, washed and separated them into two groups of about twenty grapes each. I placed them in identical bowls, one over the bionorth side of a coil from a pulsing magnetic field instrument, and one over the biosouth side of a similar coil. There was a perceptible difference in taste after four minutes of treatment. At eight minutes, it was very clear, and by the time sixteen minutes had passed, the grapes treated with the biosouth pole were so sweet I wanted to gobble them all up! The ones over the bionorth did not taste good. The control grapes tasted mediocre. An independent observer verified this as well. I restrained myself from eating all the good grapes and switched polarity to see if the effect was reversible. At the end of four minutes of reversed polarity treatment, the formerly flat tasting grapes still tasted flat, and the formerly sweet grapes still tasted sweet. After eight minutes, the flat ones tasted better, and the formerly sweet ones were still good. Eleven minutes later, the formerly poor tasting ones tasted very good, and the formerly sweet ones tasted so-so.

I have done similar experiments with oranges, strawberries, and bananas (no effect noticed on bananas). Grapes are better for such tests because of their size and easy handling. Also, if they are from the same stalk, they are fairly uniform in initial taste.

I have repeated the tests with 6" diameter permanent magnets (the Magnetic Power Pads) with similar results. The effects are quite dramatic with some frozen juices, such as guava juice. The results are consistently in favor of biosouth for sweetening or improving the flavor of fruits.

At a party, I sliced apples and distributed them on bionorth, biosouth, east/west, and alternating permanent magnetic fields. The guests universally agreed that the apples treated with bio-south polarity were the best. Apples treated with alternating polarity tasted flat. Most of the people did not know the nature of the experiment.

When in doubt, I ask my six-year-old to taste-test fruit, juice, or water, since he has no preconceived ideas and much better taste sensitivity.

This simple experiment also supports the principle affirmed by Dr. Broeringmeyer that biosouth polarity treatments have value—something I have consistently observed in treating people.

A Few Case Studies

♦ David of Soquel, California, has congenital chronic back pain. Use of pulsed magnetic fields immediately stopped the pain; however, no cure is possible, so continued intermittent use is desirable for him to remain free of pain.

♦ Richard Guillement, a Reiki healer who knows the healing business, had a persistent back problem. After treatment, he wrote me the following statement:

"After using the *Pulsar* over a three-day period, I found my chronic lower back problem healed. My back had been giving me a lot of pain and was very stiff. At times I found it very difficult to even get out of bed because of the pain."

"Previously, I had been to a chiropractor, an osteopath, had taken hot tubs, and even utilized "natural" healing techniques. All of this helped somewhat, but did not give me as complete relief as the *Pulsar* did. Each day I used the *Pulsar* for fifteen to thirty minutes, three or four times a day, for several days. I now have complete relief."

That was in 1990. Three years later, Richard called to tell me that he hasn't had any back pains since his initial treatments. He now resides in Rapid City, South Dakota, and is a distributor of magnetic products as well as a Reiki healer.

♦ In March of 1994 a friend moved and paid me and another friend to move her things. Since I had been sitting endless hours working on this book, I welcomed the opportunity to get some exercise. We started about eight in the morning and finished at eight at night. There were a lot of boxes! We moved them from one second floor to another second floor miles away (we did have a big truck). Before we even started, my back hurt slightly, and my friend, half my age, kept a good pace. Fortunately, I put on a magnetic belt pad before I started lifting and kept it on for most of the day. Although I experienced some back pain during the day, I didn't have any pain or stiffness the next day. My friend and I found it pleasant work, and we were ready to go into the business of moving people as a balance for too much computer work.

♦ A chronic back pain, not helped by one chiropractic adjustment, disappeared after two twenty-minute sessions for one man.

♦ A young man called one day who had read my previous book. He told me that he had a torn cartilage in his knee from a ski injury. He used the domino-size magnets from the Biomagnetic Kit for one half-hour twice a day—sometimes two magnets held side by side with duct tape. His knee is fine now.

♦ Deborah was a participant in one of my workshops. During the course of the workshop I treated her knee, and she later wrote me a more complete statement about it: "I fell and twisted my knee in August. In December I had surgery, and after the surgeon flipped a tendon back over, repaired a tear, and cut away excess growth, I was sent on my way. I have been in more pain since the operation and not out of pain since August. Ten minutes of magnetic treatment, bionorth pole, and I was free of pain for forty minutes."

♦ Sarah complained of lower back pain. The large coil applicator of a *Power Pulsar* was placed against her back and a test made of her arm strength. Biosouth made her stronger, so that side was placed against her back. After 20 minutes of treatment the pain moved to her side, then faded away.

♦ Jake had a hard lump growing on the end joint of his thumb. It continued to grow and begin to hurt when the pressure was applied or when the thumb was bent to the maximum. After two or three weeks it was about the size of a small pea.

A muscle test showed the south pole towards the lump made him stronger. It was treated for about an hour with a $1^1/_2$ inch disk applicator from a *Pulsar* at 16 Hz pulse rate. Within a few hours it began to shrink. It was treated the next two days for 20-30 minutes and by the third day it was practically gone. No more treatments were given and it entirely disappeared in a few more days.

♦ Richard Fuge was traveling from moist Santa Cruz to dry and cool Nevada one December. He developed chapped lips after being a few days in the cool dry air. His lips were almost painful. He was treated for 1/2 hour with the pulsing biosouth field and his lips immediately improved. He said it was like magic. A second treatment the next day cleared up the remaining chapped feeling and no cracking or chapping was visible.

♦ A young woman came for a visit one afternoon who appeared to have low energy in the chest area. She was tested with the Electronic Muscle Tester, which indicated that the biosouth side of a 2"x6"x1" bar magnet strengthened her. Within a few minutes, her heart began to beat rapidly and she took the magnet away. She definitely experienced an increase in energy, but it was a bit too much. She appeared to be slightly agitated.

Since this was a big magnet, even though the force was only about 1,000 gauss at the surface, its biological effect was large. She would probably have responded better to a weaker magnet, perhaps of about 300 gauss, which she could have placed on her chest for thirty to sixty minutes. I just happened to have that large magnet handy. A neodymium magnet would not have been good, since it has a strong force and a small area. A large-area weaker ceramic magnet would have been better because she was more than usually sensitive to magnetic force. Wearing a magnetic necklace for a few days also might have been a good remedy for her.

♦ Louise, a personal friend, developed a sore elbow one day. A 1" diameter permanent disc magnet of about 300 gauss was applied to the elbow for about fifteen minutes (bionorth pole), and the soreness disappeared.

♦ Elizabeth, another friend, from San Rafael, California, used the bionorth pole on her left foot to restore a collapsed metatarsal, which had remained unhealed after eight years. Surgery had been recommended because of the intense pain and debilitating effects, but there was a chance that surgery would make the condition worse. After one week of daily bionorth treatments, she was able to switch to the biosouth to stimulate healing. A 2"x4" block magnet was placed in her car where her right foot could rest on it while she drove. After two to three months, she was able to forget that she had once had a nearly useless foot. She stopped limping, was able to carry objects without suffering a relapse, and to hike and dance again.

Elizabeth also used the bionorth pole of a 1,000 gauss magnet to treat recurrent bleeding duodenal ulcers. At the first signs of distress, she treated herself for fifteen to twenty minutes, and the pain usually went away.

Recently she returned from a two-week trip to France, successfully using this magnet to counterbalance the stress of travel and a rich diet. She stated that the freedom from pain now gives her the energy she had ten or fifteen years ago.

♦ Laura had a sudden onset of pain along the entire length of her left arm. Treatment in three places along the arm for ten to fifteen minutes each with a 2"x6" block magnet of about 1,000 gauss strength completely eliminated the pain.

♦ Some of my friends and clients tried magnetic necklaces for various ailments. Louise occasionally suffers from headaches. She wrapped a magnetic hematite necklace around her head and experienced relief within a few minutes.

♦ Angelina had a stiff shoulder that did not respond very well to chiropractic adjustments, massage, or pulsed magnetic force therapy. She wore a hematite necklace for a couple of weeks. She reported that the difference was most apparent when she took it off for a day or two, and her neck stiffened up again.

♦ Philip came to dinner one night and happened to mention that he had a sore shoulder, so I invited him to try a domino-size neodymium magnet placed with the bionorth side towards the body. Two sessions of fifteen minutes each in the course of one evening helped reduce the pain about 75 percent. A few days later, a second session helped reduce the pain another ten percent.

♦ A note came one day from the purchaser of a magnetic pillow stating, "Already the pillow has helped my back and also the stiffness in my shoulders and neck. Thanks again for sending them."

The above cases are typical of the use of magnets for minor sprains and pains. Thousands of such cases could be collected.

The results are basically the same—a person has a problem and treatment with magnets dramatically helps.

Magnets don't seem to work very well to treat acute local infections or deep-seated general infections, although they help relieve minor complaints.

♦ The first person to purchase one of my instruments called a few days later to say he had stopped a cold and sore throat by treating it immediately when it began.

♦ A friend obtained relief from a sore throat after fifteen minutes.

♦ Another friend healed his sprained finger in fifteen minutes by simply placing a magnet on it (bionorth towards the finger).

♦ A friend's wife complained of a severe headache and pain at the back of her neck. This was relieved in fifteen minutes with a bionorth magnet treatment, and she was able to go out for the evening.

♦ Someone with a sore toe obtained relief from pain after fifteen minutes of magnetic treatment.

♦ A youngster with pain in his leg (no specific cause—growing pain?) obtained relief after fifteen minutes.

There were also some cases that did not respond. Since these people self-treated with magnets, it is possible that they did not use the optimum strength or proper polarity. However, magnetic therapy does not work for everyone, even when the symptoms are apparently identical to those of someone for whom it worked.

I had a headache and magnetic treatments did not help. An acupuncturist friend put a few needles in for ten minutes; the headache disappeared. It is impossible to tell in advance whether or not a magnetic treatment will be successful; there are always other factors. Ultimately, you must experiment for yourself.

♦ Becky, the eight-year-old daughter of a friend, was visiting from New Zealand and became ill one day. A physician friend diagnosed strep throat and impetigo and gave her an antibiotic. A magnetic endocrine and organ diagnosis showed that she needed red (biosouth pole) treatment on the pituitary, thymus, and all heart points, as well as the colon and ovaries. The throat needed bionorth pole treatment. After twenty minutes she was up and as active as usual.

Several hours later she was again magnetically diagnosed. She now only needed red pole treatment on the heart, thymus, and kidneys (the kidneys were overlooked in the earlier test). Those areas were treated for twelve minutes before she went to bed. The next day she appeared to be in fine health. No doubt the antibiotic helped as well as the magnetic treatment. This was a good example of how magnetic treatments can work synergistically with mainstream medicine. Her recovery was certainly rapid!

♦ One day, Becky's mother, Shena, remarked that she felt "terrible." She was obviously ill and in an irritable mood. A magnetic diagnosis showed five glands and organs were out of balance. She needed bionorth and biosouth pole treatments in alternating order for the pineal (on top of the head), pituitary, thyroid, thymus, and so forth down her body. She was treated for fifteen minutes simultaneously with five pulsed magnetic force instruments (Pulsars). She reported that she felt energy in her legs, which she wanted to "kick out" but couldn't. I suggested she take a bath to help smooth out her energy. One hour later she was feeling fine.

I have often seen these alternating patterns of imbalance in the endocrine glands when a person is clearly ill. Perhaps this is because of interaction between the glands, such that if one becomes hyperactive, another one becomes hypoactive, then a third one attempts to compensate and becomes hyperactive. Such conditions can be brought back into balance with the aid of magnetic treatment.

♦ Isabelle came to see me as a client. She had been ill for two months, sleeping hours every day as well as nights, since she had very little energy. A complete endocrine and organ magnetic analysis was done as described in chapter 4. Three glands and four organs were out of balance, but after only one hour's magnetic treatment, she said she felt alive again. The good effect only lasted an hour or two, and the next day she was tired again. She was treated an hour each day for the next six days. The number of glands and organs needing treatment diminished each day. After each treatment, she felt better and the effects lasted longer, and by the seventh day she was back to normal and stayed that way.

♦ A man came by who had tumors in his neck. He came once a day for one hour and was treated on the neck and other glands and organs as indicated by the complete magnetic diagnostic procedure described in chapter 4. Every day he visibly improved. By the end of the fifth day he purchased an instrument and left, pleased with the results.

Following are a couple of reports from people I did not see in my practice. I include them because back pain is a problem for so many people.

♦ Bruce of Boston has had back surgery and wears a magnetic belt every time his back acts up. He has tried almost all of the available support belts that do not have magnets, and they have not helped. The magnet belt with bionorth magnets facing the body is the only one he can wear that takes the pain away. He needs to wear it only for two to three hours once every few days.

♦ Richard of Santa Cruz, California, complained of feeling grumpy and frumpy, with the beginning of a headache, and a general feeling of mild depression/anger/frustration. A quick muscle test for the pineal, pituitary gland, and chest area showed he was strengthened by a biosouth on the glands and the chest area. In about 7 minutes the feelings of malaise left and he said he felt lighter and energetic again.

These case studies could be expanded to fill pages, but they are basically all the same: so-and-so was hurt or ill and after so many treatments recovered. Of course there were a few failures as well, but they are far outnumbered by the successes!

Formal Studies

Research activity is now being carried out around the world to determine the precise mechanisms by which pulsed magnetic fields aid healing. At this point we don't yet know the optimum pulse rates, waveforms, and amplitudes to use in treatment. We need to determine the most effective treatment times. And we need to know whether magnetic forces produce actual regeneration of damaged tissue or whether there is only a temporary improvement.

There have been many formal studies on the effects of magnetic forces on healing of fractures, nerve regeneration, enzyme activity, and other topics. I have described a few that may be of general interest or that have some bearing on a particular illness or mode of treatment.

Neck and Shoulder

♦ In 1976, the Japanese physician Kyoichi Nakagawa carried out a large research study on more than 11,000 people with symptoms of stiff necks, painful muscles, rheumatism and neuralgia. The patients wore magnets about the size of a large vitamin pill, applied to specific acupressure points, with the bionorth poles oriented toward the body. More than 90 percent of the patients said the magnet treatments were effective. Beneficial results occurred within three or four days of continuous treatment.

♦ A second Japanese study used magnetic necklaces, with both poles sideways to the skin. Sixty to eighty percent of the patients reported pain relief, but not until seven to fourteen days after the treatment commenced, compared with three to four days for bionorth only towards the skin.

This study is significant because it suggests that the use of simultaneous magnetic polarities is not as effective as the use of the appropriate single pole. Unfortunately, it is difficult to design a necklace with only one pole facing the body.

A number of studies have been done on the effects of wearing magnetic necklaces. These necklaces are popular—over ten million have been sold by one Asian company.

♦ TDK, a Japanese company that manufactures biomagnetic necklaces, asked users for reports on their effectiveness. Of a total of 33,000 respondents, nearly ninety percent reported positive results. Even discounting thirteen percent of these as placebo effects, the number of positive reports is remarkable.

According to TDK's research, the beneficial effect is not usually instantaneous, but appears gradually over a two- to four-day period. No adverse side effects were reported. Since so many people get stiff necks from driving, sitting at desks all day, typing, and watching computer terminals or television screens, it seems most people would benefit from wearing a biomagnetic necklace.

♦ In a study done at the University of Tokyo (Hirose, 1976), nearly two-hundred participants wore either a dummy necklace with 200 gauss magnets or a necklace with nine tiny magnets of 1,300 gauss each for a two-week test period. Statistical analysis showed that the group which wore the strong magnetic necklaces experienced improvement, usually within two or three days. Besides stiffness, the magnetic necklaces were also effective for menstrual pains, older people's shoulder problems, and in some cases helped improve the condition of the whole body.

Several other studies have been done, and all show the same highly positive results. One researcher stated that the necklaces were more effective for healthy individuals in their everyday life than for persons with serious illness. While the necklaces helped relieve stiffness in the neck and shoulders and made work more pleasant, they did not help major ailments.

♦ In March 1984, the well-known British medical journal *The Lancet* published an article by Allan Binder and others on the results of pulsed magnetic forces on persistent rotator cuff tendonitis (shoulder pains). Although this study is now over ten years old, it is one of the best studies published and therefore well worth summarizing.

The authors begin by discussing the previous approach to shoulder pain: corticosteroid injections. This powerful hormone, naturally secreted by the adrenal glands, helped sixty-seven percent of the 138 patients treated at their clinic in Cambridge, England, but sometimes there were side effects such as facial puffiness.

Twenty-nine patients from the same clinic were chosen for experimental treatment with pulsed magnetic forces. The chosen patients were from the group that did not respond to hormone injections and had suffered shoulder pain for more than three months. At each visit, a subjective pain score was obtained for each subject, and the range of free and easy movement was checked. The twenty-nine patients were divided into control and treatment groups. A coil, 13 centimeters in diameter, was placed over the shoulder and electronic circuitry generated a 20-gauss force pulsing at 73 cycles per second. (No explanation was given for the choice of this unusual frequency.) The direction of magnetic polarity was not specified. Patients were instructed to use the coil for five to nine hours per day.

After four weeks, most of the experimental group improved, so the control group, which initially were treated with fake coils, were also given the benefit of real pulsed magnetic forces. They too, improved, and by the end of sixteen weeks, only three of the twenty-nine patients did not improve. There were no side effects. Remember, these were the twenty-nine people who did not respond to the corticosteroid injections.

The researchers in *The Lancet* study did not appear to take into account magnetic polarity. Had they done so, improvement might have been more rapid. Also, I have found (by muscle testing) that magnetic pulse rates over 30 Hz are not as strengthening as rates around 14-20 Hz. Drs. Lau and Warnke (see p. 145) found 16 Hz. to be close to optimum for maximum blood flow and increased blood oxygen. (Permanent magnets of the right polarity will also work for treating shoulder pain, although perhaps more slowly.)

Miscellaneous Studies

♦ In India, researchers showed that month-long pretreatment of an unstated number of albino rats with 0.1 Hz pulsed magnetic forces almost completely prevented injury from exposure to cold. Rats pretreated with pulsed magnetic forces recovered ten to twelve days after exposure to cold; untreated rats took twenty-four to thirty days to recover, and three died.

♦ In China, researchers studied the use of tiny magnets placed on acupuncture points of 300 people who had not previously responded well to either needles, Western medication, or Chinese medication. Positive effects occurred in 72 percent of the patients, and when a rotating magnet was used in addition, the efficacy rate increased to 85 percent. (Rotating magnets have been used in the past. Apparently, this was discovered to be helpful by some practitioners many years ago. It may be an archaic means of alternating polarities, or creating pulsed magnetic forces that can now be produced much more easily by electronic means.)

Cancer

Although there are many positive accounts of cancer remissions in humans, most of the formal research studies have been carried out on mice.

♦ Chinese M.D. Y.S. Kim (1976) wrote a review of a few of the latter. He noted that cancer cells are more susceptible to magnetic treatments than normal cells, and that in most of the studies, cancer cell growth was retarded. In the studies he reviewed, both magnetic polarities were often applied to the cells. Magnet therapists generally advocate the use of bionorth for cancer.

♦ In studies not reviewed by Dr. Kim, Weber and Cerilli (1971) found that tumor growth in mice was inhibited by a factor of two by magnetic treatment. They used a very strong static electromagnetic field (38 kilogauss) but did not state the polarity used.

♦ Jeno Barnothy at the Biomagnetics Research Foundation in Evanston, Illinois, also found that magnetic forces inhibited tumor growth in mice. Barthony apparently did not take polarity into account.

♦ One Soviet study found positive results for lung cancer. Another study used magnetically treated water to reduce the growth of cancer tumors. Unfortunately, the abstracts I have give no details.

Oxygen and Blood Flow

When magnets are applied to the body, the blood flow increases, and the oxygen absorbed by the tissues is increased. This is probably one of the mechanisms by which magnets promote healing and one of the reasons they are helpful for many different kinds of ailments.

♦ German physician Ulrich Warnke utilized a pulsing magnetic force with a repetition rate of 20 Hz and an intensity of five gauss applied to the head area. Infrared radiation from local areas of the body was detected by a process known as a thermogram (infrared photograph).

Dr. Warnke found an increase in blood flow in the arms and hands within two minutes in some subjects. In a variation of his study, he measured the oxygen partial pressure at the skin. This increased on the average by 200 percent in a study of fifty-eight subjects. There were large individual differences.

The type of magnetic impulse he used was apparently an alternation of both north and south polarity, although that's not clear in the article I have. Polarity could be an important variable. Within each pulse interval of about 1/40 of a second were 4 sub-pulses

This pattern may have been more complex than was needed, particularly if the sub-pulses produced alternating polarities. At this point we really don't know enough about the effects of magnetism on the body to know precisely what is needed).

Dr. Warnke concluded that the large blood vessels dilated as well as capillaries in the periphery. He also found that only when the pulsating forces were applied to the head was there an increase in blood flow.

In a study on frogs and fishes, Warnke found that their capillary action was changed by magnetic forces from a "stop-and-go" pattern to a nearly uninterrupted flow.

Not only do magnetic forces help more blood to flow through human tissues, but that blood also transfers more oxygen to the cells. Dr. Warnke reported up to a **200 percent increase** in dissolved oxygen in the tissues!

In order to further confirm the dramatic results, he applied measuring probes directly to the skin. He also constructed special glass cubicles that could be filled with nitrogen and sealed around an arm and hand. The amount of oxygen diffusing from the skin into the nitrogen-filled cubicle was then measured as another indicator of the increased amount of oxygen under the influence of pulsing magnetic forces.

As of 1980, Dr. Warnke did not know exactly why the blood oxygen was increased. He listed fourteen possible mechanisms and planned further research. He found the following parameters of importance in his initial work:

- Best results were obtained with magnetic strengths of about five gauss; stronger forces did not improve the results.

- Pulse repetition rates below 6 Hz did not show any effects (same finding as Dr. Lau, see next page).

- Children often showed greater effects.

- Results were better when a person was lying down.

- Subjects who exercised vigorously for fifteen minutes before the magnetic field was applied showed large reactions.

♦ In the United States, Dr. Benjamin Lau of Loma Linda University performed a different type of study on blood oxygen using pulsed magnetic forces. Twenty-six subjects ranging in age from twelve to sixty-five years old were treated around the chest with a pulsing magnetic force that could be varied from 2 to 20 Hz and from 2 to 100 gauss. The magnetic polarity was not specified. The apparatus is a standard one manufactured by Elec Gmbh in West Germany. The researchers used a coil large enough to be placed over the head and around the chest area. If it was placed that way, the force orientation was apparently vertical in the body. An ultrasound blood flow meter was placed over the skin above the radial artery. Dr. Lau found that:

- In 60 percent of the subjects, the maximum increase in blood flow (200 to 400 percent) occurred at a magnetic pulse rate of 15 Hz.

- Blood velocity (or blood flow) was not increased when the pulse frequency was 5 or below (about the same result obtained by Dr. Warnke for blood oxygen).

- At 20 Hz, blood flow was a maximum for only 20 percent of the subjects.

- The largest response was obtained at an intensity of 5 gauss (the same as Dr. Warnke's finding in the study of increased tissue oxygen).

- Due to dilation of the arteries, there were no significant changes in blood pressure and pulse rate for the majority of the subjects.

In a second study, Dr. Lau used a transcutaneous (on the skin) electrode placed on the forearm or palm. Sixty-four subjects had pulsing magnetic forces of varying pulse rates and intensities applied to the chest. In this study he found that:

- Pulse rates below 10 Hz did not increase the measured blood oxygen partial pressure in most subjects. In fact, 40 percent of the subjects showed a decrease.

- At a pulse frequency of 12 to 20 Hz, an increase of oxygen partial pressure from 100 to 400 percent was observed in 90 percent of the subjects. This was a gradual increase, reaching a peak in ten to fifteen minutes. It persisted for several hours after the magnetic treatment.

The results found by Drs. Lau and Warnke have been substantiated in other studies and reports.

♦ Swedish engineer Ivan Troeng, who did research on people with cancer, reported that subjects treated with magnets had 30 percent more oxygen absorption at the end of three weeks compared to a control group. Another test of football players showed an increase of approximately 25 percent in their ability to absorb oxygen.

♦ A Canadian researcher measured the oxygen content in a blood sample from a horse before and after a one-hour treatment. A 52 percent increase was observed in one case.

Possible mechanisms for increased oxygen carrying capacity include:

- An increase in the electrostatic charge on the outside of the red blood cells that causes them to repel each other rather than be clumped together. When blood cells clump together, there is less surface area available to absorb oxygen.

- An increase in calcium bicarbonate in the blood. Calcium bicarbonate appears to be involved in carrying oxygen.

It is still not clear how magnetic forces could alter the charge on blood cells. More research is needed, but some fundamental research was done many years ago by Linus Pauling and other chemists.

Because iron is a basic element in hemoglobin (one atom of iron resides at the center of this complex molecule), some people have supposed that the blood cells line up in the presence of a magnet and that this can be seen with a microscope. Others dispute this, although there could be a difference depending on whether the blood cells have taken on oxygen or given it up. But if the blood cells were to respond to magnetic fields, they would clump together and lose their effectiveness to carry oxygen.

The effect of magnets on the iron in the hemoglobin molecule has proved difficult to determine. In 1845, Michael Faraday, one of the pioneers in the study of electricity and magnetism, investigated the magnetic properties

147

of dried blood. He failed to notice an effect that Linus Pauling reported many years later—that there was up to a 20 percent difference in magnetic susceptibility between completely oxygenated and completely deoxygenated blood. Deoxygenated blood has four unpaired electrons which can orient to external magnetic fields. But once hemoglobin has captured oxygen, the four free electrons are tied up and unable to react to external magnetic fields. Pauling's work on the magnetic properties of hemoglobin began in the 1930s and culminated in a Nobel Prize in 1954.

Each hemoglobin molecule consists of a central iron atom surrounded by four substructures called hemes, each of which can carry one oxygen molecule. Each oxygen molecule is composed of two oxygen atoms, so one iron atom can carry a maximum of eight oxygen atoms. Apparently, not all hemoglobin molecules carry the maximum possible number of oxygen atoms. This is where magnets and certain nutritional supplements can make a difference. Pauling discovered that when oxygen molecules attach to the hemoglobin molecule, they undergo a change in electronic structure. Oxygen loses its freedom to resist magnetic fields, and the hemoglobin molecule loses its magnetic susceptibility. Clearly, magnetic fields have some effect on unoxygenated hemoglobin that helps it capture more oxygen, but the exact mechanism is a mystery (to me).

The acid-base balance of the blood is another factor in the amount of oxygen that the hemoglobin molecule can carry. The acidity of the blood varies slightly from person to person, and from time to time within the same individual. Normal blood is just slightly alkaline. The amount of oxygen carried by the red blood cells has been found to vary with blood acidity. Linus Pauling worked out some of the descriptive equations in 1935. It is not a simple one-to-one relationship. Since magnetic fields appear to influence the structure of water and other liquids (that is, fruit juice, wine, and so forth), magnetic fields probably also can influence the blood, which will affect the amount of oxygen carried by hemoglobin molecules.

The amount of oxygen that hemoglobin can carry varies with the degree to which the cells clump. According to Keffi Bell, a Santa Cruz medical technologist who examines live blood routinely in her practice, when people eat animal products, more clumping occurs. Clumping also occurs when a person has an ailment such as bronchitis. Ms. Bell has observed that magnetic treatments can change the blood cell distribution patterns within twenty minutes.

Some years ago, before learning of the above mentioned studies, I had been experimentally treating my chest area with biosouth magnets and noticed that jogging was easier. Upon taking a ski vacation to the Rockies, I found there was no difficulty breathing at high altitude under maximum exertion during my first day, and from there on. Most people require a two or three-day adjustment period, with a month needed for full adjustment. My previous adjustment times had been three days as well. A couple of trips to mountains over 12,000 feet were also free of high-altitude adjustment. This was great! Treatment times were typically for an hour or two for two days prior to a ski trip or mountain climb, or for thirty minutes prior to jogging.

Some marathon runners now use pulsed magnetic force instruments. Probably mountain climbing expeditions will find these instruments useful.

Frequently, when people use a pulsed magnetic field, they sense a feeling of warmth around the area treated. This is likely due to an increase in blood flow.

These studies and anecdotal reports clearly demonstrate that magnetic forces increase blood oxygen. Indirectly, they promote increased stamina and endurance or increase the healing rate for injuries or diseases.

Formal Studies in Arthritis Research

Arthritis turns out to be one of the conditions that responds best to magnetic treatment.

♦ A group of Connecticut physicians, including David Trock and Richard Markoll, carried out one of the most recent formal studies. They were particularly interested in osteoarthritis.

Drs. Trock and Markoll established the most effective magnetic force configurations empirically by trial and error determinations on 20 arthritis patients. They then made a major pilot study in Europe on 861 patients with painful arthritis conditions. When they observed 70 to 80 percent improvement with this group, they decided to carry out a more careful double-blind study in the United States as part of the FDA approval process for their magnetic pulsing instrument.

Twenty-seven patients with knee arthritis were treated eighteen times for thirty minutes each with a dc pulse that was less than 30 Hz. The force was between 10 and 20 gauss. Patients were helped between 23 and 61 percent on various improvement parameters that were measured.

Dr. Trock says over 200,000 patients, most of them in Europe, have been safely treated with pulsed magnetic forces with no toxic side effects.

♦ Sarada Subrahmanyam, M.D., and Sanker Narayan, Ph.D., of the Madras-based Institute of Magnetobiology have been studying the effect of pulsed magnetic forces in healing since 1979. In a preliminary study, they artificially produced arthritis in rats and found they could get rid of the inflammation in three to four days using pulsed magnetic forces, while it took three or four weeks for inflammation to subside without treatment.

After this success, they began systematic treatment of about 1,000 people with arthritis using sinusoidal-waveform pulsed magnetic forces of about 350 gauss strength at 0.1 Hz. Treatment time was thirty minutes per day for thirty to forty days. Patients were examined, had their blood tested, their range of movement was measured, and x-ray pictures were taken.

About 75 to 80 percent of the patients with rheumatoid arthritis and osteoarthritis recovered most of their lost movement and became free of pain. With only two exceptions, no recurrence of pain was noted after two years. Between 80 and 85 percent of the patients with spondylosis (spinal arthritis) were free of pain at the end of the thirty-day treatment period.

♦ Dr. Benjamin Lau of Loma Linda University in California treated nineteen patients with severe to moderate stiffness of joints. After about three weeks of daily treatment (time, pulse rate, and polarity not specified), sixteen of the nineteen reported no more stiffness and very little or no pain.

♦ At the Sinadecki Hospital in Wloszczowa, Poland, about 200 people with rheumatoid arthritis were treated with pulsed magnetic forces for twenty to twenty-five minutes per day. Pain generally decreased after five or six treatments, although the treatment was continued for ten to fif-

151

teen sessions. Magnetic therapy was judged to be 73 percent effective, compared with 45 percent effectiveness for short-wave diathermy treatments carried out on a control group. The good results lasted for several months.

Both polarity and pulse repetition rate are important variables. Future studies on arthritis (and people doing treatments at home) might take this into account, thereby obtaining even better results. Each person may need his or her own particular magnetic frequency, and each case may have its own unique point where soothing bionorth forces should be superceded by stimulating biosouth forces. Muscle testing provides a way to quickly test for these factors.

Many more studies need to be done before we have a good grasp of the basics of magnetic healing—what works best and why. In the meantime, you have a good chance of discovering something new by experimenting at home.

You are not likely to experience any adverse side effects, especially if you follow the general principles and guidelines described in chapter 4. Magnetic treatments work; it's only a question of how well, or how quickly, they work.

Chapter X
Magnetism and Spin

Some Semantics

What is magnetism? To ask that question in that form does not lead to clear thinking. No mere verbal answer can ever satisfy us. Instead, we will gain more understanding by asking questions about how magnetism operates. What are the observations that lead to the inference that there is such a thing as magnetism?

Part of the confusion about magnetism arises from an historical and uncritical use of the word itself. Once a word is put into common practice, clouds of ideas, prejudices, and associations form around it, which can lead to incorrect perceptions.

Because the term *magnetism* is a noun in our language, we tend to think of it as a **thing**. After all, we were taught that a noun is either a person, place, or thing. This is a subtle yet powerful kind of mental programming that is built into our language, making it difficult to comprehend dynamic structures in the actual world. The language structure acts like a "meta-mind" that does some of our thinking for us. We are often unaware that this is happening, for we unconsciously or uncritically take the structure and use of language **as the truth**, without realizing it is only a vague guideline for "**reality.**"

With this notion of magnetism as a "thing," then, following the logic of how *things* are built into the grammar of the language, we are automatically led to the notion that magnetism is something added to a substance like a coat of paint, so we look for it.

As Anton Mesmer said, "I observe with regret that people flippantly abuse this name: Once having become familiar with the word *magnetism*, they flatter themselves that they have the idea of the thing, whereas they merely have the idea of a word." This is as true today as it was two hundred years ago in Mesmer's time.

The Observations

As described in chapter 3, (p.16), Hans Oersted made some of the first observations associating electric current with the movements of a compass needle. It was inferred from his discovery that an electric current produces a magnetic force just like the one observed between lodestones (in his time there were no artificial permanent magnets, only lodestones and compasses).

> **The magnetic force *direction* changes continuously around the wire in a circular form; it is not simply a north force on the top and a south force on the bottom.**

Oersted's discovery was made seventy-five years before the discovery of the particles called electrons and served as a basis for the mathematical formulations of James Clerk Maxwell stating the equivalence of electricity and magnetism. Nowadays, it is known that electrons moving in the vicinity of a current-carrying wire will spiral around the wire in a circular or helical path. **Magnetic force acts at a right angle to the electric force** and the result is that charged particles move in an orbit rather than being pushed or pulled.

Now that more is known about the nature of electrons and protons, **we can say that neither magnetism nor electricity are things or properties added to something. They appear to be intrinsic aspects of electrons and protons and other subatomic particles.** In fact, elementary particles are now considered to be more like spinning fuzzy clouds or vortices rather than discrete little balls.

Electric charge, magnetic force, spin, and mass are merely abstractions which physicists have extracted from experimental observations that bring out one or the other of these aspects.

The Classical Forces of Physics

The term force is introduced in the language to account for an observed change in movement. Force is a word used to cover our ignorance. Although this may seem like a semantic trick, it is just how the game of physics is played.

When electrons are gathered together, for example, on the surface of a metal sphere, and electrons are gathered on a piece of foil which moves when placed near the sphere, an electric force is said to be present. When electrons move in a beam or within a wire, the change in direction of other electrons moving around the wire is presumed to be due to a magnetic force. When objects are held above the ground and released, their fall is said to be due to the force of gravity. Using these terms does not explain the movements; it merely gives us a way to talk about them.

In the classical science of physics, a force is said to be present if an object moves or changes direction.

In the case of magnetic forces, there is an alternative way of explaining them. Each electron can be thought of as if it

155

were a tiny whirling vortex. When a large number of electrons spin in the same direction, which happens when a piece of iron is magnetized, the aggregate whirling motion imparts a drag-along spinning motion to other electrons in the vicinity, and we say the piece of iron has magnetic force.

When electrons move in a wire, their individual spins apparently become more organized in such a way that an external spin force, a summation of all their individual spin forces, is evident in the space around the wire. If two wires carrying electric currents are placed parallel and near one another, and if the current is in the same direction, the two wires will seek to move closer together so that the spins of the multitudes of moving electrons in the wires can align (Fig. 4, p. 15). Two magnets, seeming to attract or repel, behave like two coils of wire.

From these examples, and any others you care to imagine, you can see that there is a relationship between **magnetism** and spin.

Discovery of a Biological Spin Force

In 1978, I discovered the presence of a biological force around the human body that appears to be a special type of spin force. It manifests as a torque exerted on a hanging frame. The force was also observed around a cat, a plant, a watermelon, and a grapefruit, and presumably it exists around all living things. This force is not magnetic in the usual sense of iron magnetism, but its amplitude varies with changes in Earth's magnetic field, being larger when there are magnetic storms, so it must have some connection with magnetism. The force acts like a spin force in that it causes hanging objects to rotate around the body, rather than swing to and fro. It usually moves clockwise as seen from

156

above the head. It also varies with the emotional state or vitality of the person. The force is estimated to be over one million times as large as the body's magnetic field! Healers were observed to have large spin forces around them since they could usually make my devices rotate more than normal people. When people are ill or meditate, the spin force around them decreases. This force may be related to what people have called *chi, prana, life energy, odic force*, etc. For more information, see chapter 3 in *The Body Magnetic* or *The American Journal of Acupuncture*, Dec. 83. A simple device to detect the spin force is available for a nominal cost.

The spin force, or aura, appears to be an entirely new kind of force. Magnetism may only be a special case or lower order of spin force. Tesla referred to the existence of a *higher octave* of magnetism. (See chapter 12.) In Denmark, this discovery was also made by Dr. Bjoorn Vlistigk, who made a large hanging structure with heavy magnets on it. When a person sits under this structure, the weights revolve and drive an electric generator, which he claims could produce over 1,000 watts!

Spin—A Fifth Force?

Based on my discovery, which has been verified or independently discovered by others, I propose that we should consider spin to be a fundamental force along with the other fundamental forces. Spin is everywhere. Spin is observed around nearly every object in the universe from galaxies to subatomic particles. If this assumption is made, the forces of physics can be seen to be interconnected, for spin complements gravity. Electricity and magnetism are aspects of stationary and moving particles, and magnetism appears to be a special case of spin. The existence of spin forces around suns and planets helps to organize solar and satellite systems. Galactic spirals appear to be spin-organized. The existence of spin forces around electrons and protons may help to account for the stability of atoms.

The acceptance of spin as a force in its own right would account for the reason why the universe has not come together in clumps, and perhaps solve the missing mass problem, for it could account for the observation that stars distant from their galactic centers rotate faster than would be expected by gravitational forces alone. (See Chapter 4 of *The Body Magnetic* for more information.)

The acceptance of spin, especially the spin force around living organisms, would help unite the science of physics with the science of biology. The forces of physics are summarized in the table on the next page. This table does not include the other two forces, called the strong and weak nuclear forces, which are inferred to exist to keep nuclear particles from dispersing due to electric repulsion.

The Forces of the Universe

Note that each force subsumes the lower ones; that is, spin forces produce rotation, magnetic forces twist, push, and pull, electric ones push or pull, and gravity only pulls. In this model, the forces help to structure the universe in ever more complex ways. If magnetic forces weren't operating, electrons and protons would eventually find one another and annihilate in a flash of light. If there were no spin forces, gravity would eventually draw everything together. Even light is influenced by gravity. **Spin is not antigravity; it is the complement to gravity**, keeping particles orbiting around whether or not they are electrically charged. Undoubtedly there are yet higher forces, such as a universal *force of organization* or a *life force*. Perhaps there is even a *force of love* (See my little book, *The Quantum Theory of Love*) and a *force of creation*.

FORCE	LEVEL OF OPERATION	EFFECTS
Gravity	Operates between all matter.	Pulls matter together.
Electric	Only manifests between charged particles.	Pushes or pulls.
Magnetic	Manifests when charged particles move.	Twists, then pushes or pulls at right angles to the direction of motion. Only sensed by other charged particles. Causes moving charged particles to move in circles, spirals, or helixes.
Spin	Possibly present around all bodies—much larger around living organisms.	Causes all bodies to spin around one another. Counter-acts gravity. Produces complex forms or structures.

Note that the spin force related to magnetism is not in the same direction as the spin force which makes planets and stars spin around their axes. The Earth spins around what we call the north pole. The magnetic curves or moves almost at right angles to this, entering into one pole and leaving the other. For Earth, the magnetic pole is a few degrees off the spin axis. For some rapidly spinning planets such as Uranus and Neptune, the magnetic pole is about 45° different from the rotational axis. If this all makes your head spin, don't worry; I don't completely understand it myself just yet or I could explain it more clearly. Perhaps some reader more knowledgeable than I about nuclear spins can add clarity.

Magnetism and Monopoles— More Semantic Confusion

One reason magnetism has been lumped together with electricity may be because of a semantic error, arising from an early misunderstanding of the nature of magnetism. Initially it was believed, because of the words used, that there were two poles to a magnet—north and south. These two poles were thought to be different. Now it is clear that these poles are only two directions of a continuously changing **direction**. Magnets are made from coils which are usually formed into flat or cylindrical forms. This form accentuates two directions, which by convention were called north and south. When permanent magnets were initially made in the form of horseshoes or cylinders, this accentuated the two directions of magnetic force. However, the magnetic force change makes a circle around a coil, as shown in Figure 7 on p. 22.

North and south are convenient two-valued abstractions, accentuated by the flat shape of the coil, but there are also east and west magnetic forces, and all directions in between. The north and south direction has sometimes been called negative and positive, further mystifying the notion of magnetism, and giving rise to the erroneous conclusion that there could be a magnetic current between the two poles of a magnet.

A flat or cylindrical coil accentuates two directions of magnetic force, either into or out of the coil face, but by making coils in other forms we can accentuate other directions of the magnetic force.

The structure of coils and their use to form permanent magnets has misled people to speak and write about the north pole or the south pole, forgetting that these are merely directions. From this came the notion of magnetic monopoles, a convenient abstraction devised by physicists to make their calculations simpler. The notion of two separate aspects of magnetism became crystallized in the language and it is hard to remove. It has led to much wasted money spent looking for magnetic monopoles, which may be as foolish as looking for the back of a hand separate from the front. (The time might be better spent contemplating the sound of one hand clapping, as Zen monks do.)

Types of Spin and Magnetism

The table on the next page lists common objects in the universe from small to large. Spin appears to be a common property of these elements, but whether or not these are really different types of spin or just aspects of the same spin force remains to be clarified. Although the property of magnetism is associated with all of these objects, it may be useful to consider that there are different types of magnetism, at least for a while, until more experiments and observations bring greater clarity.

Electron spin resonance is a whole field of study which involves changing electron spins by the application of magnetic forces. MRI, or nuclear magnetic resonance imaging, which uses changes in proton spins, is also a big field of study. Both of these processes may be important in understanding how magnetic forces heal, which is the subject of the next section.

POSSIBLE TYPES OF MAGNETISM

Electron	Present around all electrons. Electron magnetism may be different from proton magnetism.
Proton	Present around all protons.
Iron	Present in iron and some other metals under certain conditions. Manifests from spin **directions** that normally cancel each other out in most materials, but not in iron.
Electro-	Manifests when charged particles move together in an organized manner.
Animal	A special type of spin force present around living organisms which interacts with other types of magnetism.
Planetary	Known to be present around Earth and possibly other planets. Origin unknown.
Stellar	Present around stars. Origin unknown.
Galactic	Present around galactic centers to help form the structure of galaxies.

Chapter XI
How Magnetic Forces Heal

People always ask how magnets work—a simple ques- tion with a complex answer. Much is known, more is being constantly discovered, and questions will prob- ably always remain, for we are dealing with the most com- plicated instrument in the world—the human body. A com- plete answer would involve details from atomic physics, biophysics, biochemistry, molecular chemistry, biology, physiology, neuroscience, and psychology. The average per- son who asks that question probably doesn't really want to know, or may not feel like learning, all the details. An entire book could be written on this subject and the writer of such a book would scarcely be able to keep up with the literature. Nevertheless I'll sketch a few salient mechanisms in approx- imate order of importance, and let the interested reader fol- low up some of the references listed. But please note that if you have an injury, disease, or condition, magnetic therapy has greater than a 50% chance of working, so don't wait until you 'understand' how it works to try it for yourself.

Blood Flow

This may be one of the most important mechanisms by which magnetic fields heal. The work of Dr. Warnke and Dr. Lau on oxygen absorption and blood flow was discussed in chapter 9 (page 143). If diseased or injured cells receive more oxygen, it seems natural to expect faster healing.

Hemoglobin has iron, but not in a form that is much affected by external magnetic forces. If the blood cells were affected by a magnet they might collect together and form a clot where a magnet was applied. Fortunately that doesn't happen. What does seem to happen is that the blood cells separate after a magnet is applied. This can be seen with Live Cell Blood Analysis where a sample of blood is placed under a microscope and shown on a large screen. People who have some diseased condition often have clumped blood cells which presumably can't carry and distribute oxygen as effectively.

Enzyme Activity

Enzymes are complex molecules which are fundamental to cell biology. They are the workhorses, carrying nutrients into the cells from the blood and carrying end products out to be swept away by the lymph. In 1994 Charles Grisson, a chemist from the University of Utah reported in *Science Magazine* that magnetic fields can alter the activity of enzyme molecules. A similar finding was reported many years ago by Justine Smith and R. Cook using a 5,000 gauss permanent magnet. They found the enzymes did not disintegrate as quickly as control samples.

Jan Walleczek, founder of a Bioelectromagnetics Laboratory at Stanford, and his associates developed a computer model of what could be happening at the molecular level of enzymes. They made use of the well-known fact that in any chemical reaction, molecules may pass through an intermediate state where they have 'free' electrons which can be influenced by magnetic fields. During this brief time interval a magnetic field can influence an enzyme reaction or other biochemical operations. Usually all the electrons in molecules are paired off with other electrons and aren't much affected by external magnetic fields. Depending on what the reactions are, and what the external magnetic fields are like, this can be beneficial or harmful. Several interesting studies have been published by Jan Walleczek (see references) and more are on the way.

Calcium Ions

At the same Bioelectromagnetics laboratory another researcher, Pam Killoran, found that calcium ions moving into and out of cells can be influenced by magnetic fields. This is important because the concentration of calcium rises and falls according to a cell's needs. Ross Adey, a researcher at Loma Linda University found some years ago that magnetic fields pulsing at 16 hertz strongly affected calcium ions in nerve axons.

As mentioned previously, Warnke and Lau, working independently in Germany and Loma Linda University, both found that a 16 Hz pulsed field was optimum for pulses of magnetic force to increase blood flow and absorbed oxygen. By muscle testing I found many years ago that 16 Hz pulses seemed to be the most strengthening pulse rate for the body. These observations are beginning to form a pattern.

Magnetic Matter in Cells

Many years ago Dr. Joseph Kirschvink, a researcher at UCLA, discovered the presence of magnetite, a form of iron oxide that is sensitive to magnetic fields, in bacteria. Later he found magnetite in human brains, and at the 1998 conference on magnet therapy in Los Angeles he announced that he had found it in many cells of the human body. Exactly how this responds to applied magnetic fields to produce changes in the cell is as yet unknown, but at least there is the possibility of an interaction.

Wound Healing-Cell Division Rate

When skin is cut, the cells begin dividing and growing to fill in the cut. Magnetic fields increase the cell division rate and also appear to reduce scarring. Japan Life,

165

International, an early manufacturer of magnetic beds, published microscope pictures of the cell structure with and without magnetic treatment. Apparently the presence of magnetic fields stimulate cell growth and help the cells reorganize after a wound.

Nerve Regeneration

At the same conference, Betty Sisken reported on research done by herself and Jane Wolker at the University of Kentucky, on nerve regeneration in the spinal cord of rats. An earlier study by Basset also reported successful nerve regeneration in rats. A San Diego magnetic therapist, Richard Hopkins, has succeded in helping several people recover movement after paralyzing injuries to the spinal cord. These people used diffeerent types of magnetic forces, yet all got positive results.

Magnetism at the Atomic Level

All matter responds to the presence of magnetic forces. Each atom, with its circulating electrons, will resist being pushed out of pattern by an external magnetic force. This was dramatically demonstrated in April of 1997 at the Magnet Laboratory of Massachusetts Institute of Technology when researchers published a photograph of a tiny frog floating in a magnetiic field (*Science News*, Vol. 152, Dec. 1997). The effect has been known for years; in fact, the *Handbook of Physics* lists tables of the magnetic reponse for every element, but this was the first picture of a living organism levitated at room temperature. Previous levitation demonstrations have used superconductors at liquid helium temperaturess or used iron which responds a billion times more strongly than other elements. (Iron in our blood won't respond to a magnetic field like iron in a magnet however, as it is in a different molecular form.) What part this atomic magnetic effect plays in magnetic therapy is currently unknown, but it does exist.

Subatomic Magnetic Effects—Proton Magnetism

Besides the effects of electrons in iron and orbiting electrons in other elements, protons, those particles which reside at the center of atoms, also repond to external magnetic fields. A proton, similar to an electron but much larger, may be thought of as a topologically closed vortex. That is, like a little spinning fuzzy cloud which has a direction of spin, and associated magnetic polarity as discussed in the chapter on Magnetism and Spin.

Another means by which magnetic forces affect the body could be what I call *proton magnetism*, not electron magnetism. One proton is at the center of every hydrogen atom, and 92 percent of the atoms in the body are hydrogen atoms. Hydrogen protons are known to respond to magnetic forces by emitting radio waves, which range from a few cycles to thousands of cycles per second, depending on the strength of the external magnetic force.

Since the hydrogen protons are fixed in atoms that in turn are embedded in molecules, they are not free to jump out of the body and clamp to an external magnet. In this respect, they are somewhat analogous to a compass needle that is fixed on a pivot. The protons can turn either towards or away from the applied magnetic force. How much they turn depends on the strength of the applied magnetic force. Usually they only turn a little bit, they do not flip completely around like little toy magnets do when a large magnet is placed nearby. After the external magnetic force is removed, the proton reverts to its original position. As it does so, it generates a radio signal. This effect has been known and used for 100 years. It was first discovered by a physicist named Larmour in 1895 and is called the Larmour precession effect. Scientists use this effect to measure small magnetic force changes. The instruments are called proton magnetometers and are sometimes flown in planes or dragged by ships so geologists can look for magnetic anomalies that might indicate the presence of oil.

All atoms other than hydrogen have more than one proton in the nucleus. Every pair of protons will couple with each other and will not be influenced by external magnetic forces. Only atoms with an odd number of protons, therefore, will be affected by external magnetic forces. Nitrogen, sodium, and potassium are three of the major elements in the body which have an odd number of protons in their nuclei. These odd protons are free to twist and emit radio signals when an external magnetic force is applied. The behavior of these protons is the basis of Nuclear Magnetic Resonance Imaging in which the radio signals generated by the protons are detected and processed by a computer to generate an internal image of the body.

The Earth's magnetic field of about 1 gauss is a steady background. Changes in the Earth's field can induce proton wobbles which in turn can produce radio signals of only a few cycles, but these small changes can be detected by sensitive radio frequency amplifiers. Such small changes can also be significant for people, for it is well known that humans respond markedly to changes in the Earth's magnetic field. When external magnetic forces of about 1 gauss are applied, hydrogen protons will produce a radio frequency wave (called the precession frequency) of around 430 Hz, well within the audible range if there were a suitable transducer present. Protons may be literally singing to one another all the time. As magnets applied to the body are moved, or as blood and lymph carries hydrogen protons past a fixed magnet, the hydrogen protons emit varying frequencies, apparently slightly changing the biochemistry. **Such variations would occur no matter what the polarity of the applied magnet—north, south, alternating, or pulsed**. Unless an applied magnet is larger than the entire body, there will always be edge effects where the direction of the magnetic changes from in or out to sideways and all degrees in between. When alternating magnetic pole faces are applied to the body, there will be rapid changes of proton spin orientation. Pulsed magnetic fields are often in the form of a square wave, so there are abrupt off-and-on pulses which produce effects somewhat like alternating pole faces.

This type of mechanism may account for the observation that practically all types of magnets, strengths, and directional patterns have effects on the body, although exactly how changing proton spin orientations can change the biochemistry is unknown (to me).

Perhaps a result of an injury or illness at the smallest structural level is a dislocation of the normal organized pattern of protons. When an external force is applied, it may shake them loose from their abnormal pattern, thereby allowing the organizing force of the body to more quickly bring them back to the optimum state. If so, this model might give us some clues to providing optimum magnetic *returning* forces. It should be possible to apply a pulsed magnetic force to, for example, an injured hand, detect the proton precession frequencies generated, and tune the applied pulse rate to produce maximum precession amplitude, or tune to produce a pattern which is similar to one generated from a healthy hand. The instrumentation for doing this already exists in Nuclear Magnetic Resonance Imaging devices.

Proton precession frequency changes may account for the observation that pulsed magnetic forces are more biologically effective than permanent magnets. To produce the most powerful biological effects, the pulses may need to be in some kind of resonance with the proton frequencies.

Italian engineer Antoine Priore (Bird, 1993) used both radio waves and magnetic forces in his remarkably effective healing instruments. Perhaps the fields from his instruments were tickling the nuclear spins more effectively than magnetic forces alone. Appaarently his technology was never duplicated.

The work of Carleton Hazlewood and his associates provides additional information of possible connections between magnetic therapy and the proton relaxation times (a term used by MRI technicians to describe how quickly protons return to their original states when perturbed by a magnetic field and radio wave). These relaxation times are longer for diseased tissue than healthy cells. Hazlewood's work goes back twenty yeaars when MRI was first being used for cancer diagnosis. The connection between magnetism was therapy and findings of Hazlewood and others with MRI technology is unknown, at least to me, but suggests that more attention should be given to the findings of biophysicists engaged in MRI research. Probably MRI instruments could be modified to provide healing pulses as well as diagnostic pictures.

Acid-Base Balance

One aspect of the interaction between magnetism and biological processes may be a change in the acid-base balance. A liquid is said to be more acidic if there are more hydrogen ions in the solution. A hydrogen ion is just another name for the proton which constitutes the center of a hydrogen atom. If two hydrogen ions combine with one another and attract a couple of free electrons to form hydrogen gas (H_2), the gas can escape the liquid, leaving it less acidic. Protons with different spin orientations are more likely to combine than protons with the same spin orientations. (Like poles repel; unlike poles attract.) In a normal ionic solution, some hydrogen protons are constantly changing, combining with one another and dissociating. Apparently, small external magnetic forces can alter this random equilibrium. Changes in Earth's magnetic force can probably affect the process, slightly changing the acid-base balance of the body and thereby affecting the biochemistry, glandular secretion, brain waves, and ultimately our emotions, thoughts, health, and behavior. Although such changes in behavior do happen, it is only speculation, not proven fact, that they arise from changes in the acid-base balance.

How applying magnets to the body can help regulate the pH is not at all clear. When I made measurements on the acidity of water with a sensitive pH meter, I could not detect a change in pH, regardless of whether I used north, south, alternating, or pulsing magnetic fields. Several other people told me they also couldn't find any changes, even with the strongest magnets. Although William Philpott and others have claimed a pH change is only apparent in the body's fluid, I have never seen a formal study on this or even any informal data. I did notice the pH in water left standing overnight with no applied magnetic force changes. Water in the organism is sometimes referred to as 'living water' by biologists. Perhaps this makes a difference.

171

Other Magnetic Mechanisms

When an electron moves in a magnetic field its motion is deflected. This is the key to making television tubes which shoot electrons at the screen and direct their movements with magnets to obtain pictures. You can demonstrate this effect for yourself by placing a small magnet on your TV screen. In the body there are often some atoms within molecules which are said to be ionized; that is, they temporarily have an extra electron or have lost an electron. This means that the course of the entire molecule can be slightly changed by applying a magnetic force. The moving blood and lymph carries ions which can be so affected. These small effects can possibly result in triggering changes which would show up at the macroscopic level.

Other mechanisms include ion transport across cellular membranes, resonance and piezoelectro effects and electron spin resonance. These are succintly described in an excellent article by Lynn Surgalla (see references and look at all the issues of the *Journal of Bioelectromagnetics* for more and more and more...)

Chapter XII
Frontier Views on Magnetism

S everal years ago, I was presenting a paper at a conference organized by the American Holistic Medical Society. As I passed by an exhibit table, a little book practically jumped out for me to see. The author, Dr. Robert Leichtman, a physician from Ohio, was also presenting a paper at the conference. The book, entitled *Tesla Returns* (see References), was channeled by Dr. Leichtman. Nikola Tesla was a scientific giant. He made major contributions to the development of our electric technology, and, even today, some of his work has not been duplicated. This book was purported to be statements of Tesla from "the other side," channeled by a medium. At that time, I was struggling to understand my discovery of the biological force around the body and its relationship to magnetism. The book *Tesla Returns* had relevant information for that puzzle, whether the source was in fact Tesla in spirit or the astute thoughts of Dr. Leichtman. I was delighted with my purchase, because it gave me fresh thoughts about my research. Another book channeled by Dr. Leichtman was called *Einstein Returns*. It also had new information for expanding my understanding of magnetism. Consequently, I have included a few paragraphs of relevance from each of these delightful little books.

Einstein Returns

"One of the discoveries that researchers in psychology and medicine will eventually make is that nonferrous matter also has the magnetic properties which ferrous matter does. This includes the matter which goes into the substance of human thought and feeling.

"It is not the type of magnetism which attracts iron filings, of course, but it is most definitely a species of magnetism. It attracts other substances in harmony with it. Indeed, there is a whole science of magnetism waiting to be discovered and applied to physical and psychological health.

"The magnetic properties I am referring to here are more likely to be found in the bodies of higher plants, animals, and humans."

Comment: This may be what I discovered and described as the biofield in chapter 3 of *The Body Magnetic*. It can be detected by a device called an Aura Meter. (See resources.) Einstein continues:

"Emotions must be dealt with both as highly magnetic nonphysical matter and as an aspect of consciousness. The difficulty in treating many emotional illnesses stems, in part, from the fact that the emotions which cause these problems tend to be magnetically responsive to a kind of astral matter which easily glues itself both to our own feelings and to more of its own kind. This magnetic action makes it very difficult to get rid of the "bad" astral matter— and the emotional problem.

"I suspect that some of these ideas about the magnetic aspects of physical and emotional sickness will be the focus for some real breakthroughs in medicine, and perhaps inspire similar breakthroughs in other scientific disciplines."

A related statement was found in the book about Tesla:

Tesla Returns

"Electromagnetic phenomena are enhanced at the time of the full moon. That is why the emotions are intensified then. As you know, emotions carry a kind of magnetic charge."

Comment: This suggests that whole body magnetic treatments ought to accompany psychotherapy. People who are highly emotional exhibit larger biofields as measured by the Aura Meter, and the direction of the biofield usually reverses around the time of the new or full moon.

"Therefore, by manipulating the electromagnetic forces around the body one can alter the emotional states of humans as well as other aspects of body functioning. I'm talking about a higher octave than physical magnetism. It's important to understand that all matter is magnetized and can carry some form of current. The earth carries a magnetic charge—indeed, a very heavy magnetic charge.

"The real physical body is basically a magnetic gridwork. Acupuncturists work with this magnetic gridwork of the physical body. By adjusting the electrical flow or magnetic potential at various points within the body's distribution system, you can augment either health or disease.

"The etheric matter has a magnetic charge which is the real "body" holding together the dense physical, flesh body.

"The more evolved animals and plants have a measure of sensitivity which could be called "psychic." They are certainly aware of human thought. We live in the magnetic atmosphere of the planet,

175

after all. And this magnetic atmosphere is filled with human thought. That's the basis of telepathy, and telepathy exists between animals and humans, as well as between humans and humans."

Comment: Thoughts have power. Psychokinesis, the ability to move matter, has been demonstrated many times under controlled laboratory conditions. Not everyone has the overt power to move objects at a distance from the body, but everyone I have tested shows the presence of a large mechanical force that can be detected a foot or two away from the body. This force is usually not under conscious control.

Within the body, and particularly within the brain, we all have the power to alter neurons and brain chemistry. Every thought we think influences the course of millions of ions, atoms, and molecules. An original thought demonstrates psychokinesis in action. The brain amplifies thoughts and the body amplifies them even more. So thoughts can move mountains, although there are intermediate steps.

Thought may have to be carried by emotion to be transferred or sent from one brain to another, analogous to the way speech and music is "carried" by high frequency radio waves. It is emotion that has the magnetic charge according to Tesla. One experiment has been done showing that telepathy increased at times of increased geomagnetic activity (Persinger).

In one of the largest experiments ever done, I found that several million people meditating could apparently influence the sun (Payne, 1987). This was a $3\frac{1}{2}$-year experiment studying 18 peace meditations. The average decrease in solar activity was about 30 percent the day after the meditations, and the effect lasted for an average of two weeks. One possible explanation for this effect may be related to this *biological magnetism* mentioned by Tesla and Einstein which is in resonance with the Earth's magnetic field, which is in turn related to the Sun's magnetic field.

This experiment was undertaken because previous research by Professor Raymond Wheeler at the University of Kansas had uncovered the fact that wars occur in cycles of approximately 11 years, and have done so for over 2,500 years, matching in nearly perfect step the cycle of sunspot activity (as shown in the graph on page 178). This remarkable fact was confirmed by Edward Dewey, Director of the Foundation for the Study of Cycles, who considered it to be the most important discovery of his life. The pathological disturbance in large numbers of people which often results in warring behavior is triggered by magnetic forces arising from the Sun's activity, which in turn is a function of the positions of the planets.

The next peak in solar activity is expected about the year 2000. International battles usually increase about two years before solar activity peaks or one year after, as the magnetic activity around Earth is largest at these times.

Minute changes in Earth's magnetic field have been found to be correlated with accidents, injuries, the onset of illness, wife poisonings, psychotic episodes, and of course wars, which are basically large-scale psychotic outbreaks. Even plants and animals are affected by changes in Earth's magnetic field. (See chapter 4 in my earlier book, *The Body Magnetic*, for more information.)

If such large effects are produced by such small magnetic field disturbances, it seems reasonable that beneficial magnetic fields could have equal power to change our physical, mental, and social health. They can and they do.

The graph in chapter 3, page 30 shows the comparison between Earth's magnetic field at a normal, or undisturbed level, and the small changes or modulations of this field during times of solar flares. As can be seen in the figure, these changes, although small, are larger than the magnetic forces detected around the heart or the brain. Tesla comments directly on this in a positive manner.

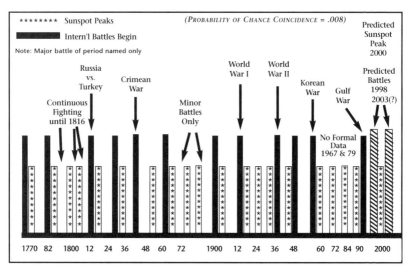

Figure 25: Sunspot Peaks and Battles

This figure was prepared from the data of Professor Raymond Wheeler of the University of Kansas. He found that international battles waxed and waned in cycles of approximately 11 years. Plotting the time that battles begin rather than the time of their peak intensity, a close correlation was found with solar activity, which in turn disturbs Earth's magnetic field and apparently changes brain rhythms and the hormone balance of human beings. Only some of the many worldwide battles are shown.

Tesla Returns (Again)

"It is perfectly reasonable to contact the energy fields of other planets and apply them. If you could tap the actual energies of different planets and work with them, then astrology would have a therapeutic application. It can be done."

Comment: When Earth is near Jupiter, which occurs approximately every thirteen months, the geomagnetic field is quieter than usual, the weather is usually warmer than normal, and people feel more optimistic and joyful. It is possible to record on a magnetic tape the different patterns of the geomagnetic field, play them into an amplifier and then direct them into a coil around the body. By recording and playing back these patterns, perhaps we could give someone a good *feeling* even on a down day. When Earth is near some of the other planets, a unique geomagnetic pattern often occurs, especially if the Moon is aligned with the planet. There are often different biological or psychological effects, just as Tesla said. It is also possible to collect emanations from stars in water and use it therapeutically. In fact, it is being done, and such water is commercially available from a company called Pegasus in Boulder, Colorado.

My research and that of others has shown that all living things are connected to some degree through the magnetic field of the planet, which in turn is connected with the Sun and, to a lesser degree, with the other planets. The Sun's magnetic field is probably connected with other stars and the galactic center, and so on throughout the universe. Magnetism, or the higher octave of magnetism as Tesla calls it in *Tesla Returns*, may be that force which links us all together with the universe.

The magnetic field of Earth is now being polluted by AM and FM radio waves, television, radar, and power line emanations, but the pollution due to violent emotions and thoughts may be even more serious. Maybe that's why enlisting the power of thought (one's own or others) in helping the body heal is so useful, and why more large-scale peace meditations could prove helpful.

In an experiment spanning a decade, years before Tesla's channeled book was published, I made an apparatus that detected *emanations* from some of the planets. These emanations were observed as an alteration in the taste of water and, when drunk, water from the different planetary emanations had different psychophysiological effects. The effect appeared to be stronger when the geomagnetic field was more active (Payne, 1990).

Some Thoughts From My Own Meditations

Often when I get up, my busy mind is relatively quiet, and I will sit at the typewriter, ask questions, tune in, and wait for an answer from my intuitive sense, higher mind, or whatever you wish to call the faculty that gives us new ideas. I have a stack of material, ideas for instruments, ideas for experiments, ideas for improving my health, wealth, relationships, and so forth. Often the ideas and suggestions obtained this way give me useful information. Sometimes it takes me months or even years to understand and act upon them. Sometimes I get immediately useful guidance for a health problem. But since it's appropriate here, I asked about magnetism.

The question was: "What is the mechanism for sensing magnetic forces in humans?"

Within each cell are DNA and other complex molecules. These have different resonance frequencies.

180

Some frequencies and patterns of electromagnetic radiations and magnetic pulses slightly change the physical properties of some molecules. This, in turn, can change the rate or type of chemical reactions in which those molecules are involved. Although this may be only a small change, it can have a large effect if the molecules altered are involved in key functions within, for example, the cells of endocrine glands.

Enzyme activity, for example, can be altered by magnetic forces. DNA molecules have a resonance at a very high frequency (3 trillion cycles per second) which is a frequency that penetrates Earth from the Sun. Each molecule has its own particular radio frequency "signature," or receptivity pattern, depending on its structure. This is one of the ways that molecules can be identified.

Whereas the other senses operate by triggered nerve impulses, magnetic and electromagnetic forces trigger chemical changes. When the special molecules in the endocrine glands are affected, the hormone balance will be altered. Small changes can alter the mood of an individual, sometimes drastically.

Therefore, the effects of magnetic forces are experienced more as changes in feelings rather than as sensations.

Because people are not used to "seeing" their personal universe in terms of feelings, they have not noticed that many feeling-sensations are externally generated and have taken them to be their own. This makes the world more confusing. People are likely to experience emotional overload, or chaos, which makes them shut down their feeling sensitivity.

Some re-education is necessary to sharpen feeling awareness.

In recent years, more emphasis has been put on the importance of feelings, but the assumption has been that people are 100 percent responsible for their own feelings and therefore they can take 100 percent control over them.

When this assumption is dropped, people may become more aware of "feeling perception" in addition to sense perception and will be able to sort out what is intrinsically theirs compared with what is externally induced by solar and planetary magnetic changes.

These ideas of Tesla, Einstein, and from my own meditations suggest that there will be an interesting and valuable future for the use of magnetic forces to produce healing not only of the physical body, but with feelings as well. Perhaps many of you readers will carry on the research.

Chapter XIII
Electromagnetic Fields from Power Lines & Appliances

lectromagnetic forces from power lines and household appliances are not healthy for human beings. These forces oscillate at 60 cycles per second and produce both magnetic polarities in rapid succession. Studies have been done, and repeated, showing that electric blankets, water beds, many types of video display terminals including television sets, other household appliances, and new cars with electronic computers all produce mildly irritating to moderately harmful electromagnetic radiation.

Sixty-cycle alternating-polarity electromagnetic fields are more damaging to growing cells; therefore, pregnant women and young children should avoid sleeping on water beds or under electric blankets, sitting more than a few hours every day in front of a computer screen, or working long hours in a copy store.

Initially, it was thought that the only biological effects from power lines were created by electromagnetic radiation heating up molecules in the body. Now it is recognized that specific frequencies and patterns of electromagnetic radiation can interact uniquely with different molecules, atoms, or even atomic nuclei within the body. Small forces can have large effects if they are of the right patterns to interact with significant molecules in key positions in glands or organs. Biological interactions appear to be based more on resonances than on simply "cooking" some molecules.

Although the field strength of electromagnetic signals is small—on the order of one hundredth to a few thousandths of a gauss for the magnetic component of the electromagnetic waves—the biological effects are significant.

In the U.S. and Canada, power lines and most household appliances operate on electricity which oscillates at 60 Hz. In Europe and Asia, power lines operate at 50 Hz.

As of 1998, more than a dozen studies have been completed, most of which showed adverse effects on people living near high-voltage power lines. Two of the most recent studies were done in Sweden. One found a higher risk of leukemia in children, but no increase in cancer in adults. This study involved nearly 500,000 people. Constant magnetic field exposures as low as 2 milligauss (oscillating, not permanent, magnets) were linked with increases in childhood leukemia. (By comparison, Earth's magnetic field is about one-half gauss; the human heart produces a field of a few microgauss. (See the chart in chapter 3, p.30.) As mentioned previously, it is the rapidly growing cells that are most sensitive to magnetic fields.

The results of studies on health of electromagnetic radiation appear similar to the studies on nuclear radiation. The more the research, the smaller the dosage is found that is linked with cancer or other adverse effects; and cancer has been definitely increasing during the past two decades. This is a serious problem! The cause of increased cancer or increased nuclear radiation is not simply 60-cycle electromagnetic radiation; there are many factors, some as yet not clearly identified. Preventive treatment with magnetic therapy may be helpful no matter whaat the cause of cancer. (See chapter 6.)

For example, the irritating effects of fluorescent lights are not widely known, although some studies have been done. Unfortunately, because fluorescent lights are cheaper than incandescent, they are coming into wider use.

I noticed that fluorescent lights in Europe and Asia, which operate at 50 Hz, were less irritating to me than our 60 Hz systems. Appliances and the proximity of power lines there might be less likely to trigger illness than those in the United States; no comparative research studies have been completed. The second Swedish study showed a link between leukemia and men who worked near high-voltage power lines.

Varieties of Harmful Effects

Genetic damage, cancer, immune system ailments, head-aches, eyestrain, and mild fatigue may be increased by exposure to some patterns of oscillating magnetic forces. The list continues to grow as research continues.

A number of studies have found adverse effects. Dr. Jerry Phillips of the Cancer Therapy and Research Foundation in Texas found that human tumor cells multiply more readily when exposed to weak pulsating electromagnetic forces (polarity and pulse rate unknown). Other researchers have discovered that weak magnetic forces can cause animals to release stress hormones. The different types of electromagnetic radiation from radio broadcasting stations and telephone microwave relay towers can also damage the immune systems of people who are close to them for hours every day. In 1986, researcher David Savitz of the University of North Carolina reported that 20 percent of childhood cancers appeared in children who had long term exposure to only a three-milligauss oscillating magnetic force.

A Swedish physician surveyed over 2,000 homes located near power lines or substations and found twice as much childhood cancer as in average homes. An Air Force study of cancer cases in Cincinnati showed clear patterns of cancer increase on hills facing the Air Force airport radar and on hills facing the civilian airport radar. (The airports are at opposite corners of the city.) People living in the valleys, where they were shielded from radar, had fewer incidents of cancer than those on the hills. The number of studies is increasing rapidly as more scientists turn their attention to this area. Many of these studies are reported in detail in books by Robert Becker, M.D., and Paul Brodeur. It may be years before we understand all possible effects—some harmful, others beneficial.

For instance, in January, 1998, *Science News* reported on research showing that melatonin production is decreased by electromagnetic fields (presumably those produced by 50 and 60 cycle house currents). If melatonin is low, breast cancer may be more likely.

In the same article reference is made to the work of Charles Graham, a physiologist at the Midwest Research Institute in Kansas City, Missouri. He found that magnetic fields from power lines can alter other hormones that increase cancer risk—estrogen and testosterone.

The next month *Science News* reported on the work of Fatih Uckun of the Wayne Hughes Institute in St. Paul, Minnesota who found that 60 cycle fields could influence enzyme production which in turn affects hormone production. This obviously relates to Jan Wallaczek's work on enzymes mentioned in chapter 11 of this book. Unbalanced hormone production can in turn lead to leukemia, lymphomas, and other cancers, as well as other physical and psychological ailments.

This is frightening! Especially in view of the fact that cancer has been increasing for the last few decades along with the widespread use of electricity. I'm considering going back to a manual typewriter! However there are remedies. Keep reading.

Harmful Versus Beneficial Fields

Magnetic forces are as varied as music. There are thousands of different types. In fact, when music is being played through a loudspeaker, it is transformed into a magnetic force within the speaker. This magnetic force causes a diaphragm to move to and fro, producing what we call sound.

Just as some types of music are discordant and other kinds harmonious, some types of magnetic forces are irritating and others harmonious. The steady, even magnetic forces produced by small permanent magnets are not harmful to the body, even if continuously applied. They can be beneficial. (Biosouth pole forces should not be applied to tumors or cancerous conditions, however.)

The pulsed magnetic instruments I use for magnetic therapy produce magnetic forces of one polarity only on each side of the applicator. As with a permanent magnet, one chooses which polarity to apply by using one side or the other of the applicator. The pulses are sixteen or less per second.

When polarized magnetic pulses occur at frequencies of fifty or sixty cycles per second, they have been found to weaken people, as indicated by muscle testing. Magnetic pulse frequencies of under 30 Hz can be strengthening for the body, depending upon their polarity and where they are applied. Although these pulsing forces are helpful for the body, they are not meant to be continuously applied. Caution and common sense should be used in their application. *More* and *bigger* does not necessarily mean better.

Protecting Yourself from Harmful Fields

Know What the Fields Are in Your Environment

Inexpensive magnetic field detectors are now available to measure the magnetic component of radiation around the home or office. One excellent instrument is called the Trifield Meter. (See resources.) By using one, you can determine the best place to put the baby's crib, your own bed, favorite chair, or desk. You can know where to work or stand so as to minimize 60 Hz fields from stoves, ovens, washers, dryers, etc.

You can also experiment with the Electronic Muscle Tester when you turn an appliance on and off, such as a conventional or microwave oven. This may tell you whether or not your individual body is being weakened by electromagnetic radiation. People differ greatly in their sensitivity to electromagnetic fields.

It is not easy to shield yourself from magnetic fields, but you can minimize exposure by keeping a reasonable distance from them. The magnetic fields decrease rapidly with distance. The Trifield Meter allows you to quickly determine at what distance the fields drop to a safe level.

As I type on my Xerox 620 Memorywriter, I am being zapped with a 10 to 30 milligauss field. Since I spend up to four hours a day, six days a week typing, this adds up to a fairly high dose rate. Looking at the screen definitely irritates my eyes. A quartz heater stands behind me. Although the Trifield Meter indicates a field of over 100 milligauss right at the wire cage, the field drops off to one milligauss within about three feet. Therefore, it is probably okay to use. A speakerphone measures 10 milligauss right at the surface, but this drops off quickly only a few inches away. However, the headset produces a 10 milligauss field at the surface of the earpiece. My compass indicates that there is also a permanent magnet of a few hundred gauss with the north pole facing the ear. Does talking on the phone for a few hours every day give you a headache or make you feel drowsy?

A field of 100+ milligauss was measured at waist level a few inches away from copy machines. My electric blanket showed a 100 milligauss field. Naturally I don't use it any longer, although I understand that the new ones have reduced fields.

Keep Healthy!

Although electromagnetic pollution is a problem, other health hazards of equal or greater importance include polluted water and air, pesticides in food, and personal vices. Dealing with these may be more important than moving your bed a few inches away from the wall. There is no need to panic and turn off the electricity! What you should do is keep as healthy as possible so stressors of any kind will have minimal impact, whether they be physical, electromagnetic, or psychological. It is always worthwhile to enlist the aid of the mind in the healing process as described in chapter 8.

Preventive Magnetic Maintenance

When stressors, including irritating magnetic fields, act upon the body, they may knock atoms and molecules out of alignment. By treating the body with beneficial magnetic forces on a regular basis you may keep healthier. Try it and see!

The Future of Magnetic Healing

Magnetic therapy as a science is in the beginning stages. How do we sort out what works? Obviously, it will take careful biophysics, and good instrumentation such as that used in MRI equipment.

Just as iron is the key element in hemoglobin, key atomic nuclei in each gland and organ may be identified. By altering these key nuclei with precise magnetic and radio frequencies, we may be able to produce powerful changes. In the case of cancer, for example, the key atoms involved in the erroneous process of runaway cell division will have to be identified (they may already be known to specialists). Magnetic forces and radio frequency signals tuned to affect those master atoms in a beneficial way might then be applied to the body to correct the condition. Precise control of the aging clock may also be possible. Forces applied in the early stages of embryonic growth might prevent some birth defects.

The technology to do these kinds of precise application is available now, and probably the knowledge is also. What is required is some completely objective way to determine the optimum application parameters and treatment times. At this time, magnetic diagnosis using muscle testing may be our best approach until something better is developed. *I have no doubt that something better will be developed, probably within the next ten years. Then we can expect a quantum jump in health care.*

Resources & Organizations

Where to get information on magnets:

Magnets can be purchased from hardware stores, hobby shops, and local industrial supply houses. If you obtain magnets from such sources, be sure to mark their polarity.

PsychoPhysics Labs manufactures and imports pulsed magnetic generators. Custom designed instruments can be obtained for research purposes.
1803 Mission Ave., Suite 24, Santa Cruz, CA 95073

On the Internet

The Author has a web page at **www.buryl.com**. and one for social projects at **www.apr.com**. Many companies are now maintaining web sites—a search for magnetic therapy or biomagnetic therapy will give you many contacts.

Publications and Associations

Bio-Electric Magnetic Institute (BEMI), 2490 West Moana Lane, Reno, NV 89509-7801; (702) 827-9099. Director: Dr. John Zimmerman. Publishes an excellent newsletter, research reviews, lists of suppliers, magnetic therapists, etc. (non-profit)

Bioelectromagnetic Society (BEMS), 120 Church St., Frederick, MD 21701. Publishes the *Journal of Electro-Magnetic Therapy* and holds annual conferences. Very technical.

Lotus Press, P.O. Box 325-AP, Twin Lakes, WI 53181; (800) 824-6396 (toll free order line); (414) 889-8561 (office phone); (414) 889-8591 (fax); e-mail: lotuspress@lotus-press.com. Publisher of books on ayurveda, herbology, althernative health modalities, spirituality and Native American studies. Extensive annotated book catalog free on request.

North American Academy of Magnetic Therapy, 28240 West Agoura, CA 91301, Ste. 202; 1 (800) 457-1853. This organization, founded in 1995, is interested in furthering research on magnetic therapy. Yearly conferences are held.

Magnetic Therapists Association of Australia, 103 Main North Road, Nailsworth, South Australia, 5083, Australia. This active organization has over 700 members, many in the United States. It is open to anyone engaged in the process of magnetic therapy.

Magnetism and Youthing Foundation, 5336 Harwood Rd., San Jose, CA 95124-5711. This organization publishes a newsletter and provides guidelines for people wishing to be part of the ongoing research project. Membership fee iis $50 and the newsletter is $25. Dewey Lipe, Ph. D., Executive Director, can be reached by fax: (408) 264-9659, or e-mail: DeweyL@ix.netcom.com.

Aromatherapy, Herb & Spice Resources

InterNatural, 33719 116th St.-AP, Twin Lakes, WI 53181; (800) 643-4221 (toll free order line); (414) 889-8581 (office phone); (414) 889-8591 (fax); e-mail: internatural@lotuspress.com; website: **www.internatural.com.**

Retail mail order and internet reseller of essential oils, herbs, spices, supplements, herbal remedies, incense, books and other supplies.

Lotus Light Enterprises, P.O. Box 1008-AP, Silver Lake, WI 53170; (800) 548-3824 (toll free order line); (414) 889-8501 (office phone); (414) 889-8591 (fax); e-mail: lotuslight@lotuspress.com. Wholesale distributor of essential oils, herbs, spices, supplements, herbal remedies, incense, books and other supplies. Must supply resale certificate number or practitioner license to obtain catalog of more than 10,000 items.

Educational Courses

Institute for Wholistic Education, 33719 116th Street, Twin Lakes, WI 53181; (414) 877-9396. Offering correspondence courses in Ayurveda.

Exercise

Aerobic and flexibility exercises also aid healing by improving general health. A healthier body is more able to heal and to fight off sickness. A healthier person feels better and has more energy, and therefore can do more exercise to get more energy. It's a positive cycle! You must make the effort to start.

The Fitness Deck

Regular exercise helps clear the body of toxins in a way that sleep never will. I developed a novel way to make exercise more fun by describing and illustrating each of fifty-two exercises on 4"x 6" cards. These exercises combine the best features of aerobics, kundalini yoga, and movement. To use them, shuffle The Fitness Deck and pick three or four cards each day to introduce variety into your exercise routine. The universe provides what you need. Available from PsychoPhysics Press

Hypnosis Instruments

Anton Mesmer, one of the people who discovered hypnosis, originally used magnets in the process of inducing a trance. Now his work has been revived, using electronically generated magnetic forces instead of crude iron ore magnets. In this technique, small pulsing magnetic forces are applied to the head area simultaneously with pulsed tones and blinking lights. The frequency of these stimuli can be systematically varied so as to gradually entrain the brain rhythms to lower and lower frequencies. These devices are still in the beginning stages of development; in the next decade their use will probably take hypnosis in new directions.

I recommend enlisting the power of the mind to help heal any condition. The power of the mind is amazing—it can keep us healthy, make us sick, or help us heal. The medical profession admits that a large percentage of illnesses are either psychosomatic in origin or have a psychosomatic component.

The Hypnosis Training System

The Hypnosis Training System integrates hypnosis, meditation, and biofeedback. Includes a GSR biofeedback instrument, a complete text, and a training tape. This is an ideal instrument for home use; equivalent to a complete course in hypnosis that might cost hundreds of dollars. Available from PsychoPhysics Labs.

A Hypnosis Training Instrument is also is available from:
Aura Imaging Company, 846A Jefferson Ave., Redwood City, CA 94063-1828; 800-321-AURA.

They also manufacture a special camera for taking photos of the aura, as well as a simple device for measuring the human aura.

References
Magnetism—Books

Badgley, Lawrence. 1992. *Energy Medicine*. Human Energy Press, 1020 Foster City Blvd., Suite 205, Foster City, CA 94404.
   A comprehensive description of various types of healing modalities, including magnetism. Dr. Badgley designed a pulsed magnetic intrument that detects the heartbeat and pulses at that frequency.

Bhattacharya, A. K., and R. U. Sierra. 1976. *Power in a Magnet to Heal*. West Bengal, India.
   An older book interesting to read for the novel and enthusiastic style.

Broeringmeyer, Richard and Mary. 1990. *Energy Training Manual*. Health Enterprises, Inc., P.O. Box 628, Murray, KY 42701.
   The function of each gland and organ is described, symptoms expected if the gland is overactive or underactive and how to treat it magnetically.

Davis, Albert R., and Rawls, Walter C. 1975. *Magnetism and its Effect on the Living System*. Smithtown, NY: Exposition Press.
   Another older book with some interesting historical information.

Hannemann, Holger. 1990. *Magnet Therapy*. Sterling, NY.
   Specific places to put tiny magnets to treat specific conditions using the acupuncture meridan system.

Jerabek, Jiri and Pawluck, William. 1998. *Magnetic Therapy: The Eastern European Research*. Dr. William Pawluck, 3530 No. Lakeshore Drive, No. 8A, Chicago, IL 60657-1894;

This is a summary of 343 studies on magnetic therapy. About 140 studies used permanent magnets, and the rest pulsing. Approximately 40 were controlled studies. The Europeans have been using magnetic therapy longer than people in the United States.

Lawrence, R. and Rosch, P. *Magnetic Therapy*, Prima Publishing, Rockland, CA 1998.

Ron Lawrence is founder of the North American Academy of Magnetic Therapy (See p. 194)

Leichtman, Robert. *The Hidden Side of Science*. Columbus, OH: Ariel Press. 800-336-7769.

This book incorporates the smaller books, *Einstein Returns* and *Tesla Returns*. Delightful, easy reading and mind expanding essays channeled by Dr. Leichtman and others. I've met this well-grounded physician and am impressed by his work.

Little, F. T., et al. 1987. *Pulsed Electro-Magnetic Field (PEMF) Therapy*. Hutton Publishing, 26 Finch Road, Ramsey, Isle of Man, British Isles.

A technical book with lots of specifics about frequencies to be used which are not clearly substantiated, though they may be correct.

Payne, Buryl. 1992. *The Body Magnetic*. Revised ed. Soquel, CA: PsychoPhysics Press. Order from 4264 Topsail Ct., Soquel, CA 95073. Also available from any

197

New Leaf Distributor bookstore.

The Body Magnetic describes the discovery of a fifth force which is easily measured and which is somehow related to magnetism. It also has information about the effects of magnetism on mass human behavior, its relation to sunspots and planetary positions, and some speculations.

Payne, Buryl. 1993. *Love and Sex Without Conflict*. Heart Books. Also available from PsychoPhysics Press.

People in relationships have ups and downs triggered by geomagnetic influences. Twenty remedial actions are described.

Santwand, M.T. 1986. *The Art of Magnetic Healing*. New Delhi, India: Jain Publishers, New Delhi.

Wall, A. *Magnetic Field Therapy*. Inner Search Foundation, P.O. Box 10382, McLean, VA 22102, 1993.

Specific points to place magnets on the body for specific conditions are clearly illustrated in this easy reading book.

Washnis, G., and R. Hricak. 1993. *Discovery of Magnetic Health*. Rockville, MD: Nova Publishing Co.

Many good anecdotal reports and summaries of studies of the value of magnetic healing are given.

Weber, M. 1992. *Therapy with Pulsating Magnetic Fields*. Biophysics & Medicine Report, Lehnenwein-garten 2, 8598 Uttwil, Switzerland.

This booklet is mostly about use of pulsed magnetic instruments sold by Elec-Biology. Over 100 refer-

ences are given, one of which (Warnke 1983) summa-
rizes 261 others.

Magnetism—Journal Articles
(Partial Listing)

Badgley, L. 1984. "A New Method for Locating
Acupuncture Points and Body Field Distortions."
American Journal of Acupuncture 12, no. 3.
    Dr. Badgley, M.D., acupuncturist, homeopathic
physician and researcher, is a genius. This article
describes a completely new technique for finding areas
of injuries. See his book, *Energy Medicine*, for more
information.

Baker, Mitzi. "The Force May Be With You." *Stanford
Medicine*, Vol. 13, No. 4, Summer, 1996.
    About the work of Jan Walleczek (see below) and
his Electrobiomagnetics Research Lab at Stanford. This
article is written in non-technical terms and clearly
describes the basic notions described in the more technical papers referenced below.

Bassett, C. 1974. "Acceleration of Fracture Repair by
Electromagnetic Fields." Annals of the New York
Academy of Sciences. 238-242.
    Dr. Basset did much of the original work on bone
healing with pulsed magnetic fields. He has published
many papers on the subject.

Binder, A. 1984. "Pulsed Electromagnetic Field Therapy of
Persistent Rotator Cuff Tendonitis." *Lancet* (March 31).

Dr. Binder's excellent work in England has yet to be duplicated formally, but informally thousands of people have benefited.

Bird, C. 1993. "The Case of Antoine Priore and His Therapeutic Machine." *Explore Magazine 5*, no. 4. Available from P.O. Box 1508, Mount Vernon, WA 98273.

Priore's instrument combines pulsed magnetic forces with radio frequencies—perhaps a valuable next step.

Blackman, C. et al. 1982. "Calcium Ion Resonance at 16 Hz Magnetic Pulsations." *Radiation Research* 92:510–520.

Both calcium ion resonance and blood flow seem to be a maximum at 16 Hz. Is this a coincidence, or is there a connection?

Boeinger, Greg. et al. "Building World-Record Magnets." *Scientific American*, June 1995.

This article is an interesting description of electromagnetic technology. A clear explanation of the fundamental nature of magnetism is given along wiith clear diagrams and descriptions of the latest successful attempts to make the biggest, strongest magnets.

Bonlie, Dean and Miller, Victor. "The Effects of Steady State 3,000 to 10,000 Gauss Magnetic Field on Patients with Brain and Brain Stem Trauma as Reported in Nine Case Studies." Magnetico Treatment Center, #109,5421-11 St. N.E. Calgary, Alberta, Canada T2E6M4.

The company made enough money selling magnetic beds to set up their own research laboratory and con-

struct excellent instruments and materials. The results of these nine patients is remarkable. This kind of work deserves worldwide attention.

Delgado, J. 1984. *Magnetic Fields in Biology.* Central Ramon y Cajal, Spain.
He found that monkeys are agitated by 60 Hz fields, therefore people probably are too.

Ellingsen, F., and H. Kristiansen. "Does Magnetic Water Treatment Influence Precipitation of Calcium Carbonate From Supersaturated Solutions?" Norwegian Institute of Water Research, P.O. Box 146, N-3201, Sandefjord, Norway.
This is one of many studies showing that magnetic treatments are useful. I put magnets on my car's water line (south pole towards the water) with good results.

Friedman, H., and R. O. Becker. 1963. "Geomagnetic Parameters and Psychiatric Hospital Admissions." *Nature* 200:626–628.
A fundamental study showing that changes in the Earth's field have strong influences on human behavior although they are only a few hundreths of a gauss.

Ferndale, R. W. 1985. "Low Frequency Pulsed Magnetic Field Enhances Collagen Production in Connective Cultures." *Bioelectrochemistry and Bioenergy* no. 14:83–91.
Collagen is fundamental for our bodies. It's now available as a food supplement. Will magnetic treatments help increase the manufacture of our natural collagen?

Graham, C. et al. "EMF Effects on Melatonin, Hormones, and Immunity in Men." Midwest Research Institute, 425 Volker Blvd., Kansas City, MO 64110.

This paper was presented at a 1996 meeting of the Bioelectromagnetics Society. There are 5 other similar papers, all published in the journal *Bioelectromagnetics* in 1998 and previous years, most showing adverse effects of 60 Hz fields on the human body.

Guseo, A. 1987. "Pulsing Electromagnetic Field Therapy of Multiple Sclerosis by the Gyuling-Bordacs Device: Double-Blind, Cross-Over and Open Studies." *Journal Bioelectricity 6*, no. 1:23–25.

A fundamental paper on MS showing good results. On the basis of his work, every person with MS is advised to begin immediate magnetic treatment.

Harwood, J. M., and S. R. C. Malin. 1977. "Sunspot Cycle Influence on the GM Field." *Geophysical Journal of the Royal Astronomical Society* 50, no. 3:605–620.

Both the planetary positions and the sunspot cycle affect the GM field which in turn affects us. Papers like this form a physical basis for a new science of astrology.

Hazleton, C. "Nuclear Magnetic Resonance Parameters of Water in Biological Tissues. Microcirculation, Endothelium and Lympathetaics." 2. pp. 597-606, 1985.

This is a non-technical paper discussing Nuclear Magnetic Resonance Studies showing the difference between healthy and cancerous tissue. Dr. Hazlewood and others have been making such studies for over 20 years; this paper will lead you to other references. His work forms an important link in understanding how magnetic therapy works at the fundamental level of the hydrogen proton.

Hirose, S. Internal Physiotherapy School, Medical Faculty, University of Tokyo. 1976. "A Study on the Treatment Effects of Magnetic Necklaces and Their Influence on Living Bodies." *TDK Magneto-Medical Publication Series* No. 2 (May).

Ito, H., and A. Bassett. 1983. "Effect of Weak, Pulsing Electromagnetic Fields on Neural Regeneration in the Rat." *Clinical Orthopedics* no. 181:283–290.
    That nerves can regenerate when treated with magnetic forces is extremely important. See also the article by Wolker.

Jafary-Asl, A. H. 1983. "Pulsing Electromagnetic Fields Induce Cellular Transcription." Science no. 220:1283, 1983.

Jenkins, R. D. 1992. "Healing Power of Magnets." *Fitness Magazine* (February).

Kokoschinegg, P. 1991. "The Application of Alternating Magnetic Fields (Foils) in Medicine." *Magnets in Your Future* 4, no. 5 (April).
    Done is Europe with thin, low gauss material. It takes a longer treatment time with such devices, but they do work.

Kurushima, K. "Effectiveness of the TDK Magnetic Lumbar Belt in the Treatment of Lumbar Pains." Department of

Orthopaedic Surgery, National Kokufudai Hospital, Japan.

Like the study of the necklaces, this one supports the use of magnetic belts, now used by thousands of people.

"Magnetic Treatment of Rheumatoid Arthritis." 1987. *Rheumatologia* 24, no. 1:41–44.

Mooney, V. 1990. "A Randomized Double-Blind Prospective Study of the Efficacy of PEMF for Interbody Lumbar Fusions." *Spine* no. 15:708–711.

Nakagawa, K. 1976. "Magnetic Field Deficiency Syndrome and Magnetic Treatment." *Japan Medical Journal* 2745 (Dec. 4).

He was the physician who did the most to develop the magnetic bed as a means of treatment. He seems to consider 'magnetism' almost like a substance, which the body needs.

Nord, V. 1992. "Understanding Hydromagnetics." *Magnets in Your Future* 11, no. 6 (November).

Ohno, Y. "The Effects of Magnetized Mineral Water on Memory Loss Delay in Alzheimer's Disease." *The Center for Frontier Sciences*, Vol. 6, No.2, Spring/summer, 1997.

A carefully done study on this devastating disease. The results were so positive that research is continuing with ever more subjects. The journal is available from Temple University, Philadelphia, PA 19122.

Pauling, Linus. 1935. "The Oxygen Equilibrium of Hemoglobin and its Structural Interpretation." *Proceedings of National Academy of Science* 21, no. 4:186–191.
    One of the original studies on magnetic effects on blood oxygen. Very clear and easy to read, even though the results are not simple.

Pauling, Linus. 1936. "The Magnetic Properties and Structure of Hemoglobin, Oxyhemoglobin and Carbonmonoxyhemo-globin." *Proceedings of National Academy of Science* 22:210–216.

Payne, Buryl. 1984. "Cycles of Peace, Sunspots, and Geomagnetic Activity." *Cycles* (May).

Payne, Buryl. 1987. "The Global Meditation Project," Interim Report. *National Council on Geocosmic Research Journal* (Spring). Available from 105 Snyder Avenue, Ramsey, NJ 07446.

Payne, Buryl. 1988. "A Higher Octave of Magnetism." *Magnets in Your Future* 3, no. 4 (April).

Payne, Buryl. 1990. "Detecting Planetary Emanations." *Journal Borderland Research* (November/December). P.O. Box 429, Garberville, CA 95440.

Payne, Buryl. 1992. "Planetary Positions and Sunspots." *National Council on Geocosmic Research Journal* (December). Available from 105 Snyder Avenue, Ramsey, NJ 07446.

Payne, Buryl. 1985. "The Sounds of Earth's Magnetic Field, Its Influence on Health and Wars." *Ear*. New Wilderness Foundation, 325 Spring Street, Room 208, New York, NY 10013.

Reprints of these borderline science studies are available from PsychoPhysics Press.

Preslock, J. P. 1984. "Review of Functions and Mechanisms of the Pineal Gland." *Endocrine Reviews* 5:282.

A general paper which really should be read in conjunction with Semm's paper. The pineal gland is a master gland; its output affects all the others.

Prince, J. P. "The Use of Low Strength Magnets on EAV Points." *American Journal of Acupuncture* 11 no. 2:125–130, and 11, no. 3:249–254.

A dentist who also knows acupuncture demonstrated good results for tooth treatments.

Rein, Glen. 1995. "Storage of Non-Hertzian Frequency Information in Water," *In Proceedings of the International Tesla Society*. Tesla Society Publishers, Colorado Springs, Colorado.

Water is not a simple substance. Healers who can change the structure of water are discussed in this paper.

Roffey, L. E. 1993. "The Bioelectronic Basis for 'Healing Energies.' " *Neuromagnetic Systems*. Write 999 E. 1 Box 28, Murray Hill, KY 42071.

A thorough discussion of why magnetism works, by a neuroscientist.

Sambasivan, M. 1988. "Pulsed Electromagnetic Field in the Management of Head Injuries." *Medical College, Trivandrum-695011*, India.

    If only people knew that magnetic treatments work so well for head injuries every emergency room would have devices, but this study published in India is not well known.

Sandyk, R. 1996. "Weak Magnetic Fields as a Novel Therapeutic Modality in Parkinson's Disease." *International Journal of Neuroscience.*

    He has broken new ground by showing that very weak magnetic forces appear to be helpful in the few cases he has studied

Sandyk, R., Anninos, P.A., Tsagas, N., and Derpapas, K. 1996. "Magnetic Fields in the Treatment of Parkinson's Disease," *ibid.*, 63, 141-150.

Semm, P. 1980. "Magnetic Sensitivity of the Pineal Gland." *Nature* no. 228:206.

    One of the few studies showing that magnetic fields can alter the endocrine glands.

Semm, P., 1992. "Pineal Function in Mammals and Birds is Altered by Earth-Strength Magnetic Fields." In M.C. Moore-Ede, S. S. Campbell & R. J. Reiter (eds.), *Electromagnetic Fields and Circadian Rhythmicity,* 53-62, Boston: Birkhauser.

Subrahmahyam, S. 1988. "Pulsed Magnetic Field in Therapy," *Journal Madras Institute of Magnetobiology* (Madras, India).

Subrahmahyam, S., and S. Narayan. 1993. "Pulsed Magnetic Field Therapy." *The International Society for the Study of Subtle Energies and Energy Medicine* 4, no. 4 (Winter).

Surgalla, Lynn A. 1988. "Molecular Mechanisms of Magnetic Medicine." *Magnets in Your Future* 3, no. 4 (April).
A general overview of possible mechanisms for magnetic healing. Technical.

Trock, D. H. et al. 1993. "A Double-Blind Trial of the Clinical Effects of Pulsed Electromagnetic Fields in Osteoarthritis." *Journal of Rhuematology*, April, 1996.
An excellent study showing the value of magnetic fields for the treatment of arthritis.

Walleczek, Jan. "Low-frequency-dependent Effects of Oscillating Magnetic Fields on Radical Pair Recombination in Enzyme Kinetics."
This is one of several papers on this topic. Others are referenced in this paper. Dr. Walleczek's work describes the influence of magnetic forces on electrons, which appears to be another fundamental elementary particle mechanism explaining how magnetic forces operate in the body.

Warnke, U. 1984. "Infrared Radiation and Oxygen Partial Pressure in Human Tissue as Indicators of the Therapeutic Effects of Pulsating Magnetic Fields." University of Saarbrucken, Veriagsgesellschaft fur Biophysik und Medizin, Sperberweg 2, 6200 Wiesbaden, West Germany.
A very thorough study—highly recommended reading.

Weber, T., and J. Cerilli. "Inhibition of Tumor Growth by the Use of Non-homogeneous Magnetic Fields." *Cancer,* August 1971.

Wolker, J. et al. "Enhancement of Functional Recovery following a Crushed Lesion to the Rat Sciatic Nerve by Exposure to Pulsed EM Field." *Experimental Neuroscience*, V. 125, pp. 302-305, 1994.
    The second paper I've seen on nerve regeneration in rats. Anecdotal reports indicate nerve regeneration happens for humans as well. This is important research of the kind that makes magnetic therapy respectable and scientifically credible.

Youthing—Books and Journal Articles

Bhattacharya, A. K., and R. U. Sierra. 1976. *Power in a Magnet to Heal.* West Bengal, India.

Broeringmeyer, R. 1990. "Miracles of Biomagnetic Healing: Arresting the Effects of Aging." *Bioenergy Health Newsletter* (May). *Bioenergy Health Newsletter,* P.O. Box 28, Murray Hill, KY 42071.

Burnet, F. M. 1970. "An Immunological Approach to Aging." *Lancet* 2:358–360.

Davis, A. R., and W. C. Rawls. 1974. *Magnetism and its Effect on the Living System.* Hicksville, NY: Exposition Press.

Dekker, A. 1992. "Magnets Iron the Wrinkles Away." *Magnets in Your Future* 6, no. 4 (April). Available from

L. H. Arizona Publishing Co., P.O. Box 250, Ash Flat, AR 72513.

The original source for this article was Gouldsmit Magnetic Systems, Fluxline News Bulletin. Contact Mrs. Peggy Ector, Petunialaan 19, P. 0. Box 18, 5580 AA Waalre, The Netherlands.

Hsu, M., and C. Fong. 1978. "The Biomagnetic Effect: Its Application to Acupuncture Therapy." *American Journal of Acupuncture* (October).

Jolley, W. B. et al. 1983. "Magnetic Field Effects on Calcium Efflux and Insulin Secretion." *Bioelectromagnetics* 4:330–337.

Nair, N. P. et al. 1986. "Plasma Melatonin: An Index of Brain Aging in Humans?" *Biological Psychiatry* 21:141–150.

Pesic, M. 1989. "Therapeutic Possibilities of Thymic Preparations." *Explore Journal* 1, no. 5. Available from P.O. Box 1508, Mt. Vernon, WA 98723.

Glossary

Note: Words in italics have their own entries

A. Symbol for ampere. Also Amp, or MA for milliampere (1,000 of an ampere)

ac. Alternating current.

acid-base balance. The degree to which something is acidic or basic. Measured in pH.; a pH of 7 is neutral. Numbers above 7 are alkaline. Blood is around 7.2.

alnico. Any of several alloys of aluminum, iron, and nickel used to make strong permanent magnets.

alternating current. An electric current that reverses direction at regular intervals, such as that found in most household wiring. Abbreviated *ac*.

biokinesiology. A method of diagnosis that uses the strength of the patient's muscles under different circumstances to determine the health of various parts of the body, and to determine what treatments will be effective. Also called muscle testing or applied kinesiology, abbreviated A.K.

biomagnetic. A catch-all term for interface effects between biology and magnetism.

bionorth pole. The pole of a magnet that calms, sedates, reduces inflammation, and retards growth. Mark this pole white, blue, or green for use in healing. It attracts the north-pointing end of a compass needle. Physicists use different nomenclature, and call this the *south pole*.

biosouth pole. The pole of a magnet that stimulates, promotes healing, growth, and activity. Color-code it red for use in healing. The biosouth pole attracts the south-

211

pointing end of a compass needle. Physicists use different nomenclature, and call this the *north pole.*

coercive force. The force required to completely demagnetize a magnetized material.

dc. *Direct current,* as supplied by a battery.

diamagnetic. Some substances do not align with an applied magnetic force. They will resist or twist away from either magnetic polarity. Oxygen is one of the strongest diamagnetic substances. The effects are small. See the illustration below.

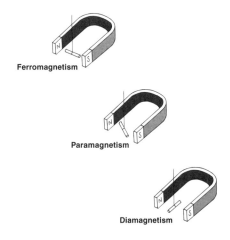

Ferromagnetism

Paramagnetism

Diamagnetism

Figure 26: Ferromagnetism, Paramagnetism, Diamagnetism

diathermy. A therapy in which high-frequency electromagnetic waves are used to generate heat inside the body.

direct current. An electrical current flowing in one direction only, such as is produced by a battery. Abbreviated *dc.*

electromagnet. A magnet made of a soft iron core surrounded by current-carrying insulated wire. The current magnetizes the core.

ferromagnetic. Ferromagnetic materials are easily magnetized when placed in a magnetic field. They include iron, cobalt, and nickel (see illustration). Ferromagnetic materials are a special class of paramagnetic materials.

gamma. One hundred-thousandth of one gauss. This term is commonly used by geophysicists in talking about variations in Earth's magnetic field. Magnetic storms may be on the order of 40 to 50 gammas. The human heart produces a magnetic field of less than one gamma, or a few millionths of a gauss. Human muscles produce about one-tenth of one gamma, and the brain neurons only about one hundred-thousandth of a gamma, or a billionth of a gauss (see illustration).

gauss. The most commonly used term for magnetic strength. Earth's field strength is about one-half of one gauss. Ordinary toy magnets have a field strength of one to two hundred gauss.

inverse square law. A formula used to describe and calculate the decreased intensity of many natural phenomena—including light, gravity, electric force, and magnetic force—at a distance from the source. The mathematical formula describing this decrease is written as: $F = 1/r^2$ where "F" is the force and "r" symbolizes the distance. The practical effect is that at twice the distance, the intensity drops to one-quarter of its former value.

Although it may sound mysterious, the inverse square law simply follows from the physical fact that if something disperses evenly in all directions from a point, it must fill an ever-expanding volume of space. The more space it has to fill, the less strong it can be at each point.

The inverse square law is only approximately accurate for magnetism because it is based on the imaginary notion that there could be a magnetic monopole (one magnetic pole without the other). It does not apply for an extended surface when you are close to that surface.

keeper. A piece of soft iron placed over the ends of alnico magnets to help them retain their magnetism.

lodestone. A naturally magnetized form of iron ore formed as volcanic eruptions cool. Also called a *natural magnet*.

magnetic current. No such thing. "Current" implies that something is moving. In fact magnetism simply exerts a force through space, much as gravity does.

magnetic energy. Nonexistent. Magnetic forces can produce changes in direction, but they do not perform work. If they did, they would run down or weaken.

magnetic field. (an abstraction) The area around a magnet or electric current in which a magnetic force can be detected. The term *magnetic force* may usually be used.

magnetic force. The twisting, pushing, or pulling force exerted on a magnetic or moving charged particle. You feel it when you hold two magnets as they try to attract or repel each other. Magnetic force, also called magnetic strength or intensity, is measured in gauss. It decreases rapidly with distance from a magnetic object.

magnetic moment. A measure of twisting force that takes the shape of the magnet into account. It is the strength of the pole multiplied by the distance between the poles.

A long skinny magnet of the same gauss strength at the poles has a larger magnetic moment than a short fat magnet. That is why compass needles are long and thin.

magnetic reluctance. The inability of a substance to become magnetized. Air has a high reluctance; it won't exhibit a magnetic effect no matter how strong a force you apply to it.

magnetic resonance. Electromagnetic waves of a specific frequency can produce a slight torque on atomic nuclei. This is the basis for Nuclear Magnetic Resonance Imaging and may be a basis for how electromagnetic pollution and planetary and solar influences affect living organisms.

magnetic susceptibility. This is the opposite of magnetic reluctance. The more susceptible a material is to magnetic spin force, the larger the number of electrons that will change their spin orientation in a magnetic field. Iron is by far the most susceptible element, but special alloys have been made which are better. One is called "Mu metal," an alloy used for magnetic shielding. Susceptible materials acquire magnetic or spin organization but won't hold it for very long; the electrons will quickly revert back to random orientations.

magnetotherapy. An older term for applying magnets to the body. Still used in India, but archaic in the U.S.

metric system. A system of measurement developed for scientific work. It can be used for very large and very small measurements. Prefixes denoting size are added to basic units designating what is being measured. Thus 1,200 gauss becomes 1.2 kilogauss (symbolized kg), while 25/1000 gauss becomes 25 milligauss (mg).

COMMON METRIC PREFIXES

Number of Units	Prefix	Symbol
1,000,000	mega	M
1,000	kilo	k
1		
1/10	deci	d
1/100	centi	c
1/1,000	milli	m
1/1,000,000	micro	μ
1/1,000,000,000	nano	n
1/1,000,000,000,000	pico	p
1/1,000,000,000,000,000	femto	f

milligauss. One thousandth of a gauss, abbreviated mg.

modality. A method of therapy.

multipole magnet. A magnet composed of two or more magnets with both poles on the face of the magnet. A common type has two magnets or many magnetic strips placed side by side with the poles alternating. Multipole magnets are often used on cards stuck on metal cabinets or refrigerators. They consist of strips of alternating north and south poles about $1/8''$ wide. They are not very effective for promoting healing.

muscle testing. A method of diagnosis which uses the strength of the patient's muscles under different circumstances to determine the health of various parts of the body, and what treatments will be effective. Also called *biokinesiology,* applied kinesiology, or A.K.

natural magnet. A magnet formed from a lump of iron ore by volcanic activity. Natural magnets are called *lodestones.*

neodymium magnet. A magnet made from a mixture of neodymium, iron, and boron. The strongest type of magnetic material yet discovered.

neo magnet. *A neodymium magnet.*

north pole. Albert Davis, who rediscovered that the two magnet poles have different biological effects, called the pole that attracts the end of a compass needle that points north the "north" pole. Unfortunately, physics and industry had already defined that pole as the "south" pole. I follow Davis, but use the term "bionorth" to avoid confusion with the physics term.

oersted. A unit of magnetic field strength used to measure the magnetizing force applied to a substance by placing it in coils carrying currents. Symbolized Oe or B. Similar to gauss.

paramagnetic. Most elements and compounds are paramagnetic, which means they are slightly attracted by a strong magnet. This happens because in some atoms in the substance, there are a few free electrons whose spins can orient to the external force and are therefore pulled into spin alignment with it. **Highly paramagnetic metals are called ferromagnetic.**

permanent magnet. A magnet that stays magnetized without a constant supply of electricity because some of the electrons of the iron atoms stay with their spin forces aligned.

pulsed magnetic force instrument. Any of various devices that generates pulsed magnetic forces. The pulse rate can vary from one to millions of times per second.

pulsed magnetic forces. Magnetic forces that vary rhythmically by getting stronger and weaker, switching polarity, or turning on and off. They are generated electrically.

south pole. Albert Davis, who rediscovered that the two magnet poles have different biological effects, called the pole that attracts the end of a compass needle that points south, the "south" pole. Unfortunately, physics and industry had already defined that pole as the "north" pole. I follow Davis, but use the term "biosouth" to avoid confusion with the physics term.

tesla. A metric unit of magnetic strength. 1 tesla = 10,000 gauss.

transducer. Any device or substance that converts input of one kind of energy into output of another kind. An ordinary radio speaker transducer converts electromagnetic waves into sound waves.

weber. an abstract term used in magnetic terminology to denote lines of magnetic force per square meter.

zipple. a transducer that changes solar magnetic energy into a form usable by humans. Not yet invented.

erbs and other natural health products and information are often available at atural food stores or metaphysical bookstores. If you cannot find what you need locally, you can contact one of the follwing sources of supply.

Sources of Supply:

The following companies have an extensive selection of useful products and a long track-record of fulfillment. They have natural body care, aromatherapy, flower essences, crystals and tumbled stones, homeopathy, herbal products, vitamins and supplements, videos, books, audio tapes, candles, incense and bulk herbs, teas, massage tools and products and numerous alternative health items across a wide range of categories.

WHOLESALE:

Wholesale suppliers sell to stores and practitioners, not to individual consumers buying for their own personal use. Individual consumers should contact the RETAIL supplier listed below. Wholesale accounts should contact with business name, resale number or practitioner license in order to obtain a wholesale catalog and set up an account.

Lotus Light Enterprises, Inc.

P O Box 1008 MH
Silver Lake, WI 53170 USA
414 889 8501 (phone)
414 889 8591 (fax)
800 548 3824 (toll free order line)

RETAIL:

Retail suppliers provide products by mail order direct to consumers for their personal use. Stores or practitioners should contact the wholesale supplier listed above.

Internatural
33719 116th Street MH
Twin Lakes, WI 53181 USA
800 643 4221 (toll free order line)
414 889 8581 office phone
WEB SITE: www.internatural.com

eb site includes an extensive annotated catalog of more than 7000 products that can be ordered "on line" for your convenience 24 hours a day, 7 days a week.

Tao and Dharma

Chinese Medicine and Ayurveda

by Robert Svoboda and Arnie Lade

Foreward by Michael Tierra, O.M.D.

"Taoism is a highly spiritual and mystical way of trandscending the human realm. Chinese medicine, whose roots embrace the Tao, provides a fundamental understanding of the reality of individual life. Ayurveda is the knowledge of life, an ancient Vedic art of balancing individual life in harmony with nature. Chinese medicine and Ayurveda are concurrent and inherent systems of healing every individual as he or she is. Together, Robert Svoboda and Arnie Lade have done remarkable work in order to bring forth the prospect of integral healing through the ancient Vedic and Oriental systems of medicine." Dr. Vasant Lad, author of Ayurveda: Science of Self Healing

"Traditional Chinese and Ayurvedic medicine constitute the two major legacies for health and healing from the ancient world....the Taoist Yin-Yang philosophy and the three Doshas of Ayurveda...were used according to their respective cultural contexts to determine the most balanced and appropriate diet, herbs, exercise and lifestyle according to inherited constitution, life work and climate....In these times of maximum fragmentation, it is truly a miracle that the perennial truths and the healing capacities of these great ancient philosophies can arise....

"To this purpose, this valuable work should serve as an important contribution." Michael Tierra, O.M.D., author of Planetary Herbology, Chinese Traditional Herbal Medicine, and The Way of Herbs

This book's interesting and valuable comparison provides a pioneering effort in examining side by side two great systems of medicine, studying closely the historical, theoretical and practical relationships. In so doing it offers these ancient paradigms for a synergistic, inclusive approach into the practice of modern healing.

To order your copy send $12.95 plus $3.00 shipping/handling ($1.50 for each additional copy) to Lotus Press, P O Box 325, Twin Lakes, WI 53181 USA 800 824 6396 email: lotuspress@lotuspress.com website: www.lotuspress.com

Wisconsin residents add appropriate sales tax for your county. Wholesale inquiries welcome. Visa, Mastercard, American Express and Discover accepted.

Lotus Press is the publisher of a wide range of books in the field of alternative health, including ayurveda, chinese medicine, herbology, aromatherapy, and energetic healing modalities. Request our free book catalog.

ISBN 0-914955-21-7   155 pp.   trade paper $12.95

**Lotus Press, P.O. Box 325 EH, Twin Lakes, WI 53181 • 800-824-6396 (order line)
414-889-8561 (office phone) •414-889-8591 (fax line)
e-mail: lotuspress®lotuspress.com web site: www.lotuspress.com**

Walter Lübeck

The Complete Reiki Handbook

Basic Introduction and Methods of Natural Application. A Complete Guide for Reiki Practice

This handbook is a complete guide for Reiki practice and a wonderful tool for the necessary adjustment to the changes inherent in a new age. The author's style of natural simplicity, so beloved by the readers of his many bestselling books, wonderfully complements this basic method for accessing universal life energy. He shares with us, as only such a Reiki master can, the personal experience accumulated in his years of practice. The lovely illustrations of the different positons make the information as easily visually accessible, as does the author's direct and undogmatic style. This work also offers a synthesis of Reiki and many other popular forms of healing.

192 pages, $ 14.95
ISBN 0-941524-87-6

Shalila Sharamon and Bodo J. Baginski

The Chakra-Handbook

From basic understanding to practical application

Knowledge of the energy centers provides us with deep, comprehensive insight into the effects the subtle powers have on the human organism. This book vividly describes the functioning of the energy centers. For practical work with the chakras this book offers a wealth of possibilities: the application of sounds, colors, gemstones and fragrances with their own specific effects, augmented by meditation, breathing techniques, foot reflexology massage of the chakra points and the instilling of universal life energy. The description of nature experiences, yoga practices and the relationship of each indiviual chakra to the Zodiac additionally provides inspiring and valuable insight.

192 pages, $ 14,95
ISBN 0-941524-85-X

AYURVEDA AND THE MIND
The Healing of Consciousness

DR. DAVID FRAWLEY

"*Ayurveda and the Mind* addresses, with both sensitivity and lucidity, how to create wholeness in Body, Mind and Spirit. This book opens the door to a new energetic psychology that provides practical tools to integrate the many layers of life. Dr. Frawley has added another important volume to his many insightful books on Ayurveda and Vedic sciences."

DEEPAK CHOPRA M.D.
AUTHOR, *Ageless Body, Timeless Mind*

PUBLISHED BY LOTUS PRESS
To order your copy, send $19.95 plus $3.00 postage and handling
($1.50 each add'l copy) to:

Lotus Press
PO Box 325CTM
Twin Lakes, WI 53181 USA
Request our complete book and sidelines catalog
Wholesale inquiries welcome.

BIOMAGNETIC
and Herbal Therapy
Dr. Michael Tierra

$10.95   96 pp
5 3/8 x 8 1/2 quality trade paper
ISBN 0-914955-33-0

Magnetic energy is the structural force of the universe. In this book the respected herbalist and healer, Dr. Michael Tierra enlightens us on the healing influence of commercially available magnets for many conditions and describes the sometimes miraculous relief from such problems as joint pain, skin diseases, acidity, blood pressure, tumors, kidney, liver and thyroid problems, and more. Magnetizing herbs, teas, water and their usage in conjunction with direct placement of magnets for synergistic effectiveness is presented in a systematic, succinct and practical manner for the benefit of the professional and lay person alike. Replete with diagrams, and appendices, this is a "how to do" practical handbook for augmenting health and obtaining relief from pain.

The paradigm of health in the future is based on energy flow. This paradigm reaches back to the ancient healing arts of the traditional Chinese, the Ayurvedic and the Native American cultures. It is connected to the work of Hippocrates, the "father" of Western medicine, in ancient Greek culture, and found its way through the herbal and homeopathic science that has flourished in Europe over the last few hundred years.

Dr. Tierra is the author of the all-time best selling herbal *The Way of Herbs* as well as the synthesizing work *Planetary Herbology*. He is a practicing herbalist and educator in the field with a background of studies spanning the Chinese and Ayurvedic, the Native American and the European herbal traditions.

To order your copy, ask your local bookseller or send
$10.95 + 3.00 (s/h) to:
Lotus Press
P O Box 325PH
Twin Lakes, Wi 53181 USA

Request our complete book and alternative health products catalogs
of over 7000 items. Wholesale inquiries welcome.